The IMF Crisis of 1976 and British Politics

KEVIN HICKSON

TAURIS ACADEMIC STUDIES
LONDON • NEW YORK

Published in 2005 by Tauris Academic Studies
an imprint of I.B. Tauris & Co Ltd
6 Salem Road, London W2 4BU
175 Fifth Avenue, New York NY 10010
www.ibtauris.com

In the United States of America and in Canada distributed by
Palgrave Macmillan, a division of St Martins Press, 175 Fifth
Avenue, New York NY 10010

International Library of Political Studies 3

ISBN 1 85043 725 4
EAN 978 1 85043 725 3

A full CIP record for this book is available from the British
Library
A full CIP record for this book is available from the Library of Congress

Library of Congress catalog card: available

Printed and bound in Great Britain by
TJ International Ltd, Padstow, Cornwall
from camera-ready copy supplied by the author

THE IMF CRISIS OF 1976 AND BRITISH POLITICS

To Nan

Contents

List of Figures

ACKNOWLEDGEMENTS

This book began life as a PhD thesis completed at the University of Southampton in 2002. I am therefore particularly indebted to my two supervisors for all of their support and advice, Raymond Plant who is a true source of intellectual inspiration and Graham Smith who provided much advice and enthusiasm. I would also like to thank my examiners Andrew Gamble, who has continued to give me the benefit of his considerable knowledge since the examination, and Dilys Hill.

Particular individuals require my thanks for reading and commenting on parts or all of the work. These include Samuel Brittan, Steve Ludlam, Tony McGrew and Anthony Seldon. Matt Beech, Clare Dubois and Jane Parker have been a source of much practical help. I am also very grateful for all those who agreed to be interviewed or who supplied written information without which the book could not have been written. All permissions have been granted.

Any remaining errors of fact or interpretation are of course my own.

I am especially grateful to the Thorneycroft Memorial Trust, who kindly gave me a scholarship without which I could not have undertaken my PhD. Thanks in particular to Stanley Crooks.

I am also grateful for all the help and encouragement of Lester Crook.

Last, but certainly by no means least, I wish to thank my family and friends. The book is dedicated to my grandmother with love.

CHAPTER 1

INTRODUCTION

OVERVIEW

The 1976 IMF Crisis remains one of those particularly rare occurrences in British economic policy, a dramatic series of events which captured public attention. Normally, I think it is fair to say, economic policy is conducted by a narrow political elite with little outside involvement. Not so in 1976 when the collapse of sterling, and the near collapse of the Labour Government maintained the public interest and debate was, relatively, open. But what was the real significance of these events? In what ways did these events mark a turning point in economic policy? Do these events have any contemporary significance? It is with these questions that this book wrestles.

The book is a study of the 1976 IMF Crisis. The term '1976 IMF Crisis' is used here to refer to the economic crisis of 1974-76 following the OPEC price-shocks of 1972 and 1973. The book therefore covers the whole of the period 1974-76. In a strict sense, this is incorrect since the 'IMF Crisis' can only refer to the period from October to December 1976, during which time the British Government negotiated the terms of the loan with the IMF. However, I still wish to keep the label 'the 1976 IMF Crisis' to cover the whole of the period since it acts as a convenient shorthand label for the conduct of policy between 1974-76. Moreover, the term is accurate in the sense that the events set in chain by the OPEC crisis led to the IMF loan in December 1976. It would be misleading to cover the events of October-December 1976 only, since this misses the long and short-term origins of the Crisis.

In the book, I make several original contributions, but in order to show what these are it is first necessary to examine the existing literature on the IMF Crisis.[1] I do not intend, at this stage, to provide a detailed literature review since the texts are discussed in more detail in the remainder of the book. Instead,

I merely wish to give a brief synopsis and to point to some of the gaps in the existing literature. The Cabinet discussions were some of the most open in postwar British history, with the result that much of what happened became public knowledge within a very short space of time. Much of the content of the Cabinet debates was leaked to the press. In early 1977 there was the first television documentary, a reconstruction of the Cabinet debates.[2] The first serious study appeared in 1978. This took the form of three long articles in the Sunday Times by Stephen Fay and Hugo Young, which were then published in book format as *The Day the £ Nearly Died*.[3] With the exception of several chapters in different books[4], this was all that existed in the historiography of the 1976 IMF Crisis.

All this changed from the late-1980s with the publication of the memoirs of the leading participants.[5] This new material led to a reassessment of the IMF Crisis. Under the auspices of the Institute of Contemporary British History, a witness seminar was held.[6] This brought together several participants to discuss the events. The most comprehensive British text on the IMF Crisis was published in 1992[7], and an important article by Steve Ludlam, which demonstrated that the policy reforms that were alleged to have been introduced in December 1976 had all been accepted by the Labour Government prior to IMF intervention, was published in the same year.[8]

Internationally, there have also been a number of studies on the IMF. Public records in the US have not been subject to the strict controls of the British records. It was therefore possible for Karen Bernstein to use these records in her PhD, completed in 1983.[9] Further research in America was conducted by Mark Harmon in the 1990s.[10] The official position of the IMF is also well known through the work of the Fund's historian.[11] These works are of great importance for researchers in Britain who do not have the time or financial resources to visit Washington. There is now little need to visit the US to examine these records since they are widely accessible through these texts.

The existing literature is therefore very extensive. However, there are several 'holes' in the literature which the book intends to 'fill'. The first is the broad point that the existing literature takes the form, almost exclusively, of narratives. There has been little serious attempt to analyse the period 1974-76 in terms of the extent to which it resulted in a shift in economic thought in Britain.[12] The main objective of the book is therefore to analyse the extent to which there was a shift in economic thinking. This falls into two parts. The first is the nature of political economy in the postwar era, up to 1974. The second is the extent to which this changed after 1976. Two dominant paradigms are said to have existed in British economic policy since 1945: Keynesianism and monetarism.[13] In fact, there are difficult questions relating to the nature of Keynesianism and monetarism, and I return to this point in the next section. The thesis therefore deals directly with the issue of policy shift, and makes contributions to the nature of economic thought post-1945, the shift in thought in the mid-1970s, and the nature of monetarism.

The existing literature also contains several gaps in the narrative of events. These can be alluded to briefly here, and dealt with in the remainder of the book. I have conducted an extensive range of interviews with some of the leading participants. I have been able to interview a wider range and greater number of individuals than earlier studies. The book therefore adds to existing knowledge of a number of events. These include the conduct of monetary policy in March 1976 which led to the fall in the value of sterling, the Labour Party leadership contest in April, the fiscal measures of July, Callaghan's speech to the Labour Party Conference in September and the activities of the Tony Crosland and Tony Benn groups in October-November.

The book contributes to understanding in four ways. Firstly, it reasserts the notion of the postwar consensus, which has been criticised extensively in the recent literature. Secondly, the book incorporates original material and perspectives in the discussion of events outlined above. The third contribution is in the discussion of economic liberalism, which is based on a much more detailed analysis of the relevant literature than previous studies on the IMF Crisis. Finally, the book challenges the commonly held assertion that the Labour Government embraced monetarism in 1976. Instead it is argued that the Government explicitly rejected monetarism, but did accept other aspects of economic liberalism including crowding-out and supply-side theories. Throughout, the argument is based on extensive interview notes.

Research Aims and Questions

In order to construct an intelligible narrative of events it is necessary to have clear research questions. Without such questions it is not possible to construct a narrative. This point has been made by W.R. Borg: "unless the student's attention is aimed at information relating to specific questions...(s)he has little chance of extracting a body of data from the available documents that can be synthesised to provide new knowledge or new understanding of the topic studied."[14]

My main aim is to assess the extent to which the IMF Crisis resulted in a decisive shift in the economic thinking of the Government. The central question therefore concerns a shift in British political economy, which can be expressed as:

> To what extent did the IMF Crisis lead to a change in the dominant approach to political economy after 1976?

In fact, this is a fairly imprecise question. This is so because it only leads to further questions, rather than to a clear answer. It is widely assumed that the dominant approach after 1945 was Keynesianism, and from 1979 was monetarist. However, both of these assumptions have been questioned, and so it is necessary to examine these issues.

The first point which has to be clarified is the extent to which there was a postwar consensus. The term 'postwar consensus' was used as a shorthand definition of British politics from 1945 to the 1970s. It was argued that there was a consensus between both of the major political parties over the welfare state, Keynesian demand-management and the mixed economy.[15] More recent literature, in contrast, has challenged the orthodoxy. The challenge is made on two distinct grounds. The first is that there was not a postwar consensus since the political parties held distinct ideologies, that they maintained the adversarial style of parliamentary debate and that there were significant policy differences between the parties.[16] The second is that the economic framework pursued after 1945 was not Keynesian, since there were significant differences between the theories developed by Keynes and the 'Keynesian' position adopted after 1945 and that the institutional conditions did not support Keynesian policies.[17] Two questions therefore emerge from this discussion:

1. Was there a postwar consensus, and if so, what did it include and what form did it take?
2. Was postwar economic policy 'Keynesian'?

Both of these questions are important since they cover the first part of the main aim of the book. Namely, that they clarify what went before the 1976 IMF Crisis, which is necessary if we are to ask what actually happened after 1976. Following the election of the first Thatcher administration in 1979, it is possible to clearly see a commitment to a new dominant policy paradigm.[18] The nature of economic policy paradigms is complex, and will be discussed below (Chapter 6). This is often shortened to the term 'monetarism'. Again, however, this shorthand term has been challenged. This challenge also takes two forms. The first is to argue that monetarism is but one part of a wider economic liberal approach, which consisted of monetarism and other such theories such as 'crowding out' and 'supply side' theory and was a general reaction against state intervention, and a general account of the role of the state and its relationship to the economic market. The second point goes beyond this. Some commentators have argued that it is possible to detect two distinct forms of monetarism. One is the broad political, often pejorative, form common to political debate at that time. The other is a strict, narrow sense of monetarism, which is a technical theory of the monetary causes of inflation. The technical theory is, according to these commentators, politically neutral between left and right.[19] The analysis leads to three further questions:

1. What is the relationship between monetarism and economic liberalism?
2. Did the Government adopt economic liberalism in 1976?
3. Did the Government adopt monetarism in 1976, and if so, did this necessarily mean a shift to the right?

These questions cover the latter half of the main aim of the thesis since they are all concerned with the outcomes of the IMF Crisis. The central research question can now be rewritten as:

> To what extent did the 1976 IMF Crisis result in a shift away from Keynesianism towards economic liberalism?

Methodology

The broad methodological framework that I follow here is hermeneutical. Hermeneutics is concerned with the recovery of the meaning and understanding of the historical actors' own beliefs and interpretations and the understanding of the context in which they operated. It is not possible to obtain a full understanding of an individuals' actions without reference to the values of that individual because they shape both the behaviour of an individual and the individual's self-interpretation of his/her behaviour. Hence a correct interpretation of human behaviour requires an understanding of beliefs. Alasdair MacIntyre argues that, "actions, as much as utterances, belong to the realm of statements, concepts and beliefs; and the relation of belief to action is not external and contingent, but internal and conceptual."[20] This is so for two reasons. The first is that an individual may act for a particular reason, different from another individual who performs the same act. In another context an individual may act differently in order to achieve the same objective. The second reason is that the beliefs of an individual will change over time. It is therefore necessary to obtain an understanding of the beliefs of an individual. Since beliefs exist as states of consciousness, it is necessary to understand the self-interpretation by an individual of their own values and conduct at the time of the events in which the researcher is interested, in this case the IMF Crisis. Hence, as MacIntyre goes on to say, "actions are uninterpretable and unidentifiable apart from beliefs."[21]

This process of interpretation is further complicated by the need to understand fully the context in which a decision is made. It is necessary to obtain an accurate interpretation of the beliefs of historical actors. In turn this requires an awareness of the range of possible descriptions available to historical actors.[22]

An actor can only describe his/her actions in terms of the range of descriptions available to them at the time in which they acted. This point has been emphasised by Stuart Hampshire: "reading history, I learn that to ascribe certain intentions, now familiar, to men living in earlier centuries would be to put words into their mouths and minds which could not possibly have occurred there."[23] It is possible to illustrate this point by drawing upon the now famous example of Martin Luther who nailed his critique of the practices of the Catholic Church to the church door. In so doing, Luther started the Reformation. However, it was not possible for Luther to describe his action in this way, whether or not he could perceive the full consequences of his action, because the term 'Reformation' was not one available to him at that time. It is clear that his action requires more than just the description of his physical movement. His action is therefore best described in terms of a reference to his beliefs since he was motivated by his opposition to the Catholic Church. Such a description has two elements. The first is that it makes reference to his beliefs which both shape his self-interpretation of the way he acts, and the interpretation of his actions by others. Secondly, it is a description which would have been comprehensible to Luther, as part of the range of meanings then available.[24] The difficulty in the understanding of context declines with more contemporary case studies since there have been fewer opportunities for the range of meanings to increase, but the difficulty remains. Moreover, there is a need to be aware of the possibility that the self-interpretation of the actor may be different in later accounts such as memoirs than they were at the time of the events in question. I return to the discussion of the evaluation of sources below.

Finally, there is a need to obtain an accurate understanding of the beliefs of actors in a given historical context because in any given context the actor will have to make choices.[25] The capacity to make choices is crucial since action is the way in which actors realise their beliefs. Moreover, the nature of the action taken allows others to understand the beliefs of the actor. This point has been argued by MacIntyre: "the explanation of a choice between alternatives is a matter of making clear what the agent's criterion was and why he made use of this criterion rather than another and to explain why the use of this criterion appears rational to those who invoke it."[26]

In holding to a hermeneutical framework, I do not intend to be critical of other methodological approaches. Instead, I wish to argue that a hermeneutical approach is the best approach to take to lead to a full understanding of the IMF Crisis. Moreover, other research strategies, such as the analysis of policy networks for example, would first require such a study as this one in order to understand what happened in the particular case study, to which networks analysis is applied. In addition to having validity in itself, therefore, the work is also relevant for further research. The attachment to hermeneutics has two implications for the thesis. The first is that the study has to be interpretative in the sense of arriving at an account of the common understandings of the actors. Secondly, it has to be narrative in the sense of constructing an intelligible story about the people with particular beliefs and interests. It is therefore historical in the sense that it discusses one particular event and the wider context in which it occurred. An historical account which follows the hermeneutical framework is capable of holding the status of greater validity. Validity requires a critical and comprehensive use of the range of sources available to the researcher. I therefore intend to spend some time discussing the various sources used in order to demonstrate the validity of such research techniques.

There are several types of source materials used in this book. Stated briefly these are books and articles, autobiographies, memoirs and diaries, biographies, parliamentary papers, public papers, the press, private papers and interviews. I wish to examine each briefly. The first is books and articles.[27] There is now an extensive list of published books and articles. These were discussed above, and form the main evidence base of the book.[28] They fall into three distinct sections. The first is the literature on the postwar consensus thesis. There are general histories of postwar British politics, together with more specific works on the thesis. The second is the literature on the IMF crisis, which takes the form of general histories of the 1970s and the Labour Party, together with the more specific work on the IMF Crisis. The final set of books and articles used are more theoretical texts used in the analytical chapter, which deal with the nature of economic policymaking and economic thought, including the texts of the leading theorists themselves.

The second set of sources used in the book is autobiographies, memoirs and diaries.[29] These are important since the outcomes of the IMF Crisis are, as I will show, closely related to the role of individuals. Nigel Hamilton writes that, "by excising all mention of individuals we run the risk of writing non-history."[30] Biographical research is closely related to hermeneutical understanding by emphasising the importance of the self-construction of individual interpretations and meanings.[31] This is particularly true in the case of the IMF Crisis. There exist a number of autobiographies, memoirs and diaries. Again, effective use of these sources depends on careful selection and evaluation. The most effective use is to compare and contrast different biographical accounts against each other and against other sources. Brian Roberts argues that the validity and reliability of biographical sources rests on the detailed use of sources within a given context.[32] This allows for a more balanced interpretation of the sources and removes the affects of bias within the sources. Diaries are very useful for obtaining an understanding of the contemporary perspective of an individual, but lack a sense of reflection.[33] The reverse is true of memoirs. Michael Kandiah also argues that the most effective memoirs are ones which are based on other sources and which are open and honest.[34] In this sense Denis Healey's account is rather poor because it avoids any statement of direct responsibility, limiting itself to the judgement of others.[35] Another factor is that a personal account may overemphasise the role of the author, as may be the case with Tony Benn's diaries.[36] Biographies have many of the same advantages and disadvantages. They are useful to gain an understanding of the character and motivation of the subject, but may tend to distort the relationship between the individual and the context in which they operated. Alternatively, they may be overly critical or praising. Kandiah therefore argues that biographies are best used as a source rather than a record.[37]

Parliamentary papers relevant to the IMF Crisis include legislative and financial records published in the form of Command Papers, and House of Commons and House of Lords debates published in 'Hansard'. All public papers are still subject to the thirty-year rule, and will not be released until 2007 at the earliest. This has implications for future research on the IMF Crisis, and I return to this point in the conclusion.

The press also adds to the study of the IMF Crisis, although its use is limited.[38] I have not cited the press directly in the references, except where there is a specific article or headline. This is because the more important articles have already been mentioned in the narrative sections of the books and articles used, and therefore I have tended to refer to the secondary literature rather than to the newspaper articles directly. Nevertheless, there are two useful purposes served by a reading of the relevant press. The first reason is that it provides a sense of 'contemporaniety' as Chris Kaul has mentioned: "it provides a window on to the past, a witness of the times, conveying something of the intangible 'atmosphere' which surrounds events."[39] Secondly, a number of articles, in the form of commentaries, are useful in examining the thinking surrounding the events. It therefore allows for an analysis of the opinions of the leading commentators.

Private papers are "the private documents accumulated by, belonging to, and subject to the dispositions of an individual person."[40] Private papers have the same benefits as diaries in that they allow the researcher to enter into the thinking of the historical actor. Papers are useful depending on the individual concerned. If the individual was an enthusiastic writer and maintained their records then the papers can be of considerable benefit. The collection can be of benefit in different ways depending on what they include. In the case of the Crosland papers, there is an extensive collection of correspondence from various individuals and a notebook containing Crosland's own reflections on the IMF Crisis.[41]

Norman Denzin argues that, "interviewing is not easy."[42] Anthony Seldon writes that elite interviewing has traditionally been viewed in a negative way by researchers.[43] Elite interviewing refers to semi-structured interviews with those who were involved in historical events, in this case the politicians, senior civil servants and others who were involved in the IMF Crisis.[44] As Lewis Dexter argues, elite interviewing tends to be semi-structured because the interviewee does not usually like to be subjected to a series of rapid-fire, short-answer questions.[45] Answers therefore tend to be qualitative rather than quantitative, unlike much of mass interview material. There are several problems associated with elite interviewing. The first is the unintentional distortion resulting from limitations to the memory of the interviewee in recalling events from many years earlier. This has been a problem with the interviews which I have conducted since the events were over twenty-five years ago. This is not an insurmountable problem, however, since it is possible to test the accuracy of the testimony of one interviewee against written documents and against other interviewees. The second problem is the intentional distortion caused by the bias or exaggeration of the interviewee. This has not tended to be a problem in my research since I knew the broad outlook of the interviewee, and they tended to be more open and honest. Other problems can include the representativeness of the sample, loaded questions, practical constraints and so forth.[46]

Seldon says that, "with all these snags of interviewing...one could be forgiven for wondering whether it would be better to dispense with it altogether. To do so, however, would be an error for it would deprive one of much insight and information, as well as sheer enjoyment."[47] Benefits of elite interviewing include the gathering of information not recorded, which I have attempted to do at particular points in the narrative. They allow the researcher to understand the perspective of the interviewee, to interpret documents and to gain a deeper understanding of the atmosphere of the event.[48] Moreover, they allow the researcher to interrogate the personal accounts of actors in their memoirs.[49] Finally, they allow the researcher to obtain types of information which cannot be obtained in other ways. This point is mentioned by Brian Harrison: "an interview can often convey types of information which of their very nature cannot be communicated in writing. The informant's gestures, innotation and manner will often be as important as the words he utters."[50] Seldon gives some practical tips which I have tried to follow.[51] Firstly, I planned the timing of the interviews so that they have occurred after I had researched the written documents. Secondly, I have ensured that my sample was representative by writing lists of those who were supporters of Crosland, Benn, Healey and so on, and then writing to each. I was fortunate to obtain written information from Callaghan and Healey who did not wish to be interviewed, while being able to interview many of the other leading figures. Seldon also writes that the interviewer needs to ask balanced questions, and to evaluate answers thoroughly.[52]

There is one final issue to be discussed as part of the methodology. This is the role of ideas in economic policy. Here I wish to draw on the work of Andrew Gamble.[53] Gamble distinguishes between three approaches to this issue. The first approach stresses the importance of broad ideology. Change follows from the climate of ideas. An example of this approach would be the rise of collectivism in the Twentieth Century, which replaced the individualism of the Nineteenth Century, and was itself replaced by the 'individualistic' New Right at the end of the Twentieth Century. Two processes were at work here. The first was the role of intellectuals in shaping ideas, and the second was the pressure for political parties to campaign on the basis of doctrine rather than sectional interests in mass democracy. The second broad approach is an interest-based approach. Public choice theory stresses that there is a competition between interest groups within the democratic process, which eventually undermines democracy. Marxists argue that the state exists to serve the interests of the dominant class. Although public choice and Marxist theories come from very different value positions, they reach the same conclusion: that the state is capable of being captured by sectional interests.

Gamble rejects both of these approaches arguing that they lead to oversimplification. Instead, there is a need to study the context within which decisions are made. Important contextual factors include institutions, personalities, current events, past decisions and so forth. Gamble therefore emphasises the importance of historical context: "the historical critique is extremely powerful and hard to refute. Casual generalisations and empty theorising are exposed by painstaking examination of the circumstances surrounding the making of decisions. A picture is built up which stresses the complexity of any actual historical situation and the multiple factors that are involved in it. Historical inquiry never furnishes the clear-cut historical examples that would be needed to test the theories of historical development."[54] However, as Gamble goes on, once empirical research is pushed beyond a certain point it becomes rather meaningless. It is necessary to provide an epistemological and methodological framework in order to construct meaning around historical events. This can be done through an ideas based approach which does not oversimplify historical events. Hence, the rationale for this particular study in which the detailed narrative of the IMF Crisis is placed within the broader shift of ideas in economic policy.

Structure of the Book

The book is divided into eight chapters including the introduction. Chapter 2 examines the nature of postwar British politics. It traces the origins of the postwar consensus thesis and outlines the critique of the thesis mounted by several writers over recent years. The chapter asks if it is possible to defend the postwar consensus thesis and also analyses the nature of economic policy after 1945.

Chapter 3 discusses three developments that are important in a fuller explanation of the IMF Crisis. These are the development of Labour's economic thought in opposition between 1970-74, the conduct of policy up until early 1976 and the changing role of the IMF.

Chapters 4 and 5 provide a detailed discussion of events from March 1976 when the pound began to fall on the foreign exchanges to the agreement of the IMF loan in January 1977. Chapter 4 discusses the monetary policy decisions in March which initiated the exchange rate crisis, the leadership contest, the April budget, the June stand-by credit facility, the July cuts and the September Labour Party Conference. Chapter 5 follows on from this by discussing the negotiations which occurred from October to December between the British, the Americans and the Germans[55], the British Government and the IMF, and within the Cabinet itself, and the granting of the loan in January 1977. I have attempted to provide a detailed narrative incorporating new information and perspectives.

Chapter 6 is a discussion of economic policy analysis. It begins by dealing with the complex nature of economic theories and how these relate to the making of policy. I then go on to discuss the relationship between Keynesianism and the Alternative Economic Strategy, the complex of ideas which constitutes collectively economic liberalism, and the spread of these ideas by 1976.

Chapter 7 relates these ideas to the conduct of policy in 1976 and Chapter 8 offers a summary of the main findings.

[1] For a shorter discussion see Hickson, K., 'Economic Thought' in Seldon, A. and Hickson, K., *New Labour, Old Labour: The Wilson and Callaghan Governments of 1974-79* (Routledge, London, 2004).

[2] 'The Cabinet In Crisis', Granada Television, February 1977. I am grateful to Brian Lapping, the producer of the programme, for sending me a free copy of the recording and for discussing the making of the programme with me.

[3] Fay, S., and Young, H., *The Day the £ Nearly Died*, Sunday Times, London, 1978

[4] Keegan, W., and Pennant-Rea, R., *Who Runs the Economy?*, (Maurice Temple Smith, London, 1979); Coates, D., *Labour In Power? A Study of the Labour Government 1974-79*, (Longman, London, 1980); Holmes, M., *The Labour Government 1974-79: Political Aims and Economic Reality*, (Macmillan, Basingstoke, 1985); Whitehead, P., *The Writing on the Wall*, (Michael Joseph, London, 1985); Whitehead, P., 'The Labour Governments 1974-79' in Hennessey, P., and Seldon, A., (Eds.), *Ruling Performance*, (Institute of Contemporary British History, London, 1987); and Browning, P., *The Treasury and Economic Policy* (Longman, London, 1986).

[5] Callaghan, J., *Time and Chance*, (Collins, London, 1987); Donoughue, B., *Prime Minister: The Conduct of Policy Under Harold Wilson and James Callaghan*, (Jonathan Cape, London, 1987); Healey, D., *The Time of My Life*, (Penguin, London, 1990, 2nd Edition); Dell, E., *A Hard Pounding: Politics and Economic Crisis 1974-76*, (Oxford University Press, Oxford, 1991); Benn, T., *Against the Tide: Diaries 1973-76*, (Arrow, London, 1989). The earlier works cited above were based on only two published accounts Pliatzky, L., *Getting and Spending: Public Expenditure, Employment and Inflation*, (Blackwell, Oxford, 1982), and Barnett, J., *Inside the Treasury*, (Andre Deutsch, London, 1982)

[6] Burk, K., et.al. 'The 1976 IMF Crisis', *Contemporary Record*, November 1989

[7] Burk, K., and Cairncross, A., *Goodbye, Great Britain: the 1976 IMF Crisis*, (Yale University Press, New Haven, 1992). See also, Burk, K., 'The Americans, the Germans and the British: the 1976 IMF Crisis', *Twentieth Century British History*, 5/3, 1994, pp.351-369

[8] Ludlam, S., 'The Gnomes of Washington: four myths of the 1976 IMF Crisis', *Political Studies*, XL, 1992, pp.713-727

[9] Bernstein, K., *The International Monetary Fund and Deficit Countries: The Case of Britain 1974-77*, (Unpublished PhD thesis, Stanford University, USA, 1983)

[10] Harmon, M.D., *The British Labour Government and the 1976 IMF Crisis*, (Macmillan, Basingstoke, 1997). See also, Harmon, M.D., 'The 1976 UK-IMF Crisis: the markets, the Americans and the IMF', *Contemporary British History*, 11/3, Autumn 1997, pp.1-17

11 De Vries, M.G., *The International Monetary Fund 1972-78: Cooperation on Trial*, 3 Vols. (International Monetary Fund, Washington D.C., 1985). See also Crawford, M., 'High Conditionality Lending: The UK', in Williamson, J., (Ed.), *IMF Conditionality*, (Institute of International Economics, Washington, 1983)

12 With the possible exception of Burk and Cairncross, but the issue does not receive as sustained focus as it does here.

13 See Hall, P., 'Policy Paradigms, Social Learning and the State: the case of economic policymaking in Britain', *Comparative Politics*, 25, April 1993, pp.275-296

14 Borg, W.R., *Educational Research: An Introduction*, (Longman, London, 1963), p.190

15 See Seldon, A., 'Consensus: A Debate Too Long?', *Parliamentary Affairs*, 1993, pp.501-514; Kavanagh, D., 'The Postwar Consensus', *Twentieth Century British History*, 3/2, 1992, pp.175-190 and Hickson, K., 'The Postwar Consensus Revisited', *Political Quarterly*, April 2004.

16 See Pimlott, B., 'The Myth of Consensus' in Smith, L.M., (Ed.), *The Making of Britain: Echoes of Greatness*, (London Weekend Television, London, 1988)

17 See Hutton, W., *The Revolution that Never Was: An Assessment of Keynesian Economics*, (Vintage, London, 2001, 3rd Edition)

18 See Hall, 'Policy Paradigms, Social Learning and the State'

19 See Hoover, K., and Plant, R., *Conservative Capitalism in Britain and the United States: A Critical Appraisal*, (Routledge, London, 1989)

20 MacIntyre, A., 'A Mistake About Causality in Social Science' in Laslett, P., and Runciman, W.G., *Philosophy, Politics and Society*, 2nd Series, (Blackwell, Oxford, 1972), pp.48-70; p.52

21 Ibid., p.70

22 Ibid., pp.58-60

23 Quoted in MacIntyre, p.60

24 See Plant, R., *Modern Political Thought*, (Blackwell, Oxford, 1991), pp.177-181

25 MacIntyre, pp.60-63

26 Ibid., p.61

27 Kandiah, M.D., 'Books and Journals', in Brivati, B., Buxton, J., and Seldon, A., (Eds.), *The Contemporary History Handbook*, (Manchester University Press, Manchester, 1996), pp.311-322

28 The writing of historical texts can be seen in terms of adding layers onto the existing literature. In this sense the thesis adds to the existing literature

29 Kandiah, pp.317-320

30 Hamilton, N., 'The Role of Biography', in Brivati et.al., p.167

31 See Roberts, B., *Biographical Research*, (Open University Press, Buckingham, 2002), pp.6-8

[32] Ibid., pp.38-39

[33] Ibid., p.68

[34] Kandiah, p.317

[35] See Healey

[36] See Benn

[37] Kandiah, p.319

[38] Kaul, C., 'The Press', in Brivati et.al., pp.298-310

[39] Ibid., p.299

[40] Quoted in Raspin, A., 'Private Papers', in Seldon (Ed.), p.89

[41] The Crosland papers are deposited in the BLPES, London

[42] Denzin, N.K., 'The Sociological Interview' in Denzin, N.K., *Sociological Methods: A Sourcebook*, (Aldine, Chicago, 1970), p.186

[43] Seldon, A., 'Elite Interviews', in Brivati, et.al. (1996) pp.353-365

[44] See Dexter, L.A., *Elite and Specialised Interviewing*, (Northwestern University Press, Evanston, 1970), pp.5-11, for a fuller definition of the elite interview.

[45] Ibid., p.56

[46] Seldon (1996) pp.355-358

[47] Ibid., p.358

[48] Ibid., pp.358-359, Stedward, G., 'On The Record: An Introduction to Interviewing', in Burnham, P., (Ed.), *Surviving the Research Process in Politics*, (Pinter, London, 1987), pp.151-165; Seldon, A., and Pappworth, J., *By Word of Mouth: 'Elite' Oral History*, (Methuen, London, 1983), pp.36-52

[49] Seldon and Pappworth p.14

[50] Quoted in Seldon and Pappworth p.15

[51] Seldon (1996) pp.359-363.   See also Stedward, pp.152-159, and Seldon and Pappworth pp.55-88

[52] See Dexter for a more detailed discussion of elite interviewing

[53] Gamble, A., 'Ideas and Interests in British Economic Policy', *Contemporary British History*, Summer 1996, 10/2, pp.1-21

[54] Ibid., pp15-16

[55] I use the term 'Germany' as a more convenient alternative to the correct term: 'West Germany'

CHAPTER 2

THE POSTWAR CONSENSUS

Introduction

The terms 'postwar consensus' and 'social democratic consensus' have been widely used as shorthand terms to cover the period from the election of the Attlee Government in 1945 to the election of the first Thatcher Government in 1979. In a similar way, the term 'Keynesian economics' has been used to describe the conduct of economic policy over the same period. In more recent literature, however, the terms 'postwar consensus' and 'Keynesian consensus' have been criticised and in some cases even rejected. The central objective of this chapter is therefore to outline the arguments made by those on both sides of the debate, and to ask if it is still possible to talk in terms of a postwar consensus incorporating a shared commitment to Keynesian economics. This is necessary since we need to understand the dominant political values and frameworks prior to 1976 in order to understand exactly what, if anything, changed with the IMF Crisis. The first section traces the origins of the postwar consensus thesis, and is then subjected to a critique. I then discuss what, if anything, can be salvaged from that critique. The final section examines postwar economic policy. The debates over Keynesianism and the postwar consensus are broadly similar, but for purposes of clarity, I intend to examine each separately.

The Origins of the Postwar Consensus Thesis

By common consent the postwar consensus thesis has only recently been developed. The core text is suggested to have been Paul Addison's 1975 book *The Road to 1945*.[1] Several critics of the postwar consensus thesis maintain this view. For example, Peter Kerr, in a recent publication, emphasises this point, which was also made by earlier writers.[2] For reasons that I will set out below, this is an important part of the postwar consensus thesis, which critics regard as a weakness. For other reasons, I think that this view is incorrect. However, before discussing these issues at greater length, it is first necessary to summarise Addison's argument and point to some possible revisions. We are then in a position to outline the key arguments of the consensus thesis.

Addison argues that wartime experience allowed for the construction of a postwar settlement. According to Addison, the war encouraged a greater sense of community and cooperation which led to the development of new policies: "the national unity of the war years gave rise to a new consensus at the top, which dominated Britain long after the last bomb had fallen."[3] This was the result of two factors. The first was the fostering of a greater sense of community within society. A number of wartime experiences produced this sentiment, according to Addison. Class privileges for the wealthy were eroded due to the impact of rationing. Moreover, the practice of evacuations encouraged a closer relationship between the urban and rural areas as children moved from the major cities to the shires. Bombing of urban areas affected middle-class and working-class areas. Addison maintains that the plight of the poor was made aware to the middle-classes so that there was a greater sense of duty and obligation to improve social welfare. Similarly, there would be an obvious need for postwar reconstruction, especially with regards to urban planning, transport and housing.[4]

The second factor was the creation of the wartime coalition in 1940. The resignation of Neville Chamberlain led to the appointment of Winston Churchill as Prime Minister. Churchill's primary concern was the conduct of the war. He therefore wished to avoid domestic policy concerns and parliamentary conflict. Churchill therefore supported the creation of a wartime coalition government. Within the Coalition, many of the domestic posts went to Labour politicians.[5] Addison therefore argues that Labour was given significant power over domestic policy, and undermined Conservative opposition to welfare reform: "the fact was that Churchill had given Labour very great power on the home front while simultaneously beheading the Conservative Party."[6]

Moreover, the civil service was transformed by wartime experience. Traditional attitudes, sympathetic to minimal welfare policy and orthodox economic policy, were transformed by the incorporation of outside advisors such as John Maynard Keynes and William Beveridge.[7]

According to Addison there was therefore widespread agreement on policy prior to the General Election of 1945, resulting from a new social and political consensus: "by the spring of 1945 a new and wide-ranging prospectus of peacetime development was at an advanced stage of preparation... All three parties went to the polls in 1945 committed to principles of social and economic reconstruction which their leaders had endorsed as members of the coalition."[8] This agreement then has implications for our understanding of the 1945-51 Labour Governments. Rather than seeing the Attlee Government as a radical departure in policy, it is instead possible to see it as merely implementing policies already agreed upon in the coalition. Hence Addison goes on: "the Attlee Governments of 1945-51 completed and consolidated the work of the Coalition by establishing a peacetime economy and the expanded welfare state envisaged by Beveridge."[9]

Arguably, however, Addison takes his thesis too far here. Others argue that the wartime Coalition was internally divided and the Conservatives acted as a barrier to the types of policies which Addison sees emerging from it. In his own study of the wartime Coalition, Kevin Jefferys argues that, "the emergence of a consensus between the parties during the war has...been overstated. Coalition government certainly blurred, but could not ultimately conceal, the deep-seated differences which continued to exist between the Conservative and Labour parties over welfare reform."[10] Churchill himself remained critical of such policies, including the Beveridge Report. Indeed, it was his opposition to the Beveridge proposals that led to the creation of the Tory Reform Committee in 1943.[11] According to W.H. Greenleaf, the Tory Reform Committee wished the Conservative Party leadership to embrace the wartime changes more wholeheartedly.[12] An important figure in the Tory Reform Committee was R.A. Butler who pushed forward some of the most progressive measures of the Coalition, including the 1944 White Paper on Education advocating a major expansion in state schools. However, other leading Conservatives were openly hostile to reform, including the Chancellor of the Exchequer, Sir John Anderson, who opposed Keynesian demand-management and wage protection; and the Health Minister, Henry Willinck, who advocated the cause of private health insurance. Hence, the Conservative Party was internally divided over domestic policy during the wartime Coalition, with Churchill himself remaining largely sceptical.

The 1945 General Election therefore emerges as a more likely starting-point in any discussion of consensus. The outcome of the election was a surprise. Churchill was widely expected to win given that he had been a highly popular war leader. Moreover, the Labour Party accepted the domestic policy proposals of the Coalition as the best that could be attained in the economic circumstances of the time, and given the expected outcome. The fact that it was the Labour Party which won that election adds to the case against Addison's thesis, for if the Conservative Party was committed to reform as he suggests then it is difficult to see why they lost. The fact the Conservative Party lost was because they were not committed to reform, or if they were then the electorate did not trust them to implement the measures. Roger Eatwell argues that the outcome was a reaction against the Conservative Party.[13] The Conservatives were too closely associated with pre-war society, characterised by mass unemployment and poverty. The reluctance of the Party to endorse the Coalition proposals with much enthusiasm and Churchill's reactionary stance during the 1945 General Election campaign further undermined public confidence. Hence, Eatwell concludes that, "people seem to have voted against the Tories as much as for Labour, to have rejected the values of the Party identified with mass unemployment and poverty...This was hardly a reforming consensus; a rejecting consensus might be more apposite."[14] This point raises a question over the extent to which the consensus was determined by the electorate or by the political elites, to which I return later.

The Labour Governments of 1945-51 therefore emerge as crucial in determining the nature of the postwar consensus, as Jefferys contends: "the precise lines upon which reform might proceed were thus left unclear by the coalition, and the manner in which social policy was to develop would owe much to the character of the postwar government."[15] There are two reasons for this. The first is that the Attlee Governments introduced the major reforms including the creation of the National Health Service, nationalisation of key industries, extension of welfare payments and the initial phase of decolonisation. The reforms form the basis of the alleged 'consensus'. Moreover, they often emerged from sources other than the Coalition. For example, Aneurin Bevan created the National Health Service on a plan based more on the proposal by critics of the Coalition proposals.

Secondly, the 1945 General Election defeat was significant for the Conservative Party. It was the shock and scale of defeat which led the Conservatives to accept reform, as Jefferys states: "the profound shock of Labour's overwhelming victory was, in short, to be of greater importance than the experience of war in shifting the Conservative Party towards a fundamental reassessment of its domestic policy."[16] The significant figure was again R.A. Butler, who became Party Chairman in 1945. It was Butler who established the committee that produced the *Industrial Charter* in 1947[17], which accepted many of the economic reforms introduced by the Attlee administration. He was also a key figure in the publication of the 1949 document *The Right Road for Britain*[18], which formed the basis of the 1950 and 1951 General Election manifestos. Butler also established the Research Department, which published pamphlets often regarded as seminal texts in the advocacy of the 'New Conservatism'. These include *The Conservative Faith in the Modern Age* by David Clarke[19] and *The Case for Conservatism* by Quintin Hogg.[20] I wish to discuss the philosophical nature of the 'New Conservatism' later. The significant point here is that, as John Ramsden argues, the Conservative Party sought to remodel itself over the period, in order to win the next general election.[21] In fact it took two attempts, but the degree of conversion can be seen in the essential continuity in public policy after 1951.

The period from 1951 to the 1970s is therefore interpreted, by some, as a period of consensus in which there was widespread continuity in policy. Dennis Kavanagh and Peter Morris argue: "in this period it is continuity rather than discontinuity that characterises the content of significant areas of public policy."[22] Consensus is said to exist in four broad areas.[23] The first broad area was economic policy. I intend to discuss this aspect in greater detail below. However, it is possible to state the consensus over economic policy briefly at this stage.   The consensus is said to include Keynesian demand management, the mixed economy including public ownership of certain key industries, and an active role for trades unions in policymaking.

The second broad area of agreement was in social policy. Both parties accepted the need for the welfare state.   The Labour Government created the National Health Service in 1946, and despite the opposition of the Conservative Party it was retained after 1951.   The National Insurance Act of 1946 introduced universal welfare payments for sickness, invalidity, unemployment and retirement.   Again, the Conservatives attacked this piece of legislation on the grounds that means-testing would have been more effective in targeting assistance to the most needy.   However, there was no shift towards means-testing after 1951.   Means-testing was associated closely with pre-war poverty, and the Conservative Party was keen to distance itself from this association.   Both parties were committed to extensive house building, although the Conservative Party was more willing to leave this to the private sector.

The other areas of agreement can be mentioned briefly.   The first was the agreement over constitutional issues.   For most of the period of consensus, issues of Scottish and Welsh nationalism were largely unimportant.   Indeed, up until the 1959 General Election, the Conservative Party had the largest number of seats in Scotland.   Only from the mid-1960s did constitutional matters in Scotland and Wales become significant.   Direct involvement in Northern Ireland was kept to a minimum until the civil rights protests of the late 1960s. Finally, there was a broad acceptance of the constitution, with little talk of reform.   The monarchy existed with very little criticism, the House of Commons was not affected by calls for constitutional reform, and the House of Lords was subject to piecemeal reform from both of the major parties.   The final area was that of foreign policy.   The economic costs of war made dependence on the United States inevitable.   Decolonisation was a gradual process conducted by both parties from 1947. Although some of the former colonies decided to sever links with Britain completely, most joined the Commonwealth.   With the exception of the period from 1955-63 during the leadership of Hugh Gaitskell, the Labour Party officially remained committed to European integration, although both parties did contain a substantial number of euro-sceptic MPs throughout the period. More significantly, both parties when in government pursued close European integration. Britain was a founder-member of the European Free Trade Area (EFTA) from 1960 and, following attempts by both parties, joined the European Economic Community in 1973. These three spheres of influence - North America, Europe and the Commonwealth - were often conflicting areas of interest, but neither party moved decisively away from, or towards, one of these three spheres when in government.

Critique of the Postwar Consensus Thesis

Essentially, there are two broad critiques of the postwar consensus. The first accepts that there was a consensus, but that consensus policies were themselves misguided. This critique takes the form of a rejection of the philosophical ideas underpinning public policy at this time. It is therefore an ideological critique, taking the form of the promotion of an alternative philosophy. The second is a critique of the 'postwar consensus' in itself, arguing that the term is an inaccurate one for describing the postwar period. This critique is therefore historical. I intend to focus on the second critique, but for reasons that will be set out below the nature of the first critique is significant to those who argue that there was not a 'postwar consensus'. The review begins by utilising the first critique.

There are three broad ideological critiques of the postwar consensus. The first is made by commentators on the right of the political spectrum. Writing in the 1970s, Keith Joseph argued that there was a 'ratchet' effect in postwar British politics.[24] Each Labour government instituted further socialist measures when elected. The intervening Conservative governments accepted these measures with the effect that by the 1970s both Labour and Conservative governments had made Britain much more 'socialist' than it was in the 1940s. There was therefore a need to break away from the ratchet effect by institutionalising neo-liberal reforms to reverse much of what had been introduced since 1945. More recently Corelli Barnett has argued that a liberal-minded elite had come to dominate policymaking in World War Two.[25] This included religious leaders such as Archbishop William Temple, middle-class intellectuals such as Beveridge, and the Labour and Liberal parties. Instead of planning for postwar economic reconstruction based on industrial efficiency, the elite planned for a 'New Jerusalem' of welfare and community. Hence from the 1940s, expenditure on welfare in Britain was higher than elsewhere, which had the effect of undermining competitiveness. Growth in Britain was much lower than elsewhere. Barnett argues that this was due to the high levels of welfare provision. Relative decline could only be reduced, according to Barnett, if welfare spending was cut and if measures to increase labour market flexibility and to encourage private sector investment were introduced. This argument was influential in the thinking of the right in Britain, but has been criticised extensively in academic circles.[26]

Commentators on the left also argue that there was a consensus. Tony Benn maintains that, "consensus politics was institutionalised during the wartime coalition... A centre party has in effect been in power for most of the time since the war...for twenty-eight years, the country has been governed by a body of people who shared a great deal of agreed doctrine."[27] Similarly, Ralph Miliband argues that since the parties agreed on many aspects of policy, electoral choices were severely limited. The consensus can be seen as an attempt by the left to manage capitalism more equitably, rather than trying to replace it with a socialist alternative. Ultimately, however, the attempt to 'manage' capitalism failed as the underlying weaknesses of the British economy, and with it the inequities of the capitalist system, re-emerged in the 1970s. What was needed therefore was a more radical socialist transformation.[28]

A novel approach is offered by David Marquand.[29] Rather than advocating a shift to the right or the left as did the various authors mentioned above, Marquand argued for a centrist position, albeit one different from the consensus. There were two underlying weaknesses in the postwar consensus. The first was that politicians had failed to outline an adequate ethical basis for their policies and had therefore been in a weak position when challenged by critics from the left and the right. Secondly, there had been a failure in economic policy, particularly the inability to reverse relative economic decline and the inability to reverse the 'stagflation' of the early-1970s.

What was required, according to Marquand, was a new form of social democracy with different policies and an underlying moral philosophy.

This is not the place to evaluate these various arguments. However, two points stand out for comment. The first is that all commentators were agreed that there was a 'consensus' in postwar British politics. That there was such a consensus was never questioned, but it was also never adequately explained. The second point is that all of the commentators were advocating a certain ideological position, be it 'New Right', 'New Left' or 'New Social Democracy'. All of the commentators believed that their positions were 'new', a break from the past, a break from the politics of 'consensus'. There was a clear ideological purpose behind talk of consensus politics, rather than an academic analysis of the particular historical period. In a similar vein, traditional 'One Nation' Conservatives used the term 'consensus' to look back nostalgically on an earlier, pre-Thatcher, period. Hence, Peter Kerr argues that, "we can infer that the postwar consensus thesis has not essentially been directed towards describing bipartisan convergence in the period after the war. Instead, it is in essence, an heuristic framework designed to highlight specific contrasts between Thatcherism and its historical antecedents."[30] So, for example, in his first discussion of consensus politics, Kavanagh argues that there was a consensus, but uses the term to distinguish the characteristics of Thatcherism.[31] Discussion of the postwar consensus thesis tends to concentrate more upon the 1980s than in the alleged period under discussion. In a similar way, Duncan Fraser emphasises the ideological motivations of the postwar consensus theorists: "the accusation of being politically motivated could, in fact, be levelled at all protagonists in the debate... No protagonist in the debate can be considered to be above the political affray."[32]

Until the late 1980s, there was widespread agreement among commentators that there was a postwar consensus. Writing in 1988, Nicholas Deakin says: "the extent to which the existence of such a consensus is currently taken as given is illustrated by the way in which discussion of new departures on policy are customarily categorised as attempts either to sustain it, overthrow it or return to it. Indeed, the usage is so automatic that only rarely is the basic notion that sustains it submitted to serious examination."[33]   More recent scholarship has tended to reject the notion of 'consensus' so that Deakin's comment can be reversed; it is now 'fashionable' to be on the side of the sceptics.[34]   The seminal text here is an article written by Ben Pimlott in 1988.[35]   Pimlott argues that the use of the term 'consensus' is misguided.   The term 'consensus' is defined literally as "a state of natural harmony."[36]   This did not exist during the period under scrutiny, nor indeed at any other. Politics is necessarily controversial, and the adversarial style of politics encouraged by the British parliamentary system makes consensus impossible.   All of the major reforms which are regarded as central parts of the consensus were in fact introduced only after considerable debate between the parties. This debate highlighted fundamental differences between the parties at an ideological level.   The level of debate was easily observable at the time, but tended to be underestimated by the consensus theorists: "it is easy to take for granted hard-won reforms, and to forget how bitterly they were contested at the time...Yet the reality of radical reform is that it has seldom been won without a fight."[37]   The divisions between the two parties at both the levels of policy and ideology can be seen in the bitterness of general election campaigns and in parliamentary debate.   Moreover, the electorate was divided with high class and partisan alignment, with only very few votes going to the Liberal Party.   If the consensus was around the centre ground then why, Pimlott asks, did the Liberal Party only record a low vote.[38]   The nature of electoral activity is necessarily adversarial as Deakin notes: "competition for office ensured that it was the differences, not the similarities, between the policies of the two major political parties that their leaders chose to stress when presenting them to the electorate."[39]

The adversarial nature of politics has been emphasised by Samuel Finer, who argued that British politics since 1945 has been marked by instability.[40]   The electoral system ensures majority government.   Once a party is elected it can implement its own policies with considerable ease.   The wish to win the next election ensures that the opposition will criticise the current government and offer alternative policies.   Finer argues that the system is an adversary one: "briefly defined, the adversary system is a stand-up fight between two adversaries for the favours of on-lookers."[41]   Finer advocated a reform of the electoral system to a form of proportional representation in order to ensure greater continuity and consensus. The relevance of Finer's argument for this discussion is that, as far as he is concerned, postwar British politics was far from consensual.

A different criticism of consensus is made by James Marlow.[42] Arguing from a more postmodernist perspective, Marlow maintains that there was not a postwar consensus. Those involved in the political process at the time were not aware that they were operating within a consensual framework, and the term 'consensus' was never used at the time. Instead, 'consensus' is an intertextual concept. That is to say that the term was first used in a secondary source, Addison's book *The Road to 1945*, and has subsequently been used in other works. However, those who seek to argue that there was a consensus can only defend their argument by citing other secondary sources; there is no independent evidence to use to support the thesis from the time of the alleged consensus. The postwar consensus therefore only exists in the pages of secondary texts.[43] This has a further implication, as Marlow makes clear: "whilst the idea of a postwar consensus is widely accepted it is not spelt out clearly and unambiguously what it amounted to."[44] A satisfactory conception of consensus would therefore need to find answers to several key questions: when did it begin, when did it end, what were the causes, what did it include and what evidence is there to support the thesis? As to the questions of timing, the origins of the postwar consensus have already been discussed and the contribution of the 1976 IMF Crisis in its collapse will be discussed in the following chapters. There is, however, much to be said on the other points.

There has therefore been a broad critique of the postwar consensus thesis, which challenges its very existence. Indeed, it has been asserted that it is best to reject the notion of consensus altogether, as Kerr maintains: "the only way to take the present debate forward is to move beyond it entirely and to redirect our focus away from the question of consensus."[45] Instead, Kerr argues that a closer examination of the postwar period demonstrates the importance of conflict in the conduct of public policy, with most of the major developments occurring out of disagreement rather than consensus.

Defending the Postwar Consensus Thesis

Taken together, the historical critique of the postwar consensus thesis is a strong one. However, it is possible to defend the notion of a postwar consensus. What the anti-consensus theorists have done is to highlight important weaknesses in the consensus literature. However, as Richard Heffernan writes, the critique points to the "need for the concept to be reformulated rather than abandoned."[46] The first problem concerns the definition of 'consensus'. Marlow contends that, "for such a taken-for-granted notion, it is...ill defined, poorly explicated and inadequately analysed."[47] This is a fair comment. However, Kavanagh provides us with a much clearer definition.[48] Kavanagh distinguishes between four possible definitions of consensus. The first applies to ends, that is to a broad agreement in policy. Secondly, that there was a consensual style of politics: agreement was reached after deliberation and compromise. Thirdly, that there was an agreement on what to exclude from the policy-making arena: a negative consensus. Finally, that there was a relative consensus: that the period under scrutiny was marked by a greater degree of agreement and continuity in policy than what went before.

Kavanagh argues that the postwar consensus was largely of the first form. Pimlott rejected the postwar consensus thesis because he argued that the correct meaning of 'consensus' relates to the style of politics. In fact, no advocate of the postwar consensus thesis has argued this point. As Heffernan points out, Pimlott did in fact construct a 'straw man' here.[49] For that reason, Pimlott's polemic fails to make an impact against the postwar consensus thesis. Debate is still possible within a consensual system for reasons I will establish below. Kavanagh also rejects the third conception of consensus, which is the one often made by the critics of postwar policy from the left and right of the political spectrum. This conception fails to allow for a positive commitment to policies on the broad centre. Instead, the political centre ground is interpreted as a position which has no distinct ideological basis of its own. Finally, Kavanagh rejects the fourth definition as inadequate. Instead, it only means that there was less conflict than before or after. A more positive conception of consensus is required. But what exactly did agreement on 'ends' constitute: was it at the level of policy or did it encourage ideological convergence? If ideologies remained distinct, what other forces shaped policy in this period?

The postwar consensus relates to the period from 1945 to the late 1970s, during which time there was a broad continuity of policy. Consensus therefore refers to this agreement and continuity in policy, as Anthony Seldon argues: "I believe that it is meaningful to talk about a postwar consensus from the 1940s to the late 1970s...in many spheres of policy. By consensus is meant a broad parameter of agreement on many key areas of policy between the leaderships of both main parties when they were in office."[50] In the same way, Kavanagh and Morris argue: "it is more appropriate to think of it as a broad set of parameters which bounded the set of policy options regarded by senior politicians and civil servants as administratively practicable, economically affordable and politically acceptable."[51]

Hence, both Kavanagh and Seldon see consensus as agreement between the party leaders and others who form the political elite. Yet what did the agreement cover? It would be going too far, I think, to argue that the leaderships of the Conservative and Labour parties were in agreement over political values, yet there was a noticeable continuity in broad areas of policy. We therefore reach a peculiar position in that there is agreement over policy, but not values. A possible explanation of this can be to use a distinction between 'means' and 'ends'. Such a distinction was made by social democratic revisionists in the Labour Party in the 1950s in an attempt to move the Party away from its central commitment to public ownership.[52] There has been little academic discussion of the means-ends distinction until recently. Raymond Plant has refocused attention on to the means-ends distinction in a recent analysis of the Blair Administration's approach to equality.[53] Tony Crosland made two points on the means-ends distinction. The first states that it is not possible to change a means – that is a policy – without changing the ends – or values – to which that policy is directed, unless an alternative means is formulated. This point is less relevant to our discussion. The second point made by Crosland is that the same means can be reached from different ends. Put another way the same policy can be defended in different ways to support contrasting values. A brief discussion of the dominant values of the Conservative and Labour parties at this time can clarify these rather abstract arguments.

It has already been mentioned that the scale of the electoral defeat in 1945 forced the Conservative Party to rethink its broad policy position. The Conservative Party had been clearly associated with free-market economic policy in the 1930s, with its concomitant widespread unemployment, poverty and inequality. However, by the time of Churchill's return to government in 1951, the Conservative Party had moved to a more collectivist position, accepting the welfare state, mixed economy and demand-management policies. The extent of this conversion can be seen by the degree of continuity in policy after 1951.[54] On the major nationalisations, to which the Conservative Party was strongly opposed in 1945, only iron and steel was privatised. However, this one act was significant, for it pointed to a deeper division between the Conservative and Labour parties. The shift in attitude towards nationalisation within the Conservative Party can be detected in a number of policy statements over the course of the period from 1945-51. For example the *Industrial Charter* of 1947 argued that there was a need to restore industrial efficiency and competitiveness in the postwar period, and that the public sector had a legitimate role to play in this including nationalisation.[55] Similarly, Leo Amery emphasised the importance of economic efficiency: "Conservatism is not concerned with capital and labour in the abstract, but with British industry as it is today, with improving its internal relations and increasing its productive efficiency."[56]

This is not to argue that the Conservative Party rejected its political values at this time. Rather that it moved from a more 'libertarian' mode of thought towards a more 'collectivist' framework. Greenleaf has demonstrated convincingly that conservatism has had both a libertarian and a collectivist strand since at least the early nineteenth century.[57] The significant point is that the collectivist strand was in the ascendancy in this period in the guise of the 'new' Conservatism of the Tory Reform Committee, most clearly personified by R.A. Butler.[58] Hence, new policies, or rather the broad acceptance of the legislation of the Attlee administration, were defended by reference to traditional Conservative values. So, for example, the welfare state was defended in terms of traditional Conservative values such as obligation or duty, humanitarian concern for the poor and the preservation of social order.

In contrast, the Labour Party was committed to social justice and equality. It can be argued that the Labour Government of 1945-51 nationalised key industries such as coal, railways and so forth for reasons of economic efficiency. However, the Labour Party's commitment to nationalisation went beyond that of the Conservative Party, as can be seen by the renationalisation of iron and steel by the 1964-70 Labour Government and by the debate over shipbuilding in the 1970s. Moreover, the Labour Government of 1945-51 created the National Health Service, raised social security payments and extended education provision in the pursuit of social justice and equality. In contrast, the Conservative Party rejected the notion of equality, as David Clarke wrote in his 1947 pamphlet *The Conservative Faith in the Modern Age*: "inequality of natural ability results in class. Some men will always rise superior to others. In a group of men pursuing the common purpose, whether it be a nation or a family, a factory or a farm, there must be those who exercise authority and those who obey."[59]

It is possible to argue for a notion of consensus as broad continuity of policy, therefore, while allowing for dissent over the underlying values. Such an interpretation allows for a confrontational style of politics since debate can occur for one of two reasons. The first is that the political parties will tend to emphasise the differences between themselves and their opponents in order to compete for votes. Secondly, because the parties still maintain different philosophical values. It is therefore incorrect to refer to the postwar consensus as being 'social democratic' since only the Labour Party was committed to social democracy. 'One Nation' Conservatism remained ideologically distinct. Hence, Deakin argues that it would be misguided to use the term 'social democratic' to "describe Conservative politicians who would themselves have neither recognised or accepted it."[60] The means-ends distinction can explain both policy continuity and policy reversals. Political parties may reject policies, or means, which are not a part of their values, or ends. Hence the initial nationalisation of iron and steel, followed by privatisation, followed by renationalisation. It can also be used to explain the initial controversy in the 1960s over comprehensive education since the Labour Party argued in favour on the grounds of social justice and greater equality, whereas the Conservative Party did not, at least initially, accept education reform as it was not a part of their values.

A similar interpretation has been offered by Heffernan, who argues that consensus can be defined as a broad position on the ideological spectrum.[61]   Senior politicians ruled out both libertarian right-wing positions and more radical left-wing positions, which they regarded as impractical and electorally unpopular.   Debate between the Conservative and Labour parties was limited to the 'middle ground' in British politics. However, rather than seeing the 'middle ground' as a fixed ideological position in British politics, it is better to regard it as the middle point between the current position of the two major parties.   The 'middle ground' is therefore distinct from the 'centre ground'.   In this sense, the 'middle ground' can itself shift as both parties move along the ideological spectrum in a leftward or rightward direction. The 'middle ground' during the postwar consensus was based around the welfare state and the mixed economy. The Labour and Conservative parties maintain their distinct values, but felt constrained by a set of factors to maintain a position close to the 'middle ground'. The Labour Party will be to the left of the 'middle ground' because of its own values, and the Conservative Party will be to the right.   The 'middle ground' is therefore an accommodation between the most right-wing position taken by the Labour Party, and the most left-wing position taken by the Conservative Party.   A number of factors have been discussed, which had the effect of limiting the range of options available to politicians.

Firstly, the civil service has been cited as a cause of policy continuity. After the upheaval of the Second World War, the civil service was permeated with Keynesian and welfarist ideas, which were then institutionalised.   The civil service has been criticised by commentators on the left and right of the political spectrum for failing to develop new and alternative policies. On the left Brian Sedgemore argues that, "the civil service machine was, as I saw it then, rather like a huge steamroller which was moving out of control down a gentle incline.   Although there was nothing malicious in its movement it crushed everything that came in its unstoppable way."[62] Sedgemore, who had been an assistant to Tony Benn in government, goes on to say that any attempt to introduce constitutional reform to achieve more open government was stopped due to the culture of secrecy. Similarly commentators on the right argued that the civil service had an interest in increasing the role of the public sector as this would increase their power. The only way to introduce 'New Right' policies was to reform the civil service, as John Hoskyns argues: "after three years working in Whitehall I am now convinced that the people and the organisation are indeed wrong."[63]   At the very least the civil service consolidated the policies agreed between the two major parties.

Secondly, all governments face a number of domestic constraints in addition to the activities of the civil service. A government inherits an array of legislative measures and spending commitments to which its own contribution is only a small part of the whole.   According to Richard Rose, governments face financial constraints and limited legislative time, much of which is taken up with uncontroversial, routine administrative measures.   The tendency is towards broad continuity rather than change despite the apparent adversarial nature of politics emphasised by Finer.[64]   In addition, certain policies are adopted due to structural constraints, so that, as Kerr argues, the mixed economy and greater extent of state planning were inevitable in the aftermath of war.[65]   Moreover, the existence of previous legislation places limits on the range of options deemed practicable to present government; what can be termed 'path dependency'.

Thirdly, governments face a number of international constraints in addition to the domestic pressures mentioned above.   The Bretton Woods system of fixed exchange rates stabilised international finance, so that there was a lack of external shocks to the system.   Economic policy could therefore continue with little external pressure.   Moreover, many countries adopted a similar economic and welfare strategy. Harriet Jones argues that this was due to the international context of the Cold War, since there was a common enemy and a need to unite around a common purpose. The democratic left was keen to emphasise its differences from Communism, and the right wished to resolve working-class grievances within the capitalist system.[66]   Hence, Jones concludes that, "the collectivist values associated with the war economy, combined with the emergence of the Cold War, created a domestic climate in the postwar period which made the resolution of class conflict within a capitalist framework an overriding imperative of elite policy formulation."[67]

Finally, the elite's conception of voter preferences tended to encourage consensus. Parties seek to win elections and therefore seek to maximise their vote. During the period of consensus, the median voter corresponded to the mixed economy-welfare state position. Fraser argues that this was the key to explaining the consensus: "the electorate was...the guiding light in the consensus. For the parties it was not a case of what should be done, but of how it should be done."[68] The structure of the electorate explains why there was a consensus, since the elites were limited to the advocacy of certain policies which were deemed to be electorally viable. The ability of the Conservative and Labour parties to appeal to the median voter explains why the Liberal Party was marginalized in the postwar period. Between 1945-70, the Liberal vote was on average less than 10%. The Liberal Party held no more than twelve seats during this period. This is in contrast to the post-1974 period when the Liberal Party was able to attract more votes. As mentioned above, Pimlott sees this as evidence that there was not a consensus. Had there been a consensus, then the Liberal Party would have done much better in postwar general elections. However, it is possible to see this the other way. The Liberal vote was effectively squeezed by the two major parties. Only after 1974, when the parties started to move away from the middle ground and when the electorate started to become disillusioned with the record of the two major parties when in office, did the Liberal Party vote increase. In contrast to Pimlott, therefore, it is possible to argue that the increase in the share of the Liberal vote after 1974 can be seen as evidence of the breakdown of consensus.

We can therefore say that there was a postwar consensus, defined as broad continuity in policy. The two major parties were able to promote certain policies despite the continuation of their differing ideologies, and against the background of a set of constraints on action. The consensus can be regarded as a 'middle ground' in which debate was constrained, with policy options to the right and the left of the 'middle ground' being ruled out by the party hierarchies. For most of the postwar period the party leaders were themselves within the 'middle ground', and so actually sought to implement policies with which they had broad sympathy. Before going on to examine the economic policy of the postwar period, one other point needs to be discussed. As mentioned above, Marlow argues that the postwar consensus thesis only emerged from the mid-1970s, with the publication of Addison's *The Road to 1945*. However, it is possible to reject this argument. A number of earlier studies pointed to the degree of continuity. In 1956, Crosland was able to argue that the Conservative Party had changed substantially since the 1930s.[69] Similarly, Robert McKenzie observed that the parties were similar in terms of both organisation and policy.[70] Sam Beer also observed a strong degree of continuity, arguing that: "when we make an overall assessment...it is the massive continuity that stands out."[71] The Conservative Government accepted the mixed economy and welfare state after 1951. Welfare expenditure increased from £1.5 million in 1950, to £3.2 million by 1959.[72] Beer argues that the parties remained distinct ideologically, but accepted similar policies due to the importance of pressure groups and electoral constraints.[73] Writing six years before Addison, Angus Calder observed many of the same policies emerging from the wartime coalition.[74] Hence, it is possible to detect the consensus thesis emerging in the literature contemporary to the period.

The Nature of Keynesian Economics

The term 'Keynesian economics', like the term 'postwar consensus', has been used to provide a shorthand definition of postwar economic policy. Indeed, the two are synonymous, since the economic policy of the 'postwar consensus' is said to have been 'Keynesian'. However, just as the term 'postwar consensus' has been criticised, so has the term 'Keynesianism'. I begin by providing a sevenfold categorisation of what Keynesian economics, in my opinion, is and then subject it to various critiques and historical events which are alleged to show that postwar economic policy was not Keynesian. Seven categories can be use to describe the major characteristics of Keynesian economics. These are: the role of the state, policy objectives, fiscal policy, monetary policy, direct intervention, industrial relations and the structure of the international economy.

Firstly, Keynesian economics emphasises the role of the state. In challenging the belief of classical economists that the economy is self-stabilising, Keynes legitimised state intervention in the economy. Under an economy based on Keynesian principles, the state had a duty to intervene in the economy, to regulate activity and to maintain full employment.[75]

Secondly, Keynesian economics, as applied post-1945, stressed the primacy of maintaining full employment as an objective of macroeconomic policy. It was not surprising that Keynes should emphasise the goal of full employment, given that he was writing during a time of high unemployment. However, it should not be assumed that Keynesian economics did not attach any importance to inflation. Full employment should be maintained within the framework of stable prices. The 1944 White Paper declared that governments have a duty to maintain full employment. For most of the 1950s and 1960s this policy objective was maintained. The emphasis placed on state intervention to attain full employment distinguishes Keynesian economics from the classical theory which preceded it and the economic liberalism which replaced it. Moreover, it fitted into the more 'collectivist' phase of politics emphasised by Greenleaf.[76] The Conservative Party could use Keynesian economics to implement its traditional values of moral obligation to the less fortunate. Similarly, Keynesian economics provided the social democratic wing of the Labour Party with a coherent economic theory, which it could use to defend the argument that public ownership and central planning were no longer necessary to manage capitalism equitably. Hence, Adam Przeworski argues: "the fact is that social democrats everywhere soon discovered in Keynes' ideas...something they urgently needed: a distinct policy for administering capitalist economies. The Keynesian revolution – and this is what it was – provided social democrats with a goal and hence the justification of their governmental role."[77]

The third feature of Keynesian economics is the emphasis placed on fiscal policy. Governments can have a strong impact on economic activity by altering levels of public expenditure and taxation. Expenditure can be used to alter the level of demand in the economy, so that higher levels of expenditure can reduce unemployment. Taxation can be used to influence private sector consumption and investment. There is little difference between borrowing and taxation as a means of financing public sector expenditure within a Keynesian framework.

Keynesians argue that the role of monetary policy is limited. The adjustment of monetary policy measures such as the interest rate, influences aggregate demand by altering private sector investment and patterns of consumer savings and expenditure. However, this influence is indirect. Therefore, monetary policy can be used to supplement fiscal policy, essentially as a means of fine-tuning the economy.

In terms of direct intervention, the Keynesian framework legitimised state action. This took the form of a much more important role for fiscal policy, but also included public ownership, regional policy and a more assertive competition policy. Public ownership, in the form taken after 1945, was not incompatible with Keynesianism since the motivation was largely pragmatic. In certain industries which were essential to overall economic performance, ownership was deemed to be the most effective means for achieving greater efficiency.

Keynesian economics co-existed with a tripartite structure of industrial relations. Although Keith Middlemas sees a corporatist bias in British economic policy[78], it is possible to argue that the corporatist structure of industrial relations was more complete in some other countries such as West Germany. There were, however, certain developments in that direction. The trades unions were granted further legal powers in the 1940s, which were maintained by the Churchill administration after 1951. Moreover, a number of new institutions were established including the National Economic Development Council in 1961 which, together with a number of sectoral organisations, was used to bring government, the trades unions and business representatives into closer cooperation.

Finally, the international economic system permitted the pursuit of Keynesian policies at a national level. The establishment of the Bretton Woods system of fixed exchange rates allowed for currency stability and reflationary domestic policies. The International Monetary Fund was initially conceived as a means of borrowing in order to finance temporary balance of payments problems, and thereby avoid domestic deflation.[79]

A number of arguments have been made which cast doubt on the existence of a Keynesian framework. R.C.O. Matthews has demonstrated convincingly that the existence of low unemployment in the postwar period – on average 1.8% between 1945-1965, compared with an average of 10.5% between 1918-39 – was not due to the use of Keynesian deficit-financing as was assumed at the time.[80] For most of the postwar period, governments ran a budget surplus.[81] Instead, the main cause was a rise in investment from a wartime low.[82] Although the study is important for providing an adequate explanation of postwar full-employment, it cannot be used to reject the notion of Keynesianism. This is so for several reasons. Matthews does show that the budget was used at certain times to reduce unemployment. Moreover, government policies contributed to the maintenance of full employment in the form of both non-Keynesian ideas such as education and training, and the specifically Keynesian idea of controlling capital exports. Finally, the analysis would need to show that the government had abandoned its commitment to full employment, which it did not do.

Jim Tomlinson goes further arguing: "there was never a thorough-going Keynesian revolution in policy...the conditions for such a revolution have never existed, and could probably never exist."[83] Tomlinson argues that Keynesian economics, like socialist economics, places too much emphasis on the importance of ideas in policy.[84] Instead, the conduct of economic policy is largely pragmatic and is subject to structural constraints.[85] Keynesian economic policies could not be implemented because of institutional and practical obstacles. The Treasury remained sceptical of Keynesian policies.[86] Moreover, demand-management required detailed information in order to make changes in the levels of economic activity. This was supposed to be the basis of the national income accounts, but Tomlinson argues that the accounts were based on factor cost calculations, against the view of Keynes. Expenditure was very difficult to calculate, and so taxation tended to be used to manipulate private consumption.[87]

There is much in Tomlinson's account of merit, particularly his emphasis on policy tools and techniques. However, it can be argued that he goes too far in his rejection of the role of ideas in economic policy. It is still possible to see a broad Keynesian framework, which lasted from 1945 through to the 1970s. This will be brought into sharper focus later in the book when it will be compared with economic liberalism. Moreover, a new technique was developed in fiscal policy. This was the 'budget-judgement', which was a review of the economic situation conducted two or three times a year by the Treasury. Recommendations for fiscal adjustment were then passed to the Chancellor of the Exchequer. Monetary policy had a minimal role in the government's management of the economy. During the 1950s, there were no adequate figures for the money supply. Monetary policy was not therefore used to control the money supply, and few commentators sought to explain inflation in terms of excess growth in the money supply. Instead, monetary policy was used to affect aggregate demand. The interest rate was used to affect private-sector investment and consumer credit. Finally, hire-purchase controls were used throughout the period. They were first introduced in 1951 and continued to be used until 1973. Hence, it is possible to detect a distinctive Keynesian economic framework after 1945, lasting until the 1970s.[88]

A further distinction is made between 'Keynesian economics' and the 'economics of Keynes'.[89] That is to say that although postwar economic policy was ascribed the name of Keynes, it differed in several crucial respects from the views of the alleged author. In particular, Keynes advocated reform of the British banking system. The key to economic growth and full employment was managed investment. In turn this required less liquidity of capital in order to make long-term investment more attractive. However, the dominance of the financial system over the industrial system in Britain, created a demand for greater liquidity in order to attain quick returns for the banking sector. It was therefore necessary to reduce liquidity, in other words to control finance capital. However, the postwar governments, supposedly following a Keynesian policy, did not introduce any reforms to achieve this. There is some truth in this argument, and the dominance of finance capital over industrial capital made the maintenance of economic growth and full employment harder to maintain. However, it must be balanced against the fact that the Bank of England was nationalised by the 1945-51 Labour Governments. The Bank of England did allow for more direct planning of investment, and reduced liquidity and raised investment compared to pre-war levels. Although it may be objected that these measures were inadequate since the rates of investment fell relative to other industrialised nations, it is still possible to detect a shift in investment policy in the postwar period as advocated by Keynes.[90]

It is not possible to discuss the development of postwar economic policy in any detail given the space available, but three events can be discussed briefly in order to cast further light on the nature of economic policy at this time.[91] The first was the resignation of Peter Thorneycroft, the Chancellor of the Exchequer, with his junior Treasury ministers in January 1958.[92] Thorneycroft argued that there was a need to cut public expenditure, which had increased substantially since 1951 when the Conservative Government came to power. Thorneycroft argued that rising public expenditure caused higher inflation. However, Harold Macmillan refused to support his Chancellor and Thorneycroft resigned. It has been alleged that Thorneycroft was the first monetarist Chancellor. Whether or not this is correct is debateable, what the episode does demonstrate is the extent to which Keynesian and welfare statist ideas had become institutionalised. In fact, the Conservative Government had continued with Keynesian ideas after 1951 as Andrew Gamble and Stuart Walkland maintain: "following the establishment of postwar inter-party agreement on Keynesian principles of economic management the potential clash between the party of capitalism and the party of socialism appeared to have been averted and the way opened for the continuation of broad consensus on economic policy."[93]

The second episode was the conduct of economic policy following the election of the Labour Government in 1964.[94] Labour inherited a difficult economic situation from the outgoing Conservative Government, with a rising balance of payments deficit. The Labour Government had the option of devaluation, but a decision taken in secret between Harold Wilson, Jim Callaghan and George Brown, the Prime Minister, Chancellor of the Exchequer and Secretary of State for Economic Affairs respectively, ruled this out. Eventually, the Government was forced to devalue under pressure from the markets in 1967. This only occurred after several deflationary budgets. According to several senior ministers, including the committed Keynesian Tony Crosland, this was a mistake.[95] It demonstrated the dominance of finance capital over other areas of policy.[96] Again, there is some truth in this and it may be possible to criticise the Government for not devaluing sooner. However, the conduct of policy demonstrates, I wish to argue, a tension within Keynesian economics, rather than a conflict between Keynesian economics and finance capital. The initial refusal to devalue was taken for two reasons. The first was the fear of political repercussions as the Labour Party could be branded as the 'party of devaluation'. The other reason was that it would undermine the Keynesian international framework. The Bretton Woods system was established, as mentioned above, to avoid exchange rate instability. It was feared that a devaluation of sterling would cause wider currency instability since it was still at the centre of the international currency markets. It was difficult for the British Government to devalue. The timing of the decision can therefore be criticised, but it is important to see it as part of a wider international system based on Keynesian ideas.[97]

One final episode requires brief discussion. This is the conduct of policy under the Conservative Government of 1970-74. Edward Heath was elected leader of the Conservative Party in 1965 and embarked on a policy review. The statement of policy was declared at the Selsdon Park Hotel in London in 1969, and formed the basis of the 1970 manifesto. The Government initially embarked on a more free-market policy and was elected on the principle of confronting vested interests which were deemed to be hampering economic performance such as the trades unions, but reversed its policy in late 1970. The Government was to go on to nationalise Rolls Royce and the Upper Clyde Shipbuilders, extend regional policy, and to introduce a highly expansionary budget in 1972. To those on the right-wing of the Conservative Party this was a betrayal of the Selsdon Park manifesto. Hence, Martin Holmes argues that: "the Heath Government can be criticised as the Government that ran away from 'confrontation', that was too eager to change its policy in the face of opposition."[98] However, others have argued that the free-market commitments of the manifesto have been exaggerated. The alleged u-turns were therefore much less significant than those on the right have tended to argue. Heath's policy from 1971 was based firmly on Keynesian ideas.[99] The significance for this discussion is that, although Heath pursued Keynesian measures for the majority of his time in government, he did inadvertently undermine the consensus by giving a hostage to fortune to the right-wing of the Conservative Party. The consensus was therefore under stress by the time the Labour Party won the General Election of February 1974.

Summary

The purpose of this chapter was to examine the nature of postwar British politics in general, and the nature of postwar British economic policy in particular. On the basis of the above discussion, it is possible to make two concluding comments. The first is that there was a postwar consensus defined as broad continuity in policy, as the reforms of the 1945-51 Labour Governments were maintained and built upon by subsequent governments. The second point is that postwar economic policy was Keynesian. By the time the Labour Party was re-elected in 1974, the consensus and the dominance of Keynesian economics were being challenged. Having established these points it is now possible to examine the conduct of economic policy from 1974-76 more accurately.

[1] Addison, P., *The Road to 1945: British Politics and the Second World War*, (Cape, London, 1975)

[2] Kerr, P., *Postwar British Politics: From Conflict to Consensus*, (Routledge, London, 2001). See also, Marlow, J.D., *Questioning the Postwar Consensus Thesis: Towards an Alternative Account*, (Dartmouth, Aldershot, 1996)

[3] Addison, p.13

[4] Ibid., pp.17-19

[5] Ibid., p.20

[6] Ibid.

[7] Ibid., p.16

[8] Ibid., p.14

[9] Ibid., p.273. Addison continues to hold to his belief that consensus emerged out of the Coalition. See Addison, P., 'Consensus Revisited', *Twentieth Century British History*, 4/1, 1993, pp.91-94

[10] Jefferys, K., 'British Politics and Social Policy During the Second World War', *Historical Journal*, 30/1, 1987, pp.123-144; p.124

[11] Ibid., pp.129-142

[12] Greenleaf, W.H., *The British Political Tradition*, Vol. II, 'The Ideological Heritage', (Methuen, London, 1983), pp.254-262

[13] Eatwell, R., *The 1945-51 Labour Governments*, (Batsford, London, 1979)

[14] Ibid., p.44

[15] Jefferys, p.143

[16] Ibid., p144

[17] Conservative Party, *The Industrial Charter: A Statement of Conservative Industrial Policy*, (Conservative Central Office, London, 1947)

[18] Conservative Party, *The Right Road for Britain*, (Conservative Central Office, London, 1949)

[19] Clarke, D., *The Conservative Faith in a Modern Age*, (Conservative Political Centre, London, 1947)

[20] Hogg, Q., *The Case for Conservatism*, (Conservative Political Centre, London, 1948)

[21] Ramsden, J., 'Adapting to the Postwar Consensus', *Contemporary Record*, November 1989, pp.11-13

[22] Kavanagh, D., and Morris, P., *Consensus Politics from Attlee to Thatcher*, (Blackwell, Oxford, 1989), p.110

[23] Ibid., Kavanagh, D., 'The Postwar Consensus' *Twentieth Century British History*, 3/2, 1992, pp.175-190; Seldon, A., 'Consensus: A Debate Too Long?' *Parliamentary Affairs*, 47/4, 1994, pp.501-514; Dutton, D., *British Politics Since 1945: The Rise and Fall of Consensus*, (Blackwell, Oxford, 1991). For an opposing view see Jones, H., and Kandiah, M., (Eds.) *The Myth of Consensus: New Visions on British History 1945-64*, (Macmillan, Basingstoke, 1996)

[24] Joseph, K., *Stranded on the Middle Ground*, (Centre for Policy Studies, London, 1976)

[25] Barnett, C., *The Audit of War*, (Macmillan, Basingstoke, 1986)

[26] See Harris, J., 'Enterprise and Welfare States: A Comparative Perspective' *Transactions of the Royal Historical Society*, 5th Series, 1990, pp.175-195

[27] Quoted in Marlow, p.1

[28] Miliband, R., *Parliamentary Socialism*, (Allen and Unwin, London, 1967)

[29] Marquand, D., *The Unprincipled Society: New Demands and Old Politics*, (Cape, London, 1988), pp.17-62

[30] Kerr, P., 'The Postwar Consensus: A Woozle That Wasn't?', in Marsh, D., (Ed.), *Postwar British Politics in Perspective*, (Polity, Cambridge, 1999), p.75

[31] Kavanagh, D., *Thatcherism and British Politics: The End of Consensus?* (Oxford University Press, Oxford, 1987)

[32] Fraser, D., 'The Postwar Consensus: A Debate Not Long Enough' *Parliamentary Affairs*, 53/2, 2000, pp.347-362

[33] Deakin, N., *In Search of the Postwar Consensus*, (Welfare State Programme, London School of Economics, London, 1988)

[34] Heffernan, R., *New Labour and Thatcherism*, (Macmillan, London, 2000), p.142. See also Heffernan, R., '"The Possible as the Art of Politics": Understanding Consensus Politics', *Political Studies*, 50/4, 2002, pp.742-760

[35] Pimlott, B., 'The Myth of Consensus', in Smith, L.M., (Ed.), *The Making of Britain: Echoes of Greatness*, (London Weekend Television, London, 1988), pp.129-147

[36] Ibid., p.130

[37] Pimlott, B., 'Is the Postwar Consensus a Myth?', *Contemporary Record*, Summer 1989, pp.12-15; p.13

[38] Ibid.

[39] Deakin, p.5

[40] Finer, S., (Ed.), *Adversary Politics and Electoral Reform*, (Wigram, London, 1975)

[41] Ibid., p.3

[42] See Marlow

[43] Ibid., pp.11-15

[44] Ibid., p.14

[45] Kerr (2001) p.51

[46] Heffernan (2000) p.142

[47] Marlow, p.5

[48] Kavanagh (1992) pp.177-178

[49] Heffernan (2000) p.144

[50] Seldon, p.508

[51] Kavanagh and Morris, p.13

[52] Crosland, C.A.R., *The Future of Socialism*, (Schocken, London, 1963, 2nd Edition), pp.61-80

[53] Plant, R., 'Blair and Ideology' in Seldon, A., (Ed.), *The Blair Effect*, (Little, Brown and Co., London, 2001)

[54] See Ramsden, and see also Evans, B. and Taylor, A., *From Salisbury to Major: Continuity and Change in Conservative Politics*, (Manchester University Press, Manchester, 1996)

[55] *The Industrial Charter*, pp.6-7

[56] Amery, L.S., *The Conservative Future: An Outline of Policy*, (Conservative Political Centre, London, 1946)

[57] Greenleaf, pp.201-254

[58] See Butler, R.A., *The Art of the Possible*, (Purnell, London, 1971), pp.126-153

[59] Clark, p.14

[60] Deakin, p.3

[61] Heffernan (2000) pp.151-154

[62] Sedgemore, B., *The Secret Constitution*, (Hodder and Stoughton, London, 1980), pp.26-27

[63] Hoskyns, J., 'Conservatism is not Enough', *Political Quarterly*, 55, 1984, pp.3-16; p.4

[64] Rose, R., *Do Parties Make A Difference?* (Macmillan, Basingstoke, 1980)

[65] Kerr (1999) pp.78-79

[66] Jones, H., 'The Postwar Consensus in Britain: Thesis, Antithesis and Synthesis' in Brivati, B., Buxton, J., and Seldon, A., (Eds.) *The Contemporary History Handbook*, (Manchester University Press, Manchester, 1996)

[67] Ibid., p.48

[68] Fraser, p.353. See also Downs, A., *An Economic Theory of Democracy*, (Harper and Row, New York, 1957)

[69] Crosland, pp.27-29

[70] McKenzie, R.T., *British Political Parties*, (Heinemann, London, 1955)

[71] Beer, S.H., *Modern British Politics*, (Faber and Faber, London, 1965), p.357

[72] Ibid., p.353

[73] Ibid., pp.359-367

[74] Calder, A., *The People's War: Britain 1939-45*, (Cape, London, 1969)

[75] For a discussion of the Keynesian view of the state see Hutton, W., *The Revolution That Never Was: An Assessment of Keynesian Economics*, (Vintage, London, 2001, 2nd Edition), pp.176-217

[76] Greenleaf, pp.254-262

[77] Przeworski, A., *Capitalism and Social Democracy*, (Cambridge University Press, Cambridge, 1985) p.36

[78] Middlemas, K., *Politics in Industrial Society*, (Andre Deutsch, London, 1979)

[79] I discuss the collapse of Bretton Woods in the next chapter

[80] Matthews, R.C.O., 'Why has Britain had Full-employment since the War', *The Economic Journal*, 78, pp.555-569; p.555

[81] Ibid., p.556

[82] Ibid., p.560

[83] Tomlinson, J., 'Why was there Never a "Keynesian Revolution" in Economic Policy?', Economy and Society, 10/1, February 1981, pp.72-87, p.73

[84] Ibid., p.85

[85] Ibid., pp.75-76

[86] Ibid.

[87] Ibid., pp.79-82

[88] Burk, A., and Cairncross, A., Goodbye, Great Britain: The 1976 IMF Crisis, (Yale University Press, New Haven, 1992), pp.132-138

[89] Leijonhufvud, A., On Keynesian Economics and the Economics of Keynes: A Study in Monetary Theory, (Oxford University Press, New York, 1968); Hutton, pp.86-110; and Gamble, A., and Walkland, S., The British Party System and Economic Policy: 1945-83, (Clarendon, Oxford, 1984), p.14. See also Longstreth, F., 'The City, Industry and the State' in Crouch, C., (Ed.), State and Economy in Contemporary Capitalism, (Croom Helm, London, 1979) who argues that the institutions of financial capital have maintained there dominant position despite economic and political change.

[90] See the discussion in Crosland, pp.288-294

[91] See Cairncross, A., The British Economy Since 1945: Economic Policy and Performance 1945-1990, (Blackwell, Oxford, 1992) for a detailed overview of postwar economic policy

[92] The following discussion is based on Brittan, S., The Treasury Under the Tories, (Penguin, Middlesex, 1964), pp.185-196

[93] Gamble and Walkland, p.14

[94] For a more detailed discussion of the economic record of the Labour Government of 1964-70 see Coopey, R., Fielding, S., and Tiratsoo, N., The Wilson Governments 1964-70, (Pinter, London, 1993)

[95] Crosland, C.A.R., 'Socialism Now', in Leonard, D., (Ed.), Socialism Now and Other Essays, (Cape, London, 1973)

[96] This view is held by Kerr (1999) pp.83-84

[97] For further views on the devaluation see Mitchell, A., and Wienir, D., Last Time Labour's Lessons from the Sixties, (Bellew, London, 1997) and Oliver, M.J., 'From Anodyne Keynesianism to Delphic Monetarism: Economic Policy-making in Britain 1960-79' Twentieth Century British History, 9/1, 1998, pp.139-150

[98] Holmes, M., Political Pressure and Economic Policy: British Government 1970-74, (Butterworth, London, 1983)

[99] See Kavanagh, D., 'The Heath Government' in Hennessy, P., and Seldon, A., Ruling Performance and Seldon, A., 'The Heath Government in History' in Ball, S., and Seldon, A., (Eds.) The Heath Government 1970-74, (Addison Wesley Londman, London, 1996)

CHAPTER 3

BACKGROUND TO THE 1976 IMF CRISIS

Introduction

This and the subsequent two chapters provide a detailed narrative of the 1976 IMF Crisis. The next chapter will discuss the period from March 1976 when the dramatic fall in the value of sterling began to September 1976 with the equally dramatic Labour Party Conference. The following chapter will then discuss the period from October 1976 to January 1977 when the IMF loan and sterling deposits were negotiated and agreements formulated. The purpose of this chapter is to examine three important developments, without which it is impossible to fully understand the IMF Crisis. The first relates to the formulation of the Labour Party's economic policy proposals in opposition between 1970-74, which explains why the manifestos of 1974 contained a number of radical left-wing proposals. The second is the initial phase of the Labour Government's economic policy between 1974 and February 1976, which shows a clear shift of approach in economic policy. Finally, the changing attitude of the IMF over the same period, which explains why the Fund acted in the way that it did in 1976. The chapter therefore begins with a discussion of the Labour Party in opposition and the development of its economic policy.

The Formulation of the Labour Party's Economic Policy: 1970-74

The key factor in explaining the formulation of economic policy in this period is the criticism of the Labour Government's record between 1964-70 from within the Labour Party. In many ways, the record of the Labour Government between 1964-70 was fairly impressive.[1] The Government managed to combine low inflation with near full employment and steady economic growth.   Moreover, there were a number of legislative achievements including liberal reforms on the laws on abortion, homosexuality, censorship, divorce and the death penalty. Education was marked by a number of reforms including the expansion of higher education, the establishment of the Open University, and the extension of the comprehensive schools system.   The Government also succeeded in reducing its military commitments east of Suez.[2]   However, the Government was later to be interpreted as a failure, or more specifically that it failed to meet the aspirations it had encouraged in 1964, with talk of the 'white heat of the technological revolution'.

The Government had been elected on the promise of transforming and modernising the British economy.   However, it was faced with an immediate balance of payments problem, which has been discussed in the earlier chapter on the postwar consensus.   The Government responded to this with orthodox measures of deflation, but was forced to accept devaluation in 1967.   Following the devaluation, the economy gradually recovered and Labour left office during a period of relative prosperity.   However, the early phase of deflation undermined the welfare programme of the Government.   Hence, when Labour left office, it did so with feelings of disappointment.[3] This was to lead to a number of criticisms being levelled against the record of the administration.

Firstly, the Prime Minister, Harold Wilson, was criticised for the style of his leadership.   In particular, Denis Healey, the Defence Secretary between 1964-70, was to criticise strongly Wilson's style.[4]   Healey argued that Wilson was concerned with maintaining his leadership of the Party against perceived conspiracies.   At various times, Wilson believed that senior ministers such as George Brown, James Callaghan, Roy Jenkins and Healey himself were plotting to overthrow him.   Wilson was keen to reshuffle his Cabinet, to outwit the alleged conspirator and to change policies in order to strengthen his leadership, and hence failed to take a long-term view of affairs.   The Government therefore lacked a sense of direction and purpose. Healey contends that, "since he had neither political principle nor much government experience to guide him, he did not give Cabinet the degree of leadership which even a less ambitious prime minister should provide.   He had no sense of direction, and rarely looked more than a few months ahead. His short-term opportunism, allied with a capacity for self-delusion...often plunged the government into chaos. Worse still, when things went wrong he imagined everyone was conspiring against him. He believed in demons, and saw most of his colleagues in this role at one time or another."[5] Wilson's style of leadership also affected the way in which policy was made. So, for example, the initial decision against devaluation was made in a secret meeting between Wilson, Callaghan and Brown in 1964, and was then effectively excluded from the Cabinet agenda until 1967.[6]

Secondly, criticism was made of the use of legislative time. Much parliamentary time was used to debate the liberal Home Office reforms mentioned above. Moreover, Wilson attempted to introduce a number of constitutional innovations including the establishment of two new Whitehall departments – the Ministry of Technology and the Department of Economic Affairs (DEA). Both of these creations were an attempt to weaken the Treasury dominance over economic policy, but resulted in policymaking getting bogged down by wrangles between the Treasury and the DEA. The National Plan, which had been drawn up by the DEA, was an attempt to produce detailed economic statistics and targets with the aim of securing higher investment and growth, but this proved increasingly difficult to implement and was largely irrelevant by 1970. Attempts to reform local government also proved difficult and costly in terms of parliamentary time. All this led Bill Rodgers, then a Labour MP and junior minister, to conclude that, "for God's sake don't get bogged down in too much constitutional change... It's the most time-wasting expensive thing you could ever do and it doesn't make friends, it makes enemies."[7] Government should instead, according to Rodgers, concern itself with economic and social policy.

Finally, some critics asserted that the Government was marked by its underlying conservatism. In his essay *Socialism Now*[8], Tony Crosland argued that the Government lapsed into economic orthodoxy, particularly in the initial phase between 1964-7. Early devaluation would have encouraged growth by which greater redistribution of income and wealth could have been implemented. Instead of seeking to achieve greater social welfare and equality as Crosland had advocated in his main work *The Future of Socialism*[9], the Government had been more concerned with international opinion and maintaining the parity of sterling. Hence, despite a number of achievements, the Government had not in the final analysis significantly advanced the cause of social democracy.

The early 1970s also witnessed the early development of the Alternative Economic Strategy (AES) by the Labour left.[10] The AES was most forcefully advocated in the document *Labour's Programme for Britain 1973*[11], and was later added to and refined so that by 1976 it had emerged as an alternative to Keynesianism. Following electoral defeat in 1970, the Labour left were significant in pushing forward new policies. The left came increasingly to dominate the policymaking committees within the Labour Party, including the National Executive Committee (NEC) and its various sub-committees. The theoretical case for the AES was made by Stuart Holland in his book *The Socialist Challenge*.[12]   Holland argued that the revisionist case promoted most strongly by Tony Crosland in *The Future of Socialism* was now outdated. This was because revisionism was based on Keynesian economics, which assumes a competitive market. However, there was evidence of a clear trend towards monopoly in each sector of the economy. Companies had gradually expanded through merger and take-over. There were a small number of business organisations which dominated each sector on an international level.

The revisionists, particularly Tony Crosland, argued that ownership no longer mattered. There had been a separation of power between the owners (shareholders) and managers of industry in which the latter had effective control. Moreover, since companies operated within competitive markets, ownership was widely dispersed. Public ownership through nationalisation was largely irrelevant.[13]   Instead, socialist objectives could be achieved through a combination of fiscal policies and regulation. Basing his argument on a Marxist[14] rather than Keynesian theory however, Holland argued that under conditions of monopoly, ownership had once again become the issue. The state needed to control industry because there was no spur to increase investment and efficiency under a condition of monopoly. Instead, companies could simply raise prices. Hence, profit-making was still the primary objective of industry.

The AES contained a number of key recommendations.[15] The first was the acceptance of the need for further reflation but, unlike revisionism, argued that this was insufficient in itself. There was also a need for nationalisation in order for the state to control investment, pricing, employment and production. The 1973 document advocated nationalisation of 25 of the top 100 companies and the establishment of a state-holding company to manage the activities of public sector organisations. The 1973 document also called for an extension of industrial democracy including worker representation on company boards and free access to corporate information. Finally, plans were developed to control the financial sector including an investment fund and public ownership of the top four clearing banks.

Following the publication of *Labour's Programme: 1973*, a number of other proposals were added. Firstly, detailed planning agreements would be formulated in order to exercise control over private companies. A National Enterprise Board would be established to regulate the activities of privately owned corporations. Financial aid would be provided to companies, but these would be subject to compulsory planning agreements. In addition, the advocates of the AES called for price controls in order to limit inflation. Limited increases in the cost of living would reduce industrial unrest and so there would be no need for wage controls. The so-called 'Social Contract' would be a basis for voluntary wage agreements and the means of imposing price controls so that the real incomes of the working-class would be protected. Finally, the AES increasingly viewed import controls as an important aspect of policy. The debate on import controls was an important part of Cabinet discussion on the IMF loan and so I return to this later.

In total, the AES was in sharp contrast, both in terms of underlying theory and policy prescription, to the dominant revisionist thesis. Social democrats were quick to criticise the theory and policies of the AES. The details of the social democratic critique of the AES are beyond the scope of the chapter, but I wish to emphasise that the leadership of the Labour Party never regarded the AES as official Party policy. Of the revisionists, only Tony Crosland was engaged in policy debate at this time. Other centre-right figures were largely uninterested in the detailed discussion on policy. This explains why the Labour left were able to exercise effective control over the policymaking structures of the Party in the early 1970s.

Labour's manifesto was formulated in such a way as to unite both of the rival factions.[16] Harold Wilson's managerial style of leadership was effective in uniting the two camps. Although he made vague concessions to the proponents of the AES, he also inserted a number of proposals made by figures on the right of the Party. As leader, Wilson had the final say in the formation of the manifesto. The manifesto remained vague on many of the proposals. Many of the terms used within the AES were maintained, but given different meanings more accommodating of social democratic approaches. Hence, Mark Wickham-Jones argues that: "it was possible for the party's factions to interpret the same policy in very different ways because aspects of Labour's proposals remained ambiguous."[17] This could be seen in the discussion on the Social Contract which had a very specific meaning as part of the AES to create a corporatist framework, remove incomes policy and introduce pricing policy, but was referred to vaguely in the manifesto as a forum in which the Government, business and trades unions could reconcile any differences.

The dilution of the AES is best seen in the establishment of the National Enterprise Board (NEB).[18] This was designed as a core component of the AES to regulate private businesses by establishing compulsory planning agreements and to manage public companies. The manifesto confirmed the commitment, albeit in vague terms, to the NEB. However, the objectives of the NEB were substantially modified in the White Paper *The Regeneration of British Industry*[19] published in August 1974. Planning agreements would be voluntary and would not be linked to state aid and investment programmes. The NEB would encourage private sector investment in profitable areas of the economy. The Industry Bill was published in January 1975. This further reduced the original intention of the NEB by placing a limit of £700 million on its annual budget. By the time the Bill became law in November 1975, it had been further amended. The Government accepted eighty-three amendments during the passing of the Bill. Hence, as Geoff Hodgson maintains, "there was little doubt, in late 1974 and early 1975, that the right-wing majority of the Labour Cabinet were saddled with a radical industrial strategy to which they had no more than minimal commitment."[20] Moreover, the original force behind the Industry Bill, Tony Benn, had been replaced by Eric Varley as Industry Secretary.   Varley was a moderate and wished to see a return to Keynesian ideas. It was Varley, with the assistance of the Chancellor of the Exchequer, Denis Healey, who was responsible for the drafting of the new White Paper *An Approach to Industrial Strategy*[21].   The new approach emphasised the primary importance of achieving private-sector profits in order to finance investment.   Hence, the original conception of the NEB as part of the AES framework was radically altered by the Government after 1974.

Two conclusions can be drawn from the above discussion. Firstly, although in theory the AES had been adopted as Labour Party policy, it was never accepted by the largely moderate centre-right leadership.   The alleged rejection of the 1974 manifestos was not therefore as surprising as the Labour left made out. Secondly, the theory of the AES formed the basis of the Labour left's alternative to the IMF loan in 1976.

The Conduct of Economic Policy 1974-February 1976

Despite some vague commitments to AES policies in the 1974 manifestos[22], the essential characteristics of macroeconomic policy after the elections of 1974 were Keynesian.[23] The Labour Party was elected in February 1974 without an overall majority. Indeed, the Conservatives were the largest single party in the House of Commons after the election.   However, the Conservative leader, Edward Heath, was unable to obtain the support of the Liberal Party and resigned on March 4, 1974. Given that no party could command an overall majority, another election was widely expected. This was held on October 10 and Labour won a small overall majority.   The period between March-October 1974 was therefore marked by a lack of policy initiatives.[24]

The Labour Government inherited a poor economic legacy from the previous Conservative Government. The first problem was the miners' strike.   Heath had refused to accept the National Union of Mineworkers' demand for higher wages leading to a prolonged conflict.   The Labour Government immediately resolved the dispute by awarding a 29% increase on March 6, and the industrial dispute was called off.   The three-day working week, which had been introduced to save energy supplies, ended the following day. On July 31, the Government repealed the controversial 1971 Industrial Relations Act, which had been introduced by the Heath administration in an attempt to place legal controls on trades unions. The Act was deeply unpopular among trades unions and had led to a series of industrial disputes in the early-1970s. The Heath Government eventually called a General Election on the issue of 'Who Governs Britain?' - the trades unions or the Government. The Labour Party argued that the industrial unrest was caused by the adversarial style of the Conservative Government. Instead, the Labour Party stated that it would be more able to work with the trades unions given their close historic relationship. The repeal of the 1971 Act and the ending of the miners' strike were seen as evidence of this relationship. The new style of industrial relations would be one based on agreement around a 'Social Contract'. The Social Contract was seen as a way of facilitating cooperation. Regular meetings would be held in order to allow the TUC and the CBI to express their opinion and to iron out differences. This was then accepted by the TUC on June 26.

The early phase of economic policy was also marked by strains in the development of the AES. The leading advocate of the AES in Cabinet was Tony Benn, then Industry Secretary. Benn immediately got to work on writing a number of reports with the aim of implementing the AES. On May 20, Benn reported these plans to the Labour Party-TUC Liaison Committee, but received little support from senior ministers including Harold Wilson and Denis Healey. Benn was also keen to provide financial assistance to a number of new projects such as the Scottish Daily News and Meriden Motorcycle Company. Financial aid was provided in order to establish worker cooperatives. But these were later to be regarded as failures, since the cooperatives were later to run into economic difficulties and the Government allowed them to go bankrupt. In fact, Benn was increasingly viewed with suspicion by many of his Cabinet colleagues.[25] Wilson himself was also sceptical of Benn. Following the referendum on the European Economic Community (EEC), which Benn had taken a key role in as one of the leading campaigners to withdraw from the EEC, Benn was moved from Industry to Energy.[26] This was seen as a demotion and the AES received little attention in future considerations on industrial policy.[27]

In contrast, the centre-right of the Labour Party advocated state intervention in the economy in order to encourage private sector growth. This was summed up in a speech delivered by Denis Healey to the CBI on May 14, 1974.[28] The state sought to provide financial aid to the private sector in order to encourage investment and profits during a time of international recession. The Government was to provide financial assistance to industry, to establish training schemes, to provide tax relief on investment and to establish the NEB as discussed above. Moreover, the Government was committed to Keynesian style reflation of the economy in order to encourage growth. In fact the net effect of budgetary measures in 1974 were strongly reflationary.

In addition to the inflation-busting wage increase given to the mineworkers, Healey's first budget on March 26 increased overall levels of taxation and spending, although Value Added Tax was cut from 10% to 8% and subsidies to the nationalised industries were cut from £1,400 million to £500 million.[29] On July 22, further budgetary measures added £200 million to aggregate demand by increasing the PSBR to £340 million.[30] Healey then added a further £800 million to the PSBR in November by granting a total of £1,500 million in aid to industry and by cutting corporation tax. Finally, the Government was to acquire shares in British Leyland and Burmah Oil in December 1974. The Government was therefore operating a Keynesian fiscal policy. The conduct of policy at this time was in conflict with the theory of the AES, and was based much more on the ideas of the centre-right revisionists.

As will be seen below, the policy of the Government in the period immediately preceding the IMF application was in marked contrast to this earlier stance. It is therefore necessary to explain why a change in policy occurred. In fact the change can be detected from early 1975, and is due to two major factors. Firstly, a growing appreciation of current economic problems, particularly inflation, public expenditure and the balance of payments. Secondly, the influence of the IMF and international opinion more generally.

There was a growing realisation that inflation was a serious problem that needed to be tackled. The major cause of inflation was seen as the rise in real wages, which had occurred in 1974. This had begun with the ending of the miners' strike as mentioned above. Other wage increases were demanded over the course of 1974. By October the moderate leader of the Transport and General Workers Union (TGWU), Jack Jones, was urging workers to accept pay restraint in order to allow inflation to fall.[31]   In fact, Jones was a key figure in the establishment of the incomes policy, as Martin Holmes argues: "it is widely believed, and rightly, that the key man in the return to incomes policy in the summer of 1975 was Jack Jones."[32] Many members of the Cabinet were willing to accept a compulsory incomes policy, but the trades unions were hostile as they held to free collective bargaining as a matter of faith. Jones had twin objectives. The first was political - that is to say that with inflation at a level of 30%, there was a threat to the existence of a Labour Government. Secondly, as Joel Barnett comments; "Jack recognised that high wage inflation was damaging to his members and that there was a simple equation that higher wages led to less employment."[33]   On February 13 1975, the NUM were granted a further pay increase of 35%. On February 19, figures were published which showed an average pay increase of 29% over the course of 1974.   During the following months, the inflation rate was to increase: 25.4% in April, 36.3% by June.[34] Jones suggested a flat-rate increase in the weekly wage of £8.   After a process of negotiation between the Government and the TUC, the level was reduced to £6, with a zero increase for those earning £8,500 or more per year.   The £6 policy was introduced on 1 August and accepted by the TUC in its September Conference.   Despite the opposition of the Labour left, it was also accepted by the Labour Party Conference on September 29.   The policy was criticised as being unjust since it restricted the growth in the real incomes of the workers, but in contrast, it is possible to argue that the measure assisted the Labour Party's historic aim to increase social justice by reducing differentials and achieving a substantial rise in the income of the lowest paid.   The extent to which the pay policy was responsible for the subsequent fall in inflation is open to some debate.[35]   However, inflation was to fall from an average of 24.05% in 1975 to 16.62% in 1976.[36]

The second major economic problem was that of public sector debt.   The Labour Government had already inherited a

PSBR deficit from the previous Conservative Government. The net effect of its reflationary budgets of 1974 was to add to the PSBR. The first sign that the Government was changing course was the introduction of a deflationary budget on April 15, 1975. The first statement by the Government of its intention to reduce public expenditure was made in the Public Expenditure White Paper in February 1975.[37] In total £1,100 million cuts in public expenditure were introduced.[38] Together with additional tax cuts, the budget was highly deflationary and reduced demand by £300 million. The budget of April 1975 was significant for two reasons. The first was that Healey used the resources argument in Cabinet for the first time. The resources argument was to be a regular defence for public expenditure cuts and will be discussed in more detail in Chapter 6. Briefly stated, the resources argument is that there is a need to cut public expenditure in order to free resources for private sector investment and exports. The second reason why the budget was significant is that it appeared to mark a shift away from Keynesian economics as practiced since the end of the Second World War. Hence, *The Times* said that Healey had "finally and totally broken with post war economic orthodoxy."[39] The budget marked a turning away from the early phase of fiscal expansion, to a process of deflationary measures ending in December 1976 with the IMF package. However, Denis Healey argued that further cuts might become necessary given the size of the PSBR.

On July 1, 1975, the Government introduced a system of 'cash limits' on public expenditure for the first time.[40] The debate over cash limits was to have an important role in Cabinet discussion on the IMF loan in 1976. I therefore intend to mention it only briefly at this stage (See Chapter 4). The Treasury had begun to formulate a policy of cash limits from December 1974, under the supervision of the then Head of the Treasury's public expenditure unit, Douglas Henley. He was then replaced as head of the public expenditure section of the Treasury by Leo Pliatzky in December 1975. It was initially seen as a technical measure with little political significance. However, it was to assume a political dimension in 1975 as the Government attempted to find a way of reducing expenditure. Public expenditure had previously been calculated in volume terms: that is in terms of the amount of expenditure required to finance particular programmes. If a scheme proved to be more expensive than originally planned, as was often the case in capital projects such as building programmes where it was common for costs to increase above those initially planned, expenditure would be increased to finance it. In contrast, cash limits set a nominal figure for each item of expenditure. It was then up to the spending department to finance the scheme out of the block allocation of funding. Cash limits were still regarded as only a minor innovation and were only applied to a small percentage of total expenditure, mainly capital projects. It was only to become a major issue of controversy in the summer of 1976 when the Treasury sought to extend the scheme in order to reduce expenditure even further.

The other major innovation at this time was a constitutional change introduced by Wilson stating that a Treasury minister could not be overruled in a Cabinet Committee on issues of public expenditure. This meant that any spending minister who disagreed with the budget had to argue in full Cabinet, and reduced the prospects of overturning a Treasury decision. Also, a decision was taken at this time that the contingency reserve - the proportion of the budget held back for emergency use - would not be increased in any financial year after the initial budget had been formulated.[41]

The major dispute over public expenditure during this period occurred during the winter of 1975-6, when the Government applied for the first IMF loan. By late 1975 many of the major economic indicators had improved, including the current account.[42] However, the Government had decided to apply for the IMF loan because of its deteriorating external payments situation.[43] Oil producing nations had been selling sterling deposits, leading to a fall in the value of the pound of almost 30% since 1971.[44] In order to finance its foreign debts, it was hoped that an IMF loan would be obtainable. The British Government made a formal application for a stand-by credit facility on December 17. Under a stand-by facility, the Government could draw upon a stated credit over a period of time. For reasons that will be discussed below, the IMF had become sceptical of fiscal expansion and would be likely to demand cuts in public expenditure. Denis Healey therefore went to Cabinet in the autumn of 1975 to request cuts in public expenditure.[45]

Cabinet divided on the issue of expenditure cuts. [46] Healey argued that cuts were needed as the growing size of public sector debt was impinging on the resources available for the private sector. Healey was planning to introduce a phased programme of cuts. There would be no cuts for the immediate financial year 1976-7, as this would damage current expenditure plans. However, there would need to be £1 billion for 1977-8 and a further £2.4 billion in 1978-9, as there would then be a period of recovery in world trade and the state needed to free-up resources for use by the private sector to invest. Arguing against this in Cabinet were two main critics – the Labour left, particularly Tony Benn, and the Keynesian revisionist Tony Crosland.

Benn advocated a break with Treasury orthodoxy and the adoption of the AES as described above. However, the strongest criticism came from Crosland. It was Crosland's contention that in a period of underemployment of economic resources, it was ridiculous to talk of wishing to reduce government expenditure in order to free resources for the private sector. There was spare capacity in the economy for the private sector to invest. A cut in government expenditure would lead to a rise in unemployment. Although Crosland was critical of Treasury thinking at this time, he did not push his case too strongly. He was not arguing that there was no need to control expenditure and had already accepted that public sector expenditure was rising too quickly and that there was a need to control its growth. On May 9, 1975, Crosland had made the 'party is over' speech in which he argued that local government expenditure was rising too quickly, and that central government controls would be increased to restrict further increases. Anyway, according to Edmund Dell, then Paymaster-General, "Healey won without too much difficulty."[47] It was however a sign of the debates which were to come in the summer and autumn of 1976. The Government accepted cuts announced in the White Paper on February 19, 1976[48], and the IMF granted a stand-by credit facility of US$2 billion on January 1, 1976.

Hence, by February 1976, before the collapse in the value of sterling began the following month, the economic policy of the Labour Government had changed. The Government had abandoned expansionary fiscal policy and introduced a compulsory incomes policy.

The Changing Role of the IMF

Before going on to examine the sterling crisis in more detail, there is one additional factor which requires some further explanation. That is the shifting attitude of the IMF between January 1974 and February 1976. This explains both the changing policy of the Labour Government described above and also why the IMF was to take a hard negotiating position with the British Government in 1976. Between 1974-6 the IMF was to move from a position advocating fiscal expansion to one of deflation and correction of balance of payments problems. This can be explained by a combination of three factors: the nature of IMF conditionality, the influence of the developing world and the influence of the United States.

As Kathleen Burk and Alec Cairncross argue: "in the case of the IMF, predominant power from the outset was exercised by the US."[49] From 1945, the United States had been the largest contributor of funds. The size of a country's contribution determined the voting rights of that country. In 1945, the United States held 33% of voting rights compared to 16% of voting rights for Britain. The share declined in the postwar period, but the United States continued to hold an effective veto in all major policy decisions. The United States argued that conditions should be placed on loans, and the IMF Executive Board accepted this as early as 1947. From 1952, there has been a strict conditionality principle.[50]

First tranche conditionality refers to the drawing of funds up to the level of quota: that is the level of the members' contribution to the IMF.[51] First tranche conditionality has no conditions attached to it, as it is in practice claiming back one's own money. Tranches beyond the first level are subject to increasing levels of conditionality. Each tranche is measured at intervals of 25% above quota. So that second tranche refers to 100-125% of quota, third tranche 125-150% of quota and so on.

In fact Britain had made several drawings from the IMF in the postwar period. The most notable occasion was in 1967 following the devaluation of that year. The devaluation has been discussed in the earlier chapter on the postwar consensus, and so it is not repeated here. What is significant for the purposes of this discussion is that Britain claimed an IMF loan of US$1.4 billion. As Burk and Cairncross note, this took

Britain into fourth tranche conditionality.[52]   This would normally require strict rules regarding repayment and adjustment of domestic targets. However, this did not happen since the IMF granted the loan without strict rules, and Britain faced only weak conditionality. In turn, this led to widespread criticism of the IMF by its Executive Directors from developing countries. The poorer countries felt that the IMF was dominated by the wealthier nations and that this led to an unfair interpretation of its rules in granting loans. In 1968, the IMF met to redraw its rules and procedures in granting loans. The IMF decided to reform its procedures. Rules would apply to all applicants, irrespective of whether the member was a developed or developing nation. Secondly, member-states borrowing from the IMF would have to remain in consultation for the full period of the loan, and would be subject to a monitoring of its domestic policy by an IMF delegation. Finally, the loan would not be granted all at once, but rather would be given in instalments with certain criteria for each instalment. As Burk and Cairncross note: "in short all members when in need, were to be treated equally."[53] When it came to the British application of 1976, many in the Government felt that the IMF was acting in an unfair and uncompromising way.[54] In fact, one of the reasons for this was the apparent ease with which the 1967 loan had been granted.

It has already been noted in the earlier chapter on the postwar consensus that the IMF was established in 1944 in order to stabilise the Bretton Woods fixed exchange rate system. However, the Bretton Woods system broke down in the early 1970s.[55]   The main cause was the growth of a private international finance market beyond the scope of national governments. In the immediate postwar period, the United States was to invest heavily in Western Europe. This in turn led to the creation of a Eurodollar market, which traded in US dollars held in European banks. The market was beyond the scope of both the US and European authorities and was liable to rapid movements of capital. By the early 1970s, the Eurodollar market had grown to such a stage of development where national authorities found it increasingly difficult to finance currency depreciations caused by movements in the international finance market.[56]   The result was that in 1971 President Nixon was forced to suspend the US dollars' convertibility against gold. Despite attempts to maintain a fixed exchange rate system[57], this effectively marked the end of managed exchange-rate policy and the US dollar, sterling and the other major currencies were left to operate in the uncertain conditions of a free currency market.[58] As Scott Lash and James Urry write, the currency market was to become increasingly volatile during the course of the 1970s.[59] In such a climate the IMF had lost its raison d'être, and was searching for a new role in the international economy. The 1976 British crisis was to be a major test case to see if the IMF still had a function that it could perform, and so the IMF was under pressure to successfully complete the loan agreement.[60]

The second major economic crisis of the early 1970s was the oil shock of 1973.[61] In response to the Arab-Israeli War of October 1973, the Arab oil-exporting countries under the umbrella of the Organisation of Petroleum Exporting Countries (OPEC) announced an embargo on the exportation of crude oil. Although the embargo only existed for a short period, the associated price increase was more permanent. Between October 1973 and January 1974, the world price of crude oil increased fourfold. This led to the twin problems of inflation and external payment deficits. World commodity prices had already increased in the early 1970s, and the oil shock was to add to general price levels. Some countries, which were net importers of crude oil, sought to pay for imports by increasing their external debt. This was particularly true in the British context. An additional problem was that oil exporters had begun to change their foreign currency deposits, which were largely held in sterling, into other currencies. This led to increased volatility in the British exchange rate on top of the problems associated with the Eurodollar market outlined above.

The increased volatility in the exchange rate undermined the domestic Keynesian economic framework. The relationships between Keynesian economics and the new floating exchange rate are numerous and complex. It was first believed that the new floating exchange rate system increased the freedom of domestic economies to operate in whichever way they chose. It soon became apparent, however, that this was not so. Fixed exchange rates provided stability, and thereby allowed the private sector to invest and export with a degree of confidence obtained from a knowledge of future trends. Floating exchange rates undermined this. Moreover, it became increasingly difficult for the Government to adjust fiscal and monetary policy to achieve domestic policy objectives. Instead, the Government became increasingly concerned with managing the exchange rate and maintaining international confidence. Increased pressure was put on the sterling balances in the more volatile exchange rate situation.[62]

The initial response of the IMF was to accept that conventional solutions to balance of payments problems - domestic deflation, import restraint and currency depreciation - were undesirable in the context of worldwide recession. At the Committee of Twenty Finance Ministers meeting in Rome in January 1974, the Managing Director of the IMF, Johannes Witteveen argued that, "attempts to eliminate the additional current deficit caused by higher oil prices through deflationary demand policies, import restrictions, and general resort to exchange rate depreciation would serve only to shift the payments problem from one oil importing country to another and to damage the world trade and economic activity."[63]

Witteveen proposed the creation of 'oil facilities'; described by Mark Harmon as, "new official borrowing arrangements administered by the Fund with looser conditionality policies that reflected the new situation."[64] The IMF would provide temporary loans to oil-importing countries as a means of financing temporary external payments problems. These would be financed by the current surpluses of the oil-exporting countries, redistributed by the IMF. After much discussion, the Executive Board of the IMF formally established oil facilities. Thirty-eight borrowers used the new oil facility in its first year of operation.[65]

When the Finance Ministers met again in September 1974 for the IMF annual meeting, a number of countries advocated renewal of the scheme. [66] Again, Johannes Witteveen supported the scheme.[67] Indeed, he argued that a higher amount would be required in 1975. Britain, France and Italy were also strongly supportive of the oil facility. The British Chancellor of the Exchequer, Denis Healey, was to advocate the establishment of a more permanent scheme; "we should see this operation as a continuing process, not simply as a once-for-all transfer."[68]

However, the position was to change during the course of 1976.[69] The earlier emphasis Witteveen had placed on sharing the burden of higher oil prices had disappeared. In his 1976 address to the IMF conference, Witteveen argued that: "the time has come to lay more stress on the adjustment of external positions and less emphasis on the mere financing of deficits."[70] Hence, Witteveen was now arguing that deficits were due to the policies of domestic governments rather than the effect of oil-exporting countries. There was a need for a reversal of policy in some countries: "payments difficulties do not arise from extraneous causes only. They are frequently due, wholly or in part, to inappropriate policies of the deficit country. Even when they are not, adjustment cannot be postponed indefinitely."[71] The change in the policy of the IMF was therefore significant, and Witteveen was advocating in 1976 what he had rejected in 1974 and 1975.

This can largely be explained by the influence of the United States.[72] The IMF lacks its own funds and is therefore dependent on its members. In this sense the term IMF loan is incorrect. Instead it is a loan from member states and international banks to an individual member administered by the IMF. As noted above, since the United States is the largest contributor, its power over the IMF is significant. From the time of the initial proposal of the oil facility in January 1974, the United States had been hostile to the scheme. The conduct of economic policy by the Americans at this time reflects the condition of their domestic economy. The extension of social programmes and the financing of the Vietnam War by deficit expenditure increased both the PSBR and inflation in the late 1960s. The US authorities were therefore concerned primarily with anti-inflationary policy. In contrast, Britain was primarily concerned with rising unemployment. The changing attitude of the IMF during this period shows a shift away from Keynesianism, to monetarism. By the late 1970s, the IMF had become an economic liberal institution. The period is therefore significant both in terms of a shift in international political economy, as well as a shift in the official British position. Under the direction of the Treasury Secretary, William Simon, the United States was critical of Witteveen's scheme. Instead, the US argued that the IMF should exert pressure on the oil-exporting countries to cut the price of oil. Moreover, oil-importers should seek to develop alternative sources of energy. If the demand for oil was reduced, prices would fall. As this would take some time to develop, deficit countries should adopt policies to reduce external debt. Germany was also critical of the oil deposits scheme. Helmut Schmidt, then German Finance Minister, argued that the scheme would have an added inflationary impact by increasing liquidity into the world economy.[73]

Simon also opposed the expansion of the scheme in the September 1974 meeting. Instead, he continued to advocate conventional policies aimed at resolving external deficits. Simon argued that, "in today's circumstances, in most countries, there is in my view no alternative to policies of balanced fiscal and monetary restraint...Some are concerned that a determined international attack on inflation by fiscal and monetary restraint might push the world into a deep recession, even depression. I recognise this concern, but I do not believe we should let it cloud our judgement."[74] At the meeting of the IMF Executive Board in November 1974, the United States was to oppose the extension of the oil facility for three reasons. Firstly, the United States was opposed to any scheme that appeared to accept the oil price increases. Secondly, the US authorities disliked the artificial separation between a country's oil and non-oil deficits. The United States believed that countries were manipulating their debt figures in order to show that debts were due more to oil than domestic policies. Finally, there was a preference for private sources of finance, so that deficit countries should seek to finance external debts by loans from private banks rather than other governments.[75] The United States advocated an alternative scheme – the Financial Support Fund. This would be used to finance external debts as a last resort after other measures had failed and would be subject to tougher conditionality.[76]

The conflicting positions of the United States and those countries, such as Britain, which supported the oil facility was clearly seen in the IMF annual meeting in the Autumn of 1974. Healey argued that there was a strong need for burden sharing and that it was desirable for the United States to adopt expansionary policies: the US had "a special responsibility to lead the world toward recovery."[77] In contrast, Simon maintained that the United States had no such role and that it was the responsibility of each country to adopt policies that would reduce external debt. Simon argued: "some have suggested that in order to help other nations out of recession, the United States should embark upon much more stimulative fiscal and monetary policies. We respectfully disagree. Too many of our current domestic troubles are rooted in such excesses in the past."[78] At this stage Witteveen continued to advocate the need for burden sharing and so was largely sympathetic to the British case. Moreover, the new German Finance Minister, Hans Apel, also had some sympathy with the British argument. Germany then had a surplus and was prepared to accept a role in stimulating world trade. However, such schemes would be limited by the inflationary effects such expansionary policies would have.

However, as has been noted above, Witteveen was to accept the argument of the United Sates during 1976. Over this period, the US financial authorities were to apply sustained pressure on the IMF, so that the IMF was forced to change its policy position. Moreover, Witteveen had become more concerned with the lack of progress made towards structural readjustment. The oil facility had proved largely incapable of forcing national governments to shift policy toward the control of inflation and the reduction of external debts. There would therefore be a need to use stronger conditionality on IMF loans.[79]

The countries which were most sceptical of the oil facility, namely the United States and Germany were to pursue a policy different from that advanced by the IMF. Rather than seeking to maintain as high a level of economic activity as possible given the international recession by allowing inflation and the balance of payments deficit to increase, the United States and, to a lesser extent, Germany responded to the oil shock with conventional policies of fiscal and monetary restraint. This was noted with some caution by Witteveen in 1975: "most of the major industrial countries followed tight financial policies during 1974, notwithstanding the deflationary threat of higher oil prices. The main purpose in adopting these policies was to counter inflation, and this was understandable, but they had important consequences for the balance of payments of other countries."[80] The result of the economic policies of the United States and Germany was to increase the balance of payments deficit in Britain. The initial rise in the British deficit was caused by the rise in oil prices. However, this was to increase still further as Healey implemented the initial IMF policy prescription. The visible balance deteriorated by £700 million between 1975-6. As was shown above, Healey then sought to change policy by placing greater emphasis on anti-inflationary and balance of payments measures.

Summary

This chapter has sought to highlight a number of key background factors, without which it is not possible to fully understand the nature of the IMF Crisis. Despite some rather vague manifesto commitments to the AES in the 1974 General Elections, the leadership of the Labour Party rejected the strategy in favour of traditional Keynesian reflationary policy. Initially, the IMF supported this policy in its efforts to avoid worldwide recession. However, by the time of the 1976 Crisis, the IMF had adopted a critical view of expansionary fiscal and monetary policy, mainly at the behest of the United States. As will be seen in the following chapters, the IMF was to take a hard line in negotiations with the British Government. This chapter has shown that this can be related to a number of factors including the low conditionality attached to British loans in the 1960s, pressure from developing countries and the interests of the United States.

[1] For a more complete discussion of the 1964-70 Labour Governments see Morgan, K.O., *The People's Peace: British History 1945-89*, (OUP, Oxford, 1990); Coopey, R., Fielding, S. and Tiratsoo, N., (Eds.), *The Wilson Governments 1964-70*, (Pinter, London, 1986); and Mitchell, A. and Wienir, D., *Last Time: Labour's Lessons From the Sixties*, (Bellew, London, 1997)

[2] For a further discussion of defence policy at this time see Healey, D., *The Time of My Life*, (Penguin, London, 1990, 2nd Edition)

[3] See Mitchell and Wienir, p.219

[4] Healey

[5] Ibid. p.331

[6] Although this was probably to do with market sensitivities as well.

[7] quoted in Mitchell and Wienir, p.220-221

[8] Crosland, C.A.R., 'Socialism Now' in Leonard, D., (Ed.) *Socialism Now and Other Essays*, (Cape, London, 1974. See also 'A Social Democratic Britain' in the same volume

[9] Crosland, C.A.R., *The Future of Socialism*, (Schocken, London, 1962, 2nd Edition)

[10] See Wickham-Jones, M., *Economic Strategy and the Labour Party: Politics and Policy-making 1970-83*, (MacMillan, Basingstoke, 1996)

[11] Labour Party *Labour's Programme for Britain: 1973* (Labour Party, London, 1973)

[12] Holland, S., *The Socialist Challenge*, (Quartet, London, 1975)

[13] Crosland was not arguing that nationalisation had no place in a democratic socialist project, but instead that it should no longer be central. Nationalisation should be limited to cases where regulation had not worked in the promotion of economic efficiency and social justice.

[14] I use the term 'Marxist' cautiously here. See Chapter 6.

[15] Wickham-Jones, pp.69-76

[16] ibid. pp.93-5

[17] ibid. p.93

[18] ibid. pp.137-150. See also Forester, T., 'Neutralising the Industrial Strategy', in Coates, K., (Ed.) *What Went Wrong: Explaining the Fall of the Labour Government*, (Spokesman, London, 1979)

[19] *The Regeneration of British Industry* (Cmnd. 5710 HMSO, London, 1974)

[20] Hodgson, G., *Labour at the Crossroads: The Political and Economic Challenge to the Labour Party in the 1980s*, (Robertson, Oxford, 1981)

[21] *An Approach to Industrial Strategy*, (Cmnd. 6315 HMSO, London, 1975)

[22] Labour Party, *Let Us Work Together: Labour's Way Out of the Crisis*, (Labour Party, London, 1974); Labour Party, *Britain Will Win With Labour*, (Labour Party, London, 1974)

[23] For a fuller discussion of economic policy in this period see Holmes, M. *The Labour Government 1974-79: Political Aims and Economic Reality*, (Macmillan, Basingstoke, 1985); and Artis, M. and Cobham,

D., *Labour's Economic Policies 1974-79*, (Manchester University Press, Manchester, 1991)

[24] See Butler, D. and Kavanagh, D., *The British General Election of January 1974*, (Macmillan, Basingstoke, 1974); and Butler, D., and Kavanagh, D. *The British General Election of October 1974*, (Macmillan, Basingstoke, 1975)

[25] Crosland once said that there was "nothing wrong with him except he's a bit cracked." quoted in Crosland, S., *Crosland*, (Coronet, London, 1983, 2nd Edition, p.204)

[26] Hodgson, pp.99-103

[27] Wickham-Jones, pp.137-150

[28] See Healey, pp.372-410 for a clear exposition of his objectives at this time.

[29] Jackson, P., 'Public Expenditure' in Artis and Cobham, pp.73-87

[30] Artis, M., and Cobham, D., 'The Background' in Artis and Cobham (1991) pp.1-18; and Wickham-Jones, M., 'A Calendar of Events' in Artis and Cobham (1991) pp.279-295

[31] See Jones, J., *Union Man: The Autobiography of Jack Jones*, (Collins, London, 1986)

[32] Holmes, p.26

[33] quoted in Holmes p.27

[34] Wickham-Jones (1991) pp.281-282

[35] See Holmes pp.26-34, who argues that incomes policy had little impact since inflation was caused by excessive growth in the money supply

[36] Artis and Cobham (Eds.) *Labour's Economic Policies*, p.301

[37] Public Expenditure White Paper (Cmnd 5879, HMSO, London, 1975)

[38] Barnett, J., *Inside the Treasury*, (Andre Deutsch, London, 1982), p66. The cuts came largely from the capital budget including transport, housing, education and health; but also from defence and food subsidies.

[39] Quoted in Wickham-Jones (1991) p281

[40] See Barnett, pp.70-71; and Pliatzky, L., *Getting and Spending: Public Expenditure, Employment and Inflation*, (Blackwell, Oxford, 1982), pp.130-134. The details are contained in 'The Attack on Inflation', Cmnd. 6151, (HMSO, London, 1975)

[41] Pliatzky, pp.134-135

[42] The current account deficit had more than halved from £3,186 million in 1974 to £1,526 million by 1975. Artis and Cobham, p.302

[43] The sterling balances held by central monetary institutions fell from £4,862 million in March 1975 to £4,100 million by December 1975. Zis, G., 'The International Status of Sterling', in Artis, M., and Cobham, D., (Eds.), *Labour's Economic Policies: 1974-79*, (Manchester University Press, Manchester, 1991), p.111

[44] Against the $ the £ fell from $2.44 in 1971 to $2.21 by 1975. Against the DM the £ fell from DM8.53 in 1971 to DM5.44 by 1975. This amounted to an effective fall of 27.9%. Artis and Cobham, p.303

45 Burk, K. and Cairncross,A., *Goodbye Great Britain: The 1976 IMF Crisis*, (Yale University Press, New Haven, 1992), pp.17-19
46 See Holmes, pp.67-73, Healey, pp.400-402, Dell, E., *A Hard Pounding: Politics and Economic Crisis 1974-6*, (OUP, Oxford, 1991) pp.186-191; Pliatzky, pp.132-3; Jefferys, K., *Anthony Crosland: A New Biography*, (Cohen, London, 1999), pp.179-187
47 Dell p.190
48 Public Expenditure White Paper (Cmnd. 6393, HMSO, London, 1976)
49 Burk and Cairncross, p.6
50 ibid. pp.7-8
51 First tranche conditionality is often called the gold tranche since members of the IMF originally deposited funds in the form of gold.
52 Burk and Cairncross, pp10-11
53 ibid. p.10
54 Tony Benn and Peter Shore felt that both protectionist measures and an IMF loan could be negotiated. They misunderstood the position of the IMF. See Chapter 5.
55 Lash, S. and Urry, J., *The End of Organised Capital*, (Polity, Cambridge, 1987). See also Britton, A., *Macroeconomic Policy In Britain 1974-87*, (Cambridge University Press, Cambridge, 1991), pp.123-131
56 In total, the Eurodollar market increased from $44 billion in 1969 to $810 billion by 1980. See Lash and Urry, p.205
57 The 'Smithsonian agreement'
58 Not totally free since capital controls remained in place until the end of the decade in Britain.
59 ibid.
60 See De Vries, M.G., *The International Monetary Fund and Deficit Countries: 1972-1978*, Vol.1 Narrative and Analysis (International Monetary Fund, Washington DC, 1985) who argues that: "several critics intimated that the Fund had outlived its usefulness." p.3
61 Harmon, M., *The British Labour Government and the 1976 IMF Crisis*, (MacMillan, Basingstoke, 1997)
62 See Britton, A., *Macroeconomic Policy In Britain 1974-87*, (Cambridge University Press, Cambridge, 1991), pp.123-131; Healey, pp.433-434; and Strange, S., *Sterling and British Policy: A Political Study of an International Currency*, (Oxford University Press, London, 1971)
63 quoted in Harmon pp.65-66. See also De Vries, p.334
64 ibid. p67
65 ibid. pp.65-69
66 ibid. pp.69-71
67 De Vries, p.334
68 quoted in Harmon p.71. See also De Vries, p.335
69 Harmon, ibid., pp.71-75 and pp.121-129
70 quoted in Harmon, p.128

[71] quoted in Harmon, p.128
[72] De Vries, pp.336-339
[73] Harmon, pp.71-75
[74] quoted in Harmon p.71
[75] This also reflects a concern with domestic economic factors. Firstly, it demonstrates the role and power of US financial interests in domestic policy. Secondly, the US was keen to redistribute its surplus in petrodollars (the increases in the balances of oil-exporting countries held in dollars, produced by the OPEC price shock). See Walter, A., *World Power and World Money: The Role of Hegemony and International Monetary Order*, (Harvester Wheatsheaf, London, 1993)
[76] ibid. pp.73-74
[77] quoted in Harmon p.122
[78] quoted in Harmon p.122
[79] ibid. pp.124-129
[80] quoted in Harmon p.122

CHAPTER 4

POLITICS AND ECONOMIC POLICY: MARCH – SEPTEMBER 1976

Introduction

The period from March to September 1976 was one when the economic situation deteriorated and the crisis that culminated in the IMF loan and public expenditure cuts in December 1976 evolved. The pound began to fall in value from March 1976, and despite several attempts by the Government to halt the slide, it continued to fall. This chapter seeks to provide a detailed narrative of the period from March to September 1976. I begin by examining the initial policy decisions that caused the pound to fall in value. The chapter then covers the 1976 Labour Party leadership contest, the initial attempts to reduce public sector borrowing and inflation in April and May, the arrangement of the June stand-by, the so-called July measures and the Labour Party Conference.[1] A narrative of these events raises several important questions. Firstly, what or who, was responsible for the initial slide in the value of sterling? Secondly, should the measures introduced by the Government between April and July have been sufficient to reverse the decline in sterling? Thirdly, what do the events demonstrate about the nature of international 'confidence'? Finally, what do these events indicate about the changing balance of power within the Labour Party, and the corresponding shift in ideas? The chapter also introduces new information and sources developed in the course of my research.

The Initial Fall in the Value of Sterling: March 1976

On March 4, 1976, the Bank of England sold sterling. The following day, the Bank then cut interest rates. This was the beginning of the 1976 sterling crisis - by the time of the Labour Party Conference, the pound had fallen from over $2 to $1.63. Toward the end of 1976, it seemed to all involved that the pound was in free-fall, and that there would be no end to its collapse. The decisions to cut the minimum lending rate and to sell sterling were therefore crucial.[2] Two separate, but to some extent interrelated questions arise. Firstly, was there a deliberate strategy to depreciate sterling? Secondly, irrespective of whether there was a deliberate strategy or not, who was responsible for the decision to cut the interest rate and to sell sterling?

The first detailed study of the 1976 IMF Crisis was made by Stephen Fay and Hugo Young for the Sunday Times in May 1978.[3] Fay and Young argued that there was a deliberate strategy of depreciation. Sir Douglas Wass, First Permanent Secretary to the Treasury, with the support of Sir Bryan Hopkin, the head of the Treasury's economic unit, advocated a policy of limited depreciation. Their argument was that an overvalued pound was hampering Britain's economic performance. The pound had been high since the autumn of 1975 when pressure on the dollar led many traders to purchase sterling. Rising unemployment would best be resolved by export-led growth, but at the current value of sterling it would be difficult to export. Moreover, high import prices were adding to industrial costs. Sir Derek Mitchell, Second Permanent Secretary with responsibility for the overseas section, argued against this, and was supported by Harold Lever, the Chancellor of the Duchy of Lancaster. Lever and Mitchell argued that the strategy would lead to a large fall in the value of sterling, as the markets would develop their own momentum.[4] Fay and Young argue that the Governor of the Bank of England, Gordon Richardson, agreed with Lever and Mitchell.[5] Despite their opposition, however, the Chancellor of the Exchequer, Denis Healey, was to eventually support the strategy of depreciation.

According to Fay and Young, however, the strategy went wrong.[6] The Bank sold sterling on March 4, at the same time as other traders, notably Nigeria, were selling sterling. The pound was already falling, therefore, when the policy was implemented. On March 5, the Bank of England and the Treasury decided to cut the minimum lending rate by a quarter of one per cent. The pound then went into a rapid fall. By March 10, the pound had fallen below $2 to $1.90. This then is the position of Fay and Young. There was a deliberate plan, which had been in place for some time, to depreciate sterling. The Treasury and the Bank of England were both responsible for making this decision. This position is largely accepted by William Keegan and R. Pennant-Rea.[7] However, Keegan and Pennant-Rea add that the decision to sell sterling on March 4, was not part of the strategy to depreciate. Instead, it was merely an attempt to halt a further appreciation. Only the cut in the minimum lending rate was a deliberate attempt to depreciate on March 5.

There was clearly much discussion in the Treasury over the issue of depreciation. As Kathleen Burk and Alec Cairncross argue, this was in marked contrast to the 1964-7 period, when Harold Wilson refused to allow discussion of devaluation.[8] Leo Pliatztky, Second Permanent Secretary at the Treasury and Head of the public expenditure unit, argued that, "a prevailing economic view in the Treasury favoured progressive depreciation in order to offset the escalation of our domestic industrial costs."[9] However, since Pliatztky was more concerned with public expenditure, he has little to say on the details of any proposed policy of depreciation. A more authoritative source on this is Edmund Dell, the Paymaster-General and a close ally of Healey's.[10] Dell argues that the Treasury was divided on many aspects of economic policy at this time, of which the debate over depreciation was just one example. This point is worth emphasising since the Treasury was to be divided throughout 1976. Dell mentions a meeting of senior Treasury ministers and officials on October 28, 1975. Wass advocated depreciation as a way of stimulating the economy. Dell argues that, "the Keynesian leadership in the official Treasury was turning towards depreciation as its preferred option."[11] However, it appears that Healey was sceptical of the plan: "such was Denis's scorn for the Treasury proposal that the meeting broke up without a thorough discussion of the options."[12]

In February 1976, Mitchell returned to the subject of depreciation by producing a memorandum setting out the disadvantages of such a strategy.[13] The report was produced for a meeting between the Treasury and the Bank of England on February 13, 1976. Fears of a significant slide in the value of sterling were raised. According to Dell, Healey again raised objections to the plan, and received support from officials in both the Treasury and the Bank of England.[14] Dell also argued that a number of measures would have had to have been taken at this time in order to have depreciated sterling. First of all, a larger depreciation than the 5% level suggested by certain writers including Keegan and Pennant-Rea would have been required. Secondly, there would have been a need for greater cuts in public expenditure in order to increase resources for greater exports. Thirdly, there would have been a need for an extension of incomes policy in order to minimise any inflationary effects of depreciation. Finally, support from international authorities would have been required in order to defend the value of sterling including an international loan. Since none of these things were developed by the time of the discussions in March 1976, Dell concludes that, "there was no plan and there could be no plan."[15] However, all of this assumes a plan for a large depreciation in March 1976. There would have been no need for these measures if the plan were to effect a minimal reduction in the value of sterling. This point is made by Hopkin: "his points would have less validity...against a proposal to take advantage of market situations to nudge the rate down a few per cent at one time and do it again some time later."[16]

What is more convincing is the widely reported view that Healey was strongly opposed to such a position.[17] This is best summed up by Dell. Since Dell was the closest minister to Healey, it is likely that Dell's view is an accurate summary of Healey's position. According to Dell, Healey was "scathing" of such a plan. He was concerned about the quality of the advice given to him by Treasury officials.[18] Moreover, Healey was convinced that holders of the sterling balances would sell the currency quickly, thus causing a rout. It also appears that Wilson was unaware of the depreciation plan. He was, according to Bernard Donoughue, the Head of the Prime Minister's Policy Unit, taken by surprise at the decline of sterling following the measures on March 4 and 5. Donoughue reveals that Wilson was planning to resign in March. Although this was not public knowledge, it was widely known in the inner-circle of 10 Downing Street. When the value of sterling began to fall, Wilson was shocked and delayed his resignation.[19] Hence, Donoughue remarks that, "there was no doubt that he was unaware and had not been made aware of what was going on in the Treasury and the Bank of England."[20]

Given that both Wilson and Healey were not supportive of such a plan, it is difficult to conceive of a deliberate policy of depreciation. Certainly there was a section of the Treasury, including Wass, which favoured depreciation. But this was never accepted by Healey, and so far as one can tell, never reached the Prime Minister. It was simply regarded as too risky. The depreciation could be larger than planned, as markets might develop their own momentum. Burk and Cairncross reach the same conclusion: "neither the Treasury nor the Bank, however, knowingly initiated the fall, nor would they have been supported in such a move by either the Prime Minister or the Chancellor, both of whom disliked the idea."[21]

Nevertheless, a decision was taken to sell sterling and then to reduce interest rates. Here the published sources have had little to say over what happened. Events moved very quickly and are difficult to interpret clearly. Here the book can add to the previous accounts by discussing information received from the Bank of England. The question of responsibility remains. In his memoirs, Healey places the blame firmly on the Bank of England. Healey writes that; "the Bank of England made two major mistakes. On March 4th, 1976 it sold sterling when the pound was already under pressure, so that the markets thought it was trying to push the pound down. Next day it lowered interest rates instead of raising them, thus appearing to confirm the market suspicions."[22] According to Healey's account, he played little, if any, part in the monetary policy decisions taken in early March. This assumes that the Bank of England had the power to decide changes in interest rates and the trading of sterling by itself. The statement is vague on whether the Treasury had intervened in the decision-making process, although Healey does concede that a section of the Treasury had been calling for depreciation for some time. At this point, it is worth re-emphasising that Bank opinion was generally sceptical of depreciation, as it was likely to get out of control. The pound was too high, but it would only stay at this level for a temporary period, and would then begin to fall to a more realistic level. It seems unlikely then, that the Bank of England would have pushed for depreciation. Hence, it is logical to assume that pressure for a cut in the minimum lending rate would be more likely to emerge from the Treasury.

By looking at the procedural rules for adjusting the minimum lending rate it becomes clear that the Treasury was involved at a senior level.[23] The Bank of England decided the minimum lending rate in line with a formula agreed with the Treasury, and linked the interest rate to the sale of Treasury Bills. The minimum lending rate was adjusted every Friday in response to the issue of Treasury Bills. However, it was possible for the Chancellor of the Exchequer to override the automatic adjustment of the minimum lending rate. The automatic adjustment was due to be made at 2PM on Friday, March 5, following the issue of Treasury Bills at 1.15pm. The decision to override would then be at the discretion of the Chancellor. According to a then Director of the Bank of England: "an override would have required the Chancellor's authority, so that formally the decision not to can be said to have been his."[24] Given the size of the cut being considered, it is difficult to believe that the Treasury would not have been consulted. It therefore seems likely that Healey, or at least some of the senior officials in the Treasury would have been consulted immediately before the minimum lending rate was cut.

In summary, therefore, it appears that although there was no official policy to depreciate sterling in March 1976, there was a decision to reduce the minimum lending rate. It seems that the Treasury, probably including Healey, was aware of this and did not attempt to stop it. The decision was taken in order to stop a further appreciation, rather than to achieve depreciation. The decision, together with the sale of sterling, was crucial in initiating the rapid fall in the pound from March 1976.

The 1976 Labour Party Leadership Contest

On March 16, 1976 the Prime Minister, Harold Wilson, resigned suddenly.[25] The following three weeks were taken up with a leadership contest. Previous studies of the IMF Crisis have underestimated the significance of the leadership contest. It is worth spending some time discussing the leadership contest for two reasons. Firstly, since the contest was at this time decided entirely on the votes of Labour MPs, it shows the balance of power between the various factions of the Parliamentary Labour Party in 1976; a factor which was to influence the Cabinet debate over the measures to reduce public expenditure in July and over the IMF loan itself later in the year. Secondly, the business of Government was effectively suspended for three weeks while the leadership of the Labour Party was fought out.[26] In total six candidates were to stand: James Callaghan, Denis Healey, Roy Jenkins and Tony Crosland from the right of the Labour Party, and Michael Foot and Tony Benn from the left.

Callaghan was to emerge as the eventual winner. Although the contest took three rounds to decide the final outcome, it can be seen that Callaghan had three distinct advantages, which were to tip the balance in his favour from the outset. Firstly, Callaghan was the only contender to know of Wilson's decision to resign. Harold Lever, a close confidant of Wilson's, had told Callaghan that the Prime Minister was going to resign during a meeting between the two in December 1975. Callaghan, however, simply did not believe this. Wilson then informed Callaghan on March 10, six days before he announced this to other ministers in Cabinet. This, as it was intended, gave Callaghan time to arrange his campaign. Secondly, Callaghan had held all of the major offices of state: Chancellor of the Exchequer (1964-7), Home Secretary (1967-70), and Foreign Secretary (1974-6). He therefore had the most popular image with the electorate at large, and could boast greater experience than the other candidates. Finally, although Callaghan was traditionally from the right of the Party, he was to present himself as a moderate, conservative candidate from the centre of the Party. He argued that he was best able to unite the Cabinet and parliamentary party. In so doing, he was able to pick up a number of votes from each broad section of the Party, as well as a number of second and third preference votes.[27]

Denis Healey's chances of winning the contest had taken a severe blow in the parliamentary debates over public expenditure on March 10.[28] The Government was attempting to introduce its Public Expenditure White Paper, involving £1,600 million of cuts for 1977/8. The left-wing Tribunite group of

Labour MPs opposed the cuts and abstained, thus causing the Government to lose the vote. The following day the Government was able to win a confidence vote. The pound fell to $1.91 on March 10, but increased the following day and remained steady. However, the episode had a lasting impact as Burk and Cairncross note: "the market saw a government unable to guarantee the support of its own backbench members when cuts in public expenditure were an issue."[29] Healey was to attack the Tribunite MPs in strong language that upset many in the Party, and therefore lost some support. Healey, in his memoirs, accepts that this was to cost him supporters: "my work as Chancellor had led many people to see me as a possible party leader. But Wilson's resignation could not have come at a more inconvenient time for my chances of succeeding him. For some days I was determined not to run at all, rightly believing that my row with my left-wing colleagues, now widely publicised, would reduce my support to a derisory level."[30]

Tony Crosland was the leading thinker on the Labour right in the postwar period. In addition, Crosland had served in several middle-ranking Cabinet jobs under Wilson since 1965, including Education where he had been responsible for developing comprehensive schools. However, Crosland had an arrogant personality, which made it difficult for other MPs to form a close relationship with him. He had little support in the Parliamentary Labour Party and his campaign consisted of a small group of close supporters led by Bruce Grocott and Peter Hardy. However, Crosland's support never seemed like going above twenty. As with Healey, Crosland was initially reluctant to enter the contest, but was eventually persuaded to stand.[31]

Roy Jenkins had, in the late 1960s and early 1970s, been considered as a likely successor to Wilson. Jenkins had been a liberal-reforming Home Secretary between 1964-7, and, had then replaced a somewhat discredited Callaghan as Chancellor of the Exchequer in 1967. As Chancellor, Jenkins was widely regarded by expert opinion to have been a success.[32] He therefore had experience of high office and was well known to the electorate. In addition, he was an effective media performer. Jenkins was undoubtedly on the right of the Party. His leadership of the Labour Party rebellion on Europe in 1973, when a number of Labour MPs voted with the Heath Government to enter the European Economic Community against the official Labour Party policy, won him the support of the pro-European Labour MPs. In addition, he was beginning to reject calls for higher public expenditure arguing that, at 60% of Gross Domestic Product, it was already too high and was a threat to liberal democracy. Although Jenkins had the support of pro-Europeans on the right of the Party, he found it difficult to extend this support to other sections of the Party.[33]

Michael Foot emerged as the representative of the moderate left of the Labour Party. Believing that Foot had enough support to win the contest outright, his supporters urged him to stand. Foot was seen as the natural heir to the Bevanite strand of the Party, which was still strong at this time. He advocated higher welfare expenditure, greater redistribution through higher levels of taxation, voluntary incomes policy and unilateral disarmament. He was therefore likely to win the support of the Tribunite MPs. Although Foot had a high level of support in the Parliamentary Labour Party, he was not well regarded by the electorate. Moreover, he had little ministerial experience as he had refused to serve in the 1964-70 Government.

The final candidate was Tony Benn. Benn had been a fairly moderate member of the 1964-70 Government and was most well known for the campaign to disclaim his peerage. However, since 1970, he had been moving rapidly to the left of the Labour Party. By 1976, he was already beginning to represent a new, different form of leftism from the Tribunites and Bevanism. As was seen in the previous chapter, Benn had been instrumental in developing the Alternative Economic Strategy. He stood in the 1976 leadership contest for two reasons. Firstly, he was keen to promote the Alternative Economic Strategy, and secondly to construct a base upon which to build in a future contest.[34]

The result of the first ballot was announced on March 25. Foot came top with 90 votes, followed closely by Jim Callaghan on 84 votes. Jenkins did less well than expected and only obtained 56 votes. Jenkins immediately withdrew from the contest. Tony Benn did better than anticipated and secured 37 votes. Benn then withdrew urging his supporters to vote for Foot. Healey faired badly and only achieved 30 votes, but refused to withdraw. Crosland came last with a mere 17 votes, and was withdrawn automatically from the contest. In the second ballot, Callaghan came top with 141 votes, Foot obtained 133 and Healey 38. The results of the second ballot were a little surprising since not all of the Jenkins and Crosland supporters moved across to the two remaining right-wing candidates. However, there was a clear momentum at this stage for Callaghan, who won on the final ballot by 176 votes to 137 for Foot, and thus became Prime Minister on April 5.[35]

So what can be said about the 1976 Labour Party Leadership Contest? Firstly, in terms of the individual candidates, the results were mixed. For Crosland, the result was particularly disappointing. Although his supporters felt that Crosland had a base upon which to build in future contests, the base was extremely small. Healey was shown to have little support in the Parliamentary Labour Party, which reflected negatively on his Chancellorship. Benn seems to have been particularly pleased with the fact that he had obtained more votes than Healey. Indeed, Benn had done well in the contest. There was now a chance for him to go on and do better in a future contest, and there was support for the Alternative Economic Strategy in the Parliamentary Labour Party. For Jenkins, the result was a disappointment. He was to leave the Cabinet in the autumn to become President of the European Commission. He maintained a core support from the pro-European right of the Labour Party, which was to re-surface in the 1981 with the formation of the SDP. Finally for Foot the result must have been good news, since he would now act as Deputy Leader and be in an excellent position to succeed Callaghan.

Taken collectively, the results show a strong position for the Labour left. Benn had captured 37 votes on the programme of the alternative strategy. Foot had won the first ballot and eventually obtained 137 votes in the straight fight with Callaghan in the final ballot. Callaghan had managed to draw widespread support by presenting himself as a centrist candidate best able to succeed Wilson. In this he had been criticised by sections of the Labour Party and the press. In particular, Peter Jenkins of the Guardian argued that what was needed was a clear ideological direction. Callaghan lacked this, and was much more of a manager and a fixer.[36] Compared to Callaghan, the three candidates clearly from the traditional right of the Party – Jenkins, Healey and Crosland – faired badly in the contest.

However, the subsequent Cabinet reshuffle marked a clear and decisive shift to the right at the senior levels of Government. Healey remained Chancellor of the Exchequer, as he was to deliver the budget the following day. Crosland was promoted to Foreign Secretary. Jenkins had let it be known that he wanted to be Foreign Secretary, but Callaghan refused to appoint him as he was too closely aligned with the pro-European wing of the Party. Instead, Jenkins continued to serve as Home Secretary until September when he became President of the European Commission and was replaced by Merlyn Rees. Foot became Leader of the House of Commons and Benn stayed at the Department for Energy despite his success in the leadership contest. According to Healey, "the firm decisiveness of that first reshuffle gave a foretaste of Jim's quality as Prime Minister."[37] However, it also highlighted the differences that existed between a largely moderate right-wing Cabinet and a largely radical left-wing parliamentary party.

Economic Policy: April-May 1976

Callaghan recalls that one of his first meetings after becoming Prime Minister on April 5 was with his Chancellor, Healey. By his own admission, Callaghan was unaware of the measures taken to maintain the value of sterling since early March: "I was shocked when he told me how much had been spent by the Bank of England to support the sterling exchange rate."[38] Healey also informed Callaghan that the Government might have to go to the IMF for a further loan given the current state of the currency. Callaghan identified three broad economic problems in April 1976. Firstly, the need to renew the incomes policy as the agreement reached in 1975 was nearing its end. Secondly, the need to reduce the public sector borrowing requirement. Finally, the need to stabilise the value of the pound.[39] Callaghan offered to support Healey: "I asked him to bring me any major initiative he might wish to take before it went to the Cabinet, and if he and I could then agree, I would back him when such matters came before our colleagues. In proposing this, I had in mind that the Chancellor of the Exchequer is the loneliest man in the Cabinet."[40] Callaghan was keen to avoid two situations from arising. First, he wanted to avoid spending ministers from forming coalitions to protect their programmes. In addition, he was suspicious of the Treasury, and wished to stop them from bouncing new measures through Cabinet without consulting him first.

In fact, plans were already well under way to deal with the first two problems identified by Jim Callaghan – namely public sector debt and incomes policy. On April 6, the day after Callaghan became Prime Minister, Healey introduced his budget.[41] The budget contained no further cuts in public expenditure after the White Paper. Burk and Cairncross note that this, "disappointed the market"[42] Martin Holmes has been particularly critical of the Labour Government's economic policy at this time: "Denis Healey's budget in April was an opportunity to restore confidence and put the economy back into kilter, but the opportunity was missed. Although Denis Healey described it as the most crucial of the present Parliament, it failed to consolidate the greater sense of economic reality which had emanated from the February Public Expenditure White Paper."[43]   According to Holmes, the Government had missed an opportunity to introduce a further round of expenditure cuts in order to restore confidence. The budget did, however, include a novel measure. This was to introduce cuts in the standard rate of income tax from 35% to 33%, but to make this dependent on trades union agreement to the incomes policy being discussed at the same time. I return to the issue of incomes policy shortly. Again, Holmes is very critical of this measure. The Government, which had initiated the fall in the value of the pound in March 1976, had now passed responsibility for control of inflation over to the trades unions.[44]

A more significant measure was the extension of cash limits.[45] In the last chapter, it was discussed how cash limits had been introduced as a means of restricting the growth of public expenditure on capital projects.   Under existing arrangements, additional money would be provided if a scheme was found to have cost more than had previously been planned. Cash limits allotted a fixed amount of money when a scheme was initiated.   If the costs then increased, it would not be covered by additional funding.   This had initially been introduced because of the 88% increase in tenders for building projects in the early-1970s.   It was now extended to cover 75% of all public expenditure.   One area in which cash limits were introduced was in local authority expenditure.   Cash limits were placed on the Rate Support Grant; that is the funding provided by central government to local authorities in the form of a block grant on top of income from rates. It was felt that local authority expenditure was increasing too quickly: the number of people employed in local government had increased from 1.5 to 2.5 million over the course of the previous fifteen years. Cash limits were also extended to cover civil service expenditure. The main area exempt from cash limits would now be social security, since it was difficult to plan for fluctuations in expenditure in this area and unemployment was rising at that time.

As Head of the Treasury's public expenditure unit, Leo Pliatzky, had responsibility for cash limits. He sees three important consequences emerging from cash limits. Firstly, cash limits had a significant impact in reducing the growth in public expenditure. This was partly due to the actual restriction placed on the costs of the public expenditure programmes, but also in the psychological affect that they engendered. Pliatzky remarks: "rumblings began to come that cash limits were going to cause programmes to be underspent."[46] Agencies responsible for public expenditure decisions were reluctant to spend the money already allocated for fear of overshooting their budgets. They therefore sought to find new savings where they could.

Secondly, cash limits had helped to stabilise the contingency reserve fund. The fund was used to provide additional resources for spending departments if expenditure had to be increased above planned levels or if there was a need for temporary measures. The contingency reserve stood at £700 million for 1976-7, and it appeared for a while that it would be exceeded as expenditure increased. The effect of cash limits was to avoid this by reducing the growth in public expenditure.

Finally, cash limits were part of a broader attempt to define more accurately what public expenditure actually constituted. Under previous arrangements it was difficult to measure total expenditure with any degree of accuracy. Leo Pliatzky was also instrumental in redefining public expenditure. By introducing a number of technical reforms, it was possible to measure public expenditure in the same way as the Organisation of Economic Cooperation and Development (OECD) had been doing for some time. The result of this was to reduce the share of GDP consumed by the public sector from nearly 60% to 46% in one go. Healey argues that the Treasury had previously failed to do this in order to argue for further expenditure cuts: "I suspect that Treasury officials were content to overstate public spending in order to put pressure on governments which were reluctant to cut it."[47]

The specific measure introduced in the Budget on April 6, to tie tax cuts to incomes policy has already been noted. Although many commentators have been critical of this measure, it appears to have been welcomed by Jack Jones, leader of the Transport and General Workers Union. Jones argues that, "it was an ingenious approach, and to Healey's credit it was the first time that the tax elements of a budget had been the subject of previous public debate."[48] It appears that at this time, the moderate leaderships of the larger trades unions and the Trades Union Congress were broadly supportive of a continuation of incomes policy. The discussion over the course of April consisted of what form the incomes policy should take. Jack Jones and David Basnett argued for a flat-rate increase as had been introduced in the £6 policy implemented in the previous year (see previous chapter). In contrast, Hugh Scanlon advocated a percentage increase to maintain wage differentials. The eventual outcome was closer to Scanlon's position. On May 5, the agreement was published. There would be a rise of £4 per week for lower income earners, with a maximum increase of 5% for middle-income earners. On average, this would result in a 4.5% increase. The Government declared that this was an important contribution in tackling inflation, and the agreement was accepted by the trades unions.[49]

However, Martin Holmes is again critical, arguing that wages were not the cause of inflation and that the Government lacked an effective strategy for tackling inflation: "in short the Stage II agreement could not take the place of effective action against inflation by the Chancellor."[50] This view is extremely harsh. As wages had been increasing rapidly the previous year, with wage settlements averaging 30% eighteen months before, it seems unlikely that there was no relationship between inflation and wages. Moreover, the Government was not relying solely on an incomes policy, but had also introduced other measures such as public expenditure controls described above and in the previous chapter. Evidence of success was to appear on April 29, when figures showed that inflation had been reduced by over half in a

period of nine months (30% to 13%). By May, it could therefore
be said that the Government had taken action in the first two of
the three areas identified by Jim Callaghan – namely public
expenditure and wage inflation. This is emphasised by Pliatzky:
"we could feel by the summer that we had turned the corner. It
was at this point when incomes policy had stemmed the orgy of
wage claims, when control of public finance was being restored,
even if at a high level of taxation and borrowing...that a loss of
confidence which had started in the spring perversely came to a
head."[51]

The June Stand-by

The pound had continued to fall rapidly in value from $1.91
following the March decision to sell sterling and to cut the
minimum lending rate, to $1.88 at the beginning of April and
$1.72 by June 2. In an attempt to halt the slide, the Bank of
England had sold its foreign currency reserves in order to raise
the value of sterling. It will be recalled that the IMF granted a
loan of $2 billion to Britain on January 1, 1976. Throughout the
year the Bank had gradually used this in support of sterling. As
Burk and Cairncross write: "on 12 May the government quietly
purchased the final SDR 700 million from the IMF."[52] It had
therefore drawn on the remainder of the loan, and had used
almost all of its reserves by the end of May 1976. This was a
major problem for the Government, as the pound continued to
fall.

Towards the end of May, the Treasury discussed what should
be done. A number of measures were entertained including
further expenditure cuts. However, Healey appears to have
decided that an international loan was required. Pliatzky writes
that, "one opinion which was urged upon the Chancellor with
characteristic persuasiveness was that the most sensible and
also the most painless course was to borrow our way through
the situation."[53] It appeared that, politically, a loan would be
the easiest solution, since there would be no difficult Cabinet
negotiations over where expenditure cuts would fall, which the
alternative policy would clearly involve.[54] There also appeared a
clear economic rationale for a further loan. It would be an
attempt to restore confidence in the finance markets. Firstly, it
would show that international banks had confidence in sterling

as they were prepared to offer support. Secondly, it would show that the Bank of England was prepared and was able to intervene and to protect the current value of sterling. This is emphasised by Leo Pliatzky: "we should raise loans enabling us to put funds in the shop window on a scale large enough to demonstrate that there was plenty of backing for the pound and that speculators against it would burn their fingers."[55]

Burk and Cairncross note that, "by the beginning of June...the belief was widespread that the pound was now undervalued."[56]   It is not exactly clear in what order the proposed loan came about as sources differ on this point, but it seems that different people came to accept the need for international support for sterling at around the same time. Harold Lever, the Chancellor of the Duchy of Lancaster and a close ally of Callaghan, argues that both senior Treasury officials and Gordon Richardson, the Governor of the Bank of England, were opposed to the stand-by.[57]   However, this appears to be incorrect. In his memoirs, Healey argues that the credit was easily obtained.[58]   The rationale for the loan was expressed by Barnett[59] and Pliatzky.[60]   In their early study of the IMF Crisis, Fay and Young stress the point that the initiative was taken by Healey and Richardson.[61]   Following a meeting between the two on Friday June 4, Richardson contacted the Governor of the US Federal Reserve, Arthur Burns, to seek a loan. Later the same day, Dr Jelle Zijlstra, President of the Bank of International Settlements and the Netherlands Central Bank, telephoned Richardson to inform him of a loan totalling $5.3 billion. The loan was to be declared on Monday, June 7, when the markets began trading.

At first, the British Government welcomed this news. Fay and Young have written that: "when it was clear that the stand-by credit would be forthcoming, the mood in London was euphoric."[62]   It appears that the European bankers, especially Jelle Zijlstra, had acted for a combination of reasons. Firstly, they were of the conviction that the pound was now undervalued, and there was a need to push it back up. Secondly, they feared that a further decline in sterling could trigger an international currency crisis. The second motivation is emphasised by Barnett: "as ever the desire not to see sterling start an international financial crisis was the primary impetus."[63]

At this point, the activities of the US were again crucial. As Burk and Cairncross write: "the mood would change abruptly the following day."[64] Over the weekend of June 5/6, Ed Yeo, the Under-Secretary of the Treasury, visited London.[65] For some time, the US financial authorities had become increasingly critical of the macroeconomic strategy of the British Labour Government. The leading figures in both the US Treasury and the Federal Reserve were all at this time strongly orthodox in their pursuit of sound money and balanced budgets. The most explicit was Arthur Burns, Governor of the Reserve, who described himself as, "a neanderthal conservative and naturally suspicious of a Labour Government. I thought it was a profligate government."[66] As was seen in the previous chapter, the US authorities were influential in bringing about a change of attitude within the IMF. By June 1976, the US authorities were reluctant to give any assistance to Britain. This is summed up by Scott Pardee, Vice-President of the Federal Reserve Bank of New York with responsibility for foreign exchange operations: "by this time a lot of people were fed up with sterling crises."[67]

Healey writes: "I got the credit without difficulty."[68] This, however, gives the wrong impression. Normal procedure for such an arrangement would be to provide a loan for a period of three months, renewable indefinitely at three-monthly intervals. Edmund Dell argues that this was the intention of Zijlstra. However, the US insisted that the loan could only be for a period of three months, and could be renewable once only.[69] Yeo describes how Callaghan and Healey attempted to get round this commitment: "Callaghan tried everything to prevent the six-month time limit... First they didn't want any limit at all. When I wouldn't have that they wanted a long take-down, which means that the six-month period would not begin until they started drawing the money."[70] Finally, the British government played down the significance of any commitment, arguing that it didn't matter anyway.

After a dramatic weekend, the stand-by was announced on Monday, June 7.[71] $2 billion was provided by the US, $600 million from Japan, $300 million from Canada, and the remainder from European central banks and the Bank of International Settlements. A number of conditions were attached to the loan. Firstly, as mentioned, it was renewable once only. This meant that the loan had to be repaid by

December 9. If the Government could not repay the stand-by, it had to apply to the IMF and thereby be subject to conditionality. In addition, the US authorities were keen to establish monetary discipline. Although no precise targets were to be published, there was an expectation that the British authorities would seek to restrict liquidity. William Simon, the US Treasury Secretary, believed that a firm commitment had been made here. In a communication to Gerald Ford, the US President, Simon wrote that, "as a condition to our agreeing to provide financial support, the British Government has communicated to me their intention to take immediate steps to reduce the availability of domestic credit."[72] However, it appears that the Government had not taken this as seriously. It was again hoped that enough had been done. Initially, the markets were supportive and the value of sterling rose to $1.74. However, the pound was again to fall later in June. Callaghan comments that, "speculators and others soon grasped that the loan was only short-term and Britain would be required to repay it in December 1976. When they digested this, pressure on sterling reasserted itself."[73]

At this point, it is worth mentioning two issues. The first concerns a growing sense of conspiracy, which began at this time and remains a controversial issue.[74] Harold Lever argued that sections of the Treasury had cooperated closely with the US financial authorities to manipulate the British Government into accepting the June stand-by, with the likely consequence that the Government would then have to revert to the IMF at the end of the year. The IMF was now taking a hard line against governments with public-sector deficits and balance of payments problems. The loan would therefore lead to a change of policy to one which the Treasury wanted to see. In particular, Derek Mitchell, the Head of the Treasury's overseas unit, was known to favour public expenditure cuts and was working closely with the US authorities. Bernard Donoughue, the Head of the Prime Minister's Policy Unit, also argued that there had been a conspiracy, and still maintains this view.[75] Callaghan, although not convinced that there was an actual conspiracy, was also critical of the Treasury for failing to advance the case of the British Government in international negotiations with sufficient determination.[76]

Arguing against this was Edmund Dell. According to Dell there was no Treasury pressure to accept the loan.[77]

International opinion was sufficient to impose the conditions on the June stand-by. Dell argues that, "it did not require a conspiracy by Treasury officials to ensure the insertion of this humiliating condition. There was a widespread view among those in a position to insist that the stand-by was the UK's last chance to get its affairs in order and that, if it failed once again, no course should be left open to it other than IMF conditionality."[78] Given that the US was providing $2 billion, they had a legitimate right to demand conditions. There had been a section of the Treasury which had advocated the loan. However, this appears to have been advocated as a more favourable option to public expenditure cuts. I think that this is to go too far. The US authorities clearly attempted to impose conditions on the loan in addition to those advocated by Jelle Zijlstra, with the clear intention of imposing IMF conditionality when the Government could not repay in December 1976.

However, this is different from arguing that there was a conspiracy involving the British Treasury. At this point, I wish to argue that there was no conspiracy. Indeed, there is absolutely no evidence to support the conspiracy theory. There could not have been a conspiracy involving the Treasury as a whole since it was internally divided at this time. Sir Douglas Wass, First Permanent Secretary, and Leo Pliatzky, Head of the public expenditure unit, were sympathetic to the Labour Government, and of a broadly Keynesian position. Of the senior officials, only Derek Mitchell, Head of the overseas section, was advocating public expenditure cuts. However, there was no evidence for a conspiracy involving Mitchell either. His views were well known within the Treasury, but Healey did not have much sympathy for them. Mitchell's job involved talking to overseas financial authorities, particularly the US. But he was open about these discussions, and sought to promote the views of the Government in foreign negotiations.[79]

The second point that needs emphasising at this stage is the concerted effort to win over international support. As will be seen below, Callaghan sought to obtain international support for a scheme to reduce the sterling deposits. Callaghan, under the influence of Harold Lever, felt that the high level of sterling held by overseas governments in their foreign reserves was causing the instability in the pound experienced since the 1960s. Callaghan sought to reduce the amount of sterling deposits and to arrange a long-term credit facility from the international banks for use in periods of instability. Callaghan also sought to obtain international support from sympathetic governments – particularly the USA, where President Ford and Henry Kissinger, the Secretary of State, were known to be more supportive than the US financial authorities.[80]

The first attempt to achieve international support came on June 27, at the Puerto Rico Summit. Healey met Simon to discuss the possibility of replacing the $5.3 billion loan with a longer-term arrangement, but was unable to secure support for this. Callaghan also had a ninety-minute meeting with Ford. Ford and Kissinger seemed much more supportive than Simon did. However, there was no agreement, as Callaghan notes: "Puerto Rico was not a memorable meeting and we left without making any progress on the long-term stabilisation plan."[81] Callaghan's efforts to secure international support were to be a constant theme during the second half of 1976.

The 'July Measures'

It soon became clear that the June stand-by had been insufficient to restore the confidence of the financial markets. Indeed, Joel Barnett comments that, "no serious observer of our economy really thought a $5.3 billion credit was all the action needed."[82]   Therefore, the Government moved toward the strategy advocated by a section of the Treasury in June: namely, public expenditure cuts.[83] This was seen as being preferable to approaching the IMF at this stage, since the IMF would have been likely to ask for greater cuts than those being considered, to have imposed other conditions such as money supply targets and tax cuts, and assumed a monitoring role. Healey says that, "I was determined not to go to the IMF for a conditional loan if I could possibly avoid it. So in July 1976, after an appallingly difficult series of meetings with my Cabinet colleagues, I announced spending cuts of...£1 billion."[84] The rationale for choosing expenditure cuts was outlined by Leo Pliatzky: "further measures to restore confidence therefore had to be considered, and public expenditure cuts, going beyond the last White Paper cuts and starting earlier, were the front runner, since it was the size of expenditure programmes and of the borrowing to finance them which, in the eyes of the financial world, were at the heart of our problem."[85]

The first full discussion of public expenditure cuts occurred at the Cabinet sub-committee on Economic Strategy (EY Committee) on July 2.[86] This committee consisted of the Prime Minister, the Chancellor, Roy Jenkins, Tony Crosland, Michael Foot, Tony Benn, Edmund Dell and Harold Lever. Callaghan asked Healey to discuss the economic situation. At this meeting, Healey appears to have asked for £1 billion of public expenditure cuts. Healey got the support of Dell, who thought that the proposed cuts did not go far enough. Lever also appears to have supported the Chancellor, which is surprising given that he was to be one of Healey's severest critics later in the year.

At this meeting, Healey faced a number of critics. Crosland argued that the economy was fundamentally strong, that public expenditure measures introduced so far were sufficient and needed time to work, and that incomes policy was now in place for a second year. This argument was to be repeated consistently by Crosland in Cabinet debates over the IMF loan at the end of 1976, and so I do not intend to discuss it further at this stage. However, it should be noted that Crosland, as Foreign Secretary, was to be absent from a number of the Cabinet meetings held in July 1976 and therefore played little part in the discussions at this time. According to his wife, Susan Crosland, he had a "fenced-in look."[87] His commitments at the Foreign Office left him with little time to think about economic policy. He was to reflect that he had been "away and muzzled."[88] He was to attend one meeting to defend Peter Shore, the Environment Secretary, in refusing further cuts in road transport and housing. But apart from this he was to make little contribution.[89]

Arguably, of more importance at this time was Tony Benn. At the EY Committee on July 2, Benn was to advocate the Alternative Economic Strategy. Based on a paper written by his economic adviser, Francis Cripps, Benn argued that as the economy was in recession there was spare capacity for expansion. Moreover, public expenditure cuts would deepen the recession. The moderate strategy advocated by Benn at this time was based on an assumption that the IMF would be willing to provide a loan with few conditions. This was therefore the final element of Benn's argument, and it was criticised for lacking a sense of realism. The IMF would insist on public expenditure cuts, presumably of a greater amount than was currently being debated.[90]

On July 6, the first full meeting of Cabinet took place.[91] Joel Barnett, the Chief Secretary to the Treasury, along with Healey, introduced a paper calling for £1.25 billion cuts in public expenditure. In addition, they also advocated the abolition of the contingency reserve by financing extra spending from existing departmental budgets. This would add an extra £1.6 billion in cuts, bringing the total package to near £3 billion. Again, the leading critic was Benn. On this occasion, Benn outlined the full Alternative Economic Strategy including import restrictions and compulsory investment plans, in order to stimulate growth in the domestic economy. Cabinet opinion was mixed. Shirley Williams and Albert Booth, Secretaries of State for Prices and Employment respectively, were concerned about deflationary effects and undermining the social contract. Roy Jenkins (Home Secretary), Reg Prentice (Overseas Aid) and Harold Lever (Chancellor of the Duchy of Lancaster) supported the cuts, but David Ennals (Health), Michael Foot (Leader of the House of Commons) and Fred Mulley (Education) were opposed. At this stage it appears that the clearly defined groups within the Cabinet that were to be a feature of the IMF discussions had not yet formed. Barnett commented that the discussions were "good-tempered."[92] This is because Callaghan was only prepared to discuss the total package, rather than individual cuts, which would be left to bilateral meetings between Barnett and the spending ministers. Barnett was critical of Callaghan at this stage: "I suppose the Prime Minister felt that the ambiguity over where the cuts should fall was a reasonable price to pay to avoid resignations. There were times when I felt the price was a bit high, and that a little more firmness from him, indicating which Ministers should accept cuts, might have ensured earlier agreement and still without resignations, if with some disgruntlement."[93]

However, Callaghan was to be influential in persuading Roy Mason, the Defence Secretary, to accept cuts in military expenditure eventually totalling £100 million. The month of July was taken up with a number of Cabinet and bilateral meetings in an attempt to reach the £1 billion cuts agreed in the

Cabinet meeting on July 6. Two Ministers in particular were to resist efforts to cut their Departmental budgets. Shirley Williams was to consistently argue that the price subsidies should be phased out slowly in order to minimise the increased costs that would be incurred by the poor. Against this Barnett argued that the price subsidies were expensive to operate and only had a marginal affect on the retail prices index. Instead, they should be replaced by alternative schemes that redistributed income directly. The other critic was Peter Shore who refused to accept further cuts in expenditure on road transport and housing.[94]

By July 21, there had still been no agreement. The Cabinet had accepted £954 million of public expenditure cuts, which, as Barnett writes, "the Prime Minister was prepared to accept as being near enough. Denis Healey, however, continued to press to get nearer the £1 billion."[95] Cabinet then broke up, and resumed again in the evening. Healey then backed down, saying that the £954 million would cut £60 million off the debt interest repayments and would therefore cut expenditure by over the £1 billion target.[96] Barnett comments that; "this was something of a subterfuge, but that is how it was done."[97] This incident is important for two reasons. Firstly, it shows that public expenditure cuts are a somewhat artificial exercise. The ability to manipulate the figures shows that not all of the cuts were 'real'. Secondly, it shows that Callaghan was not prepared to give Healey his full support at this stage. He was reluctant to push a sceptical Cabinet too far, and so put some pressure on his Chancellor to find an alternative way to find the extra £60 million.

At this stage, Healey then requested a 1% increase in the employers' National Insurance contribution. Pliatzky explains the difficulty in obtaining a £2 billion saving from cuts in public expenditure alone: "one look at the £2 billion package was enough to rule out this consideration. Though £1 billion might be the minimum from one point of view, it looked like the maximum from the point of view of acceptability to the Cabinet."[98] A number of commentators have suggested that Cabinet was angered by Healey's attempt to bounce them into accepting another measure for which they had not had time to consider. However, Dell argues that the Cabinet discussed this measure.[99] Healey initially proposed, with the full support of

Callaghan, that there should be a 1% increase in order to make the July package more favourable to international opinion. At this stage, Crosland and Dell proposed an increase of 2% in order to reduce the PSBR by a further £1 billion in addition to the £1 billion cuts agreed that day. Initially, Callaghan and Healey were sceptical, but eventually gave way and allowed a 2% surcharge in the employers' National Insurance contribution. The following day, July 22, Healey announced the measures to Parliament. In addition to the £1 billion of public expenditure cuts and the £1 billion National Insurance increase, Healey also announced his wish to achieve a money supply target of 12% for the financial year 1976/7: "I do not intend to allow the growth of the money supply to fuel inflation this year or next."[100]

Healey felt that the measures announced were sufficient. However, the July measures have been widely interpreted as a failure. Samuel Brittan argues that, "it is probable that the July package would have been sufficient without further measures if it had been announced at the time of the April Budget and been accompanied by a firm monetary budget. Even when it was announced, it would quite likely have been enough if the Treasury had not muffed the monetary side of its measures."[101] There had not been a sufficiently clear commitment to a monetary target, as was demanded by the international authorities. This, then, is a distinct monetarist interpretation. In addition, the two fiscal measures were also criticised. Firstly, the measures to reduce public expenditure were seen as inadequate. Secondly, the increase in the employers' National Insurance contribution was criticised for adding to unemployment and for undermining market confidence still further. Dell argues that, "the two per cent increase was counter-productive. If we had reduced the 1977/8 PSBR to £9 billion by public expenditure cuts, it is possible that there would have been no autumn crisis. That it had to be done by a £1 billion tax increase convinced the market that there really was no way of persuading this Government to come to its senses."[102] The inconsistency in Dell's thinking must be pointed out here. At the time of the Cabinet discussions in July 1976, Dell had proposed the idea of raising the employers' National Insurance surcharge, but by the time he came to write his memoirs he had changed his mind.

In his study of the 1974-79 Labour Government, Martin Holmes is particularly critical of the July measures.[103] Holmes accepts the criticisms of the July measures outlined above – that there should have been a clear published monetary target, and that the PSBR should have been reduced by a £2 billion cut in public expenditure. Holmes argues that, "to the background of the pound's continued decline the July package was an unmitigated failure... Not surprisingly the Americans, anxious to see signs that effective action had been taken after the $5.3 billion loan, were disappointed."[104]   However, in a recent interview, Holmes has conceded that this interpretation was unfair.   Labour had a clear understanding of the economic situation, and they had introduced measures to deal with the problems they faced.   The Government had introduced public expenditure cuts in January and July 1976 and cash limits in the spring.   They had also formulated a wages policy, which had been in operation from 1975 and had recently been renewed. Finally, they had introduced monetary targets as part of the July measures.   Taken as a whole, Holmes now believes, these measures should have been sufficient to tackle the economic problems.   This is an important concession since it means that the Government had done enough to improve the economic situation by the summer of 1976.   Moreover, it brings us to the position advocated by Crosland, set out in July and again later in the year, that enough had already been done.[105]   I will examine Crosland's position in detail in the next chapter. I now wish to make some additional comments on the July measures.

Firstly, it is difficult to accept the argument presented by Samuel Brittan, and outlined earlier, that there should have been a clearly stated monetary target. Leo Pliatzky argues that, "the Chancellor believed that the crucial reason for the failure of the July package was the omission of any money supply targets from his statement."[106]   However, Healey did announce an intention to stick to a 12% figure. Therefore, as Dell writes, "it seems improbable that Healey really believed that the 22 July statement failed because he had not given a money supply target.   The difference between his words and the actual statement of a target was minimal."[107]

Secondly, critics of the fiscal measures introduced in July 1976, argue that they were insufficient, but fail to identify the political constraints on policy. Hence, Dell argues that, "the package failed because the target for public expenditure cuts set by Treasury Ministers was itself insufficient to satisfy the market and the Cabinet failed to accept even the Treasury proposals and, instead, increased taxation."[108]   According to Dell, the Chancellor should have proposed £2 billion of public expenditure cuts. Eventually, £1 billion of cuts were proposed, but even this was viewed sceptically. Only £954 million of cuts were agreed. Even this figure did not comprise of 'real' cuts in current expenditure. There were £157 million cuts in the capital expenditure of the nationalised industries and £200 million expenditure by the British National Oil Corporation was disregarded in public expenditure accounts. The £1 billion figure was only achieved by adding reductions in debt interest. Finally, a number of measures were introduced by Healey in the form of selective assistance to industry to reduce unemployment. Dell is critical of the fact that there was no genuine attempt to cut current expenditure.[109] However, this lacks an understanding of the political views of other Cabinet ministers, who maintained an ideological commitment to public expenditure and feared the affects such cuts would have on the Social Contract and the Labour movement more generally.

Finally, the critics fail to identify the ideological stance of the international financial authorities. Given that the PSBR was being increasingly financed by overseas investors, it could be argued that this gave them a justifiable interest in British public sector debt.   However, the opinions of the US financial authorities, in particular, were clearly political at this time. Keegan and Pennant-Rea comment that the decision to increase the employers' National Insurance contribution, "only underlined, in the eyes of overseas opinion and the financial markets, the Government's reluctance to cut public expenditure."[110] This is correct in that the July measures failed to restore confidence. But it only failed since international opinion was critical of public expenditure in itself, as distinct from merely being concerned with public sector debt. Had international opinion, specifically the US and German financial authorities, the IMF and the currency markets, only been concerned with the PSBR, it would have welcomed the National Insurance increase as this cut £1 billion from the total. It is therefore clear that international opinion was determined to see public expenditure cuts.   This raises complex questions concerning the nature and content of economic liberalism and monetarism and the relationship between the two, which will be discussed later (Chapter 6).

Decision to Apply to the IMF and the Labour Party Conference: August-September 1976

Initially, the July measures had their intended result in that sterling was stabilised. However, as August wore on, pressure was again reasserted. It is worth mentioning that at this point, market pressure began to be asserted from a different source. Until the summer, the main problem had been the declining value of the pound as the foreign exchange market sold sterling. In August, this stopped, but then recommenced in early September. An added problem was now the gilt-edged market: that is the market in the sale of public sector debt to the non-bank domestic sector. By the summer, the gilt-edged market was refusing to purchase public sector debt as it feared rising inflation and expected interest rates to rise in early-September. The gilt-edged market was therefore a part of the Government's considerations at this time.[111]

The relative period of calm in early August, was already coming under strain by the end of the month. From late August, a number of events combined to cause further downward pressure on sterling. On August 13, the figures for July's visible trade were published showing a deficit of £524 million. The hot summer of 1976 had resulted in a drought, and there was a fear that a three-day week would be introduced in an attempt to save resources. On September 4, the workers at British Leyland went on strike. Three days later, the left-wing dominated National Executive Committee of the Labour Party published a report advocating the nationalisation of the top four clearing banks as the latest stage in the development of the Alternative Economic Strategy. Fay and Young argue that the plan "inevitably sent a shudder through dealers and bankers looking for an antidote to socialism, rather than another dose of it."[112]   On September 8, the Seaman's Union called an immediate strike. All of these events worked to undermine international confidence, and it appears that the markets were very nervous at this stage, responding negatively to every event.[113]

At this point sterling was beginning to fall rapidly once again. As Burk and Cairncross write: "the policy of the Bank had been to hold the rate at about $1.77 and it had done so from June to August by utilising the stand-by credit."[114] The events of late August and early September outlined above made the markets nervous, and the sale of sterling increased. On September 9, the Bank of England stopped supporting the pound after spending $400 million since September 1.[115] It appears that this decision was made by Callaghan and Healey, as the former recalls: "the reality was that as soon as the Bank repaid the $5 billion loan, it simply would not have the resources to sustain sterling at $1.77. This seemed to both the Chancellor and me to be conclusive."[116] Instead, the minimum lending rate was increased by 1.5% to 13% on September 10, in an attempt to stimulate both the foreign exchange market and the gilt-edged market, and the Bank tightened its monetary policy on September 16. However, this did not have the intended results as sterling fell to $1.70 and the gilt-edged market failed to respond.

It was at this time, in early September, that the Government considered going to the IMF.[117] The exact point at which it was agreed to approach the IMF is unclear. Gavyn Davies, a member of the Policy Unit, says that the decision was taken in early September when the first three-month period of the June stand-by passed.[118] Dell recalls that Healey had warned that another sterling crisis was imminent and that the Government must apply to the IMF. This decision was taken at the EY Committee in the week preceding the Labour Party Conference, beginning on September 27.[119] Burk and Cairncross also note that Benn made an entry in his diary on September 23, saying that the EY Committee had agreed to approach the IMF.[120] However, a week later, when Benn was told by a delegate at the Labour Party Conference that the Government was applying for a loan, he appeared surprised by the news: "it was the first I had heard but apparently Denis had gone to the IMF and borrowed £2.5 billion and the conditions won't come out until after the Conference."[121] Two alternatives therefore emerge as to how the decision was taken. The first is that the decision to approach the IMF was taken by Callaghan and Healey, without the consent of Cabinet. However, this is unlikely given that Callaghan was always concerned to maintain Cabinet unity. A decision to apply to the IMF without full Cabinet approval would have been likely to have caused a split. Therefore, the more likely explanation is simply that Benn did not fully understand the significance of the EY Committee on September 23. Cabinet had been debating the possibility of an IMF loan since July, so that the meeting on September 23, may have appeared to be a continuation of discussions, rather than actually marking the point at which a firm decision was reached.

The Labour Party Conference opened on September 27, and the Government was immediately defeated on its public expenditure plans. The result was to put further pressure on sterling. On September 28, as Healey was due to fly to Hong Kong, to attend the meeting of the Commonwealth Finance Ministers, the pound fell to $1.63. Healey decided to return from Heathrow, as he did not want to be out of contact on his journey.[122] Callaghan supported this decision, but later regretted it: "my view was that if staying in London would make the situation easier, he should do so... I should have encouraged the Chancellor to go to Hong Kong, for as soon as the City learned that he had decided not to go, hysterical panic set in for forty-eight hours."[123]

The following day, Healey announced that the Government was to apply for the IMF loan. He then visited the Party Conference on September 30. Under the rules drawn up by the Party, Healey was only given five minutes to speak since he had been voted off the National Executive Committee. Healey argued that the IMF loan would be sought on the basis of "existing policies."[124] However, as Burk and Cairncross note: "the chances of an application on this basis being successful were virtually nil... But Healey could hardly have been expected to stand up in front of the conference in full cry on 30 September and tell them that, on behalf of Britain, he was prepared to throw over cherished policies in exchange for a handful of dollars."[125] Despite this, the mood of the Conference was still hostile. Healey was faced with boos and hisses both before and after the speech. Benn notes that: "I couldn't even clap him, his speech was so vulgar and abusive."[126]

However, the main event of the 1976 Labour Party Conference was the speech by Callaghan on the afternoon of September 28, following Healey's dramatic U-turn at Heathrow airport.[127] Callaghan's speech began by paying tribute to Harold Wilson, and then went on to list the legislative record of the

Government in its first three years, and emphasised the good state of industrial relations at that time and of the need for industrial democracy. Callaghan supported the tripartite structure of industrial relations including voluntary planning agreements and the Social Contract. The Prime Minister pledged to improve educational standards and increase resources for vocational education and training. Callaghan then went on to talk about race relations, in the only section of the speech to receive widespread applause. He supported legislation for devolution in Scotland and Wales. In foreign affairs, Callaghan emphasised the need for a settlement in Rhodesia and for greater international security. Finally, he warned of the dangers of entryism in the Labour Party from extremist left-wing organisations. However, it was the section on economic policy that caused much controversy. Since this is usually interpreted as the point when Keynesianism was abandoned, I intend to quote extensively from the text of the speech. Callaghan said:

> "The cosy world we were told would go on for ever, where full-employment would be guaranteed by a stroke of the Chancellor's pen, cutting taxes, deficit spending – that sort of cosy world is gone. Yesterday delegates pointed to the first sorry fruits: a high rate of unemployment. The rate of unemployment today – there is no need for me to say this to you – cannot be justified on any grounds, least of all the human dignity of those involved, but, Mr. Chairman and comrades, still less did I become the leader of our Party to propound shallow analyses and false remedies for fundamental economic and social problems. When we reject unemployment as an economic instrument as we do – and when we reject also superficial remedies, as socialists must, then we must ask ourselves unflinchingly: what is the cause of high unemployment? Quite simply and unequivocally it is caused by paying ourselves more than the value we produce. There are no scapegoats. This is as true in a mixed economy under a Labour Government as it is under capitalism or

communism. It is an absolute fact of life which no
Government be it left or right can alter. Of course
in Eastern Europe you cannot price yourself out of
your job, because you cannot withdraw your labour.
So the Government can at least guarantee the
appearance of full-employment. But that is not the
democratic way.

We used to think that we could spend your way out
of recession and increase employment by cutting
taxes and increasing Government spending. I tell
you in all candour that that option no longer exists,
and that insofar as it ever did exist, it only worked
on each occasion since the war by injecting a bigger
dose of inflation into the economy, followed by a
higher level of unemployment at the next step.
Higher inflation followed by higher unemployment.
We have just escaped from the highest rate of
inflation this country has known; we have not yet
escaped   from   the   consequences: high
unemployment. That is the history of the last
twenty years. Each time we did this, the twin evils
of unemployment and inflation have hit hardest
those least able to stand them. Not those with the
strongest bargaining power, no, it has not hit those.
It has hit the poor, the old and the sick. We have
struggled, as a Party, to try to maintain their
standards, and indeed to improve them, against the
strength of free collective bargaining power that we
have seen exerted as some people have tried to
maintain their standards against this economic
policy.

Now we must get back to fundamentals. First,
overcoming unemployment now unambiguously
depends on our labour costs being at least
comparable with those of our major competitors.
Second, we can only become competitive by having
the right kind of investment at the right kind of
level, and by significantly improving the
productivity of both labour and capital. Third, we
will fail – and I say this to those who have been
pressing about public expenditure...if we can think

> we can buy our way back by printing what Denis
> Healey calls 'confetti money' to pay ourselves more
> than we can produce."[128]

The speech is usually regarded as the moment when Keynesianism was rejected in favour of monetarism. David Smith, in his study of monetarist economic policy in the UK, says that the speech, "effectively sounded the death-knell for postwar Keynesian policies."[129] Similarly Anthony Seldon has commented: "in 1976 the Labour Government was forced to abandon full-employment,"[130]. This point is reiterated by Noel Thompson in his recent study of the Labour Party's political economy.[131]   David Marquand argues that the postwar Keynesian consensus came to an end with the 1976 speech.[132] Callaghan has admitted that the section of the speech concerned with economic policy was written by his son-in-law, Peter Jay. Jay was one of the leading advocates of monetarism at this time, and believes that the speech was intended to criticise Keynesianism.[133] The speech raised the Keynesian–monetarist controversy and appears to have endorsed monetarism. It was widely welcomed at an international level, and helped to stabilise the value of sterling.

However, it is possible to argue that the significance of the speech has been misunderstood. In his memoirs, Jim Callaghan writes: "I see no reason to retract a single word of what I said then."[134] Callaghan argues that the speech was not a rejection of Keynesianism. His was not arguing for a monetarist position, but merely that in the context of 1976 there was a need to reduce inflation and public sector debt.   In the speech, Callaghan goes on to argue that much progress had already been made in this area, but that more needed to be done. He also supported state intervention in the economy to reduce unemployment: "of course a Labour Government must not, and will not, stand by and do nothing about unemployment."[135] Moreover, the Prime Minister did not rule out the introduction of import deposits: "we shall continue to examine them case by case... There is no philosophical block of any sort about that."[136] As mentioned above, Callaghan also maintained the need for an incomes policy to combat inflation.   Finally, it is worth mentioning that Keynesianism did accept the need to control inflation, as well as unemployment, and that the relative importance of each of these would depend on which was the major problem at a given point. This is different from saying that the objective of full employment, which was held to be the primary objective of macroeconomic policy in the longer term by the postwar Keynesians, had been abandoned.[137]

Callaghan's own opinion on the speech has previously been unknown.[138] However, in a recent correspondence, Callaghan emphasised that the speech was primarily concerned with the immediate problems in the economy at that time. Callaghan has said that he had two objectives in making the speech.[139] Firstly, he wished to develop a positive and cooperative agenda in industrial relations, bringing the trades unions and the CBI together in order to achieve lower inflation and unemployment. His second intention was to deliver a warning to the left of the Labour Party, which was advocating policies that would make the economic situation worse. Callaghan says that he was "concerned that the left-wing majority on the National Executive Committee was proposing measures to remedy the situation that were unrealistic and would not have been successful. Inflation was the main enemy both in the UK and in other countries, and we would have been heading in the wrong direction if public expenditure had been allowed to continue to grow year by year faster than GDP as this was restricting investment in industry."[140] So the policies being advocated by the left under the banner of the Alternative Economic Strategy such as general import controls and large increases in public expenditure were wrong because they took no account of economic realities and were disliked by international financial opinion. Added to these two objectives, there was also the attempt by Callaghan to restore international confidence.[141] Callaghan needed to demonstrate that the Government was committed to reducing public sector debt and inflation still further, and that they believed that monetary targets were important in combating inflation. The objectives of the speech were therefore short-term, rather than with any concern to implement monetarism. Given this, it must therefore be seen as a mistake to have raised the issue of political economy at all. As Kenneth Morgan writes: "whether he needed to do so by raising the entire Keynesian-monetarist argument in this way and giving a hostage to Tory fortunes is another matter."[142]

It also appears that the speech was not regarded as a dramatic turning point by other senior ministers. Commenting on the speech Healey was later to remark: "never have your speeches written by your son-in-law."[143] Healey appears not to have known the content of the speech before it was delivered, and felt that it was misleading. Dell thought that the speech was unimpressive, being simply a statement of what had been happening for at least two years.[144] Similarly, Steve Ludlam, in his article on the 1976 IMF Crisis, argues that the speech was of little importance. The shift in emphasis from full employment to inflation had already occurred. In short, the speech was of minor significance.[145] Hence, there is still much controversy over the speech. Either Callaghan had endorsed monetarism, or maintained support for Keynesianism. I return to this issue in Chapter 7.

Summary

This chapter has covered the period March – September 1976. The Government had already made some public expenditure cuts in January 1976. In March, the pound began to fall rapidly in value, following a bungled attempt to stop further appreciation of sterling. The period from March to September 1976 was marked by the introduction of a series of measures to halt this decline. Following the leadership contest, the Government extended cash limits on public expenditure and implemented a second year of pay restraint. In June 1976, the Government was given a stand-by credit, and in July introduced further public expenditure cuts. By August 1976, the position appeared to have stabilised. But in early September, the depreciation of sterling resumed. The Government finally declared its intention to apply for an IMF loan during the 1976 Labour Party Conference. Given that the earlier measures were an attempt to avoid going to the IMF, they could be seen to have failed. Hence as Burk and Cairncross write: "at the end of seven months the Cabinet tacitly admitted defeat and agreed to apply to the IMF."[146] The following chapter will examine the negotiations, which occurred between October 1976 and January 1977, that led to the granting of the IMF loan and the reduction of the sterling balances. I will then return to some of the events described above in order to analyse the changes in political economy and economic policy in the mid-1970s.

[1] This chapter closely follows the studies by Burk, K. and Cairncross, A., *Goodbye Great Britain: The 1976 IMF Crisis*, (Yale University Press, New Haven, 1992) and Harmon, M.D., *The British Labour Government and the 1976 IMF Crisis*, (Macmillan, Basingstoke, 1997), while adding new information obtained from interviews and, to a lesser extent, archival research

[2] Burk and Cairncross, ibid., pp.20-21

[3] Fay, S. and Young, H., 'The Day the £ Nearly Died', *Sunday Times*, 14, 21, 28/5/78. Republished in book format in 1978.

[4] Lever first advanced the argument for reforming the structure of sterling deposits, which was to become a central part of the debate at the end of 1976. Bernstein, K., *The International Monetary Fund and Deficit Countries: The Case of Britain 1974-77*, (Unpublished PhD thesis, Stanford University, 1983)

[5] Fay and Young, pp.10-11

[6] Ibid., pp.11-12

[7] Keegan, W. and Pennant-Rea, R., *Who Runs The Economy*, (Maurice Temple Smith, London, 1979)

[8] Burk and Cairncross, p.25

[9] Pliatzky, L., *Getting and Spending: Public Expenditure, Employment and Inflation*, (Blackwell, Oxford, 1982), p.148

[10] Dell, E., *A Hard Pounding: Politics and Economic Crisis*, (Oxford University Press, Oxford, 1991)

[11] Ibid.

[12] Ibid.

[13] Burk and Cairncross, pp.28-30

[14] Dell, pp.206-208

[15] Ibid. p.209

[16] quoted in Burk and Cairncross, pp.28-29

[17] It does appear that Healey was in favour of halting further appreciation however. See Whitehead, P., *The Writing on the Wall: Britain in the Seventies*, (Michael Joseph, London, 1985), p.183

[18] Dell, pp.206-208

[19] Donoughue, B., *Prime Minister: The Conduct of Economic Policy Under Harold Wilson and James Callaghan*, (Cape, London, 1987)

[20] Burk, K., et.al., 'The 1976 IMF Crisis' *Contemporary Record*, November 1989, pp.39-45, p.42. Donoughue's account mirrors that of Wilson's. See Wilson, H., *Final Term: The Labour Government 1974-76*, (Weidenfeld and Nicolson, and Michael Joseph, London, 1979), pp.227-229

[21] Burk and Cairncross, p.29. See also Bernstein, p.328

[22] Healey, D., *The Time of My Life*, (Penguin, London, 1989, 2nd Edition), p.426. Generally, Healey is vague on his role in events throughout the course of 1976

[23] Private information from a former Bank of England official (10/06/2000)

24 Ibid. Dell also says that: "it would be remarkable if Healey was not himself consulted about the drop in interest rates even though it would be normal for him not to be consulted about the day to day details of operations on the exchanges," p.207

25 Wilson's resignation was the source of much controversy given that the decision appeared to have been made suddenly. In fact, we now know that Wilson had been planning to resign for some time. See Wilson, pp.228-239, and Donoughue, pp.86-87. See also Pimlott, B., *Harold Wilson*, (Harper Collins, London, 1992)

26 The leadership contest is discussed only very briefly in Burk and Cairncross. I think that this is unfortunate since the contest is important to a fuller understanding of the 1976 sterling/IMF Crisis. See Burk and Cairncross, p.31

27 See Kellner, P. and Hitchens, C., *Callaghan: The Road to Number 10*, (Cassell, London, 1976), for a critical appraisal of Callaghan's record as a minister. See Morgan, K.O., *Callaghan: A Life*, (Oxford University Press, Oxford, 1997) for a more favourable interpretation.

28 Burk and Cairncross, p.33, Healey, pp.446-447

29 Burk and Cairncross, p.33

30 Healey, p.446

31 See Crosland, S., *Tony Crosland*, (Coronet, London, 1983, 2nd Edition), pp.311-321; and Jefferys, K., *Anthony Crosland: A New Biography*, (Cohen, London, 1999), pp.187-199. There is some degree of uncertainty in placing Crosland within the Labour Party's ideological spectrum. It is possible to argue that by the 1970s, Crosland was no longer on the right of the Party. See Crosland, p.71: " in later years as many on the right became readier to compromise with existing social structures, his impatience bordered on hostility. He said he was an egalitarian and he meant it. Those who knew him best thought his position on Labour's spectrum between the 1950s and 1977 was centre-right, centre, centre-left. His view was that he moved from the far left of his pre-war years to the centre of the Party and stayed there."

32 Although many on the left of the Party thought that he had been too orthodox, and may have contributed to Labour's General Election defeat in 1970.

33 See Jenkins, R., *A Life at the Centre*, (Macmillan, London, 1991)

34 Benn, T., *Against the Tide: Diaries 1973-6*, (Arrow, London, 1989), 2/7/76, pp.588-590. See also Adams, J., *Tony Benn*, (Pan, London, 1993)

35 See Morgan, pp.469-484; and Kellner, P., 'Anatomy of the Vote', *New Statesman*, 9 April 1976, for a discussion of the results

36 Jefferys, p.189

37 Healey, p.447. See also Morgan, pp.485-552 for a discussion of Callaghan's style as Prime Minister.

38 Callaghan, J., *Time and Chance*, (Collins, London, 1987) p.414

39 Ibid., pp.413-4

40 Ibid., pp.414-5

[41] Burk and Cairncross, p.35, Dell, pp.216-8, Barnett, J., *Inside The Treasury*, (Andre Deutsch, London, 1982) pp.87-8

[42] Burk and Cairncross, p.35

[43] Holmes, M., *The Labour Government 1974-79: Political Aims and Economic Reality*, (Macmillan, Basingstoke, 1985) p.84

[44] Ibid.

[45] See Pliatzky, pp.143-7, for a full discussion of cash limits. See also 'The Attack on Inflation: The Second Year', Cmnd.6507, (HMSO, London, 1976); and 'Cash Limits on Public Expenditure', Cmnd.6440 (HMSO, London, 1976)

[46] Ibid. p.144

[47] Healey, p.402

[48] Jones, J., *Union Man: The Autobiography of Jack Jones*, (Collins, London, 1986) p.35

[49] Holmes, pp.85-6, Healey, p.397, Dell, p.217, Burk and Cairncross, p.35

[50] Holmes, p.86

[51] Pliatzky, p.142

[52] Burk and Cairncross, p.35

[53] Pliatzky, p.148. Dell suggests that the leading advocate of the loan at this stage was Harold Lever. Dell, p.218

[54] Only two alternatives appear to have been given serious consideration. Other policy proposals such as the Alternative Economic Strategy were not considered within the Treasury. This probably shows how little importance was attached to the AES within the Treasury.

[55] Pliatzky, p.148

[56] Burk and Cairncross, p.40

[57] Ibid.

[58] Healey, p.427

[59] Barnett, p.89

[60] Pliatzky, pp.148-9

[61] Fay and Young, p.14. See also Burk and Cairncross, pp.40-1

[62] Fay and Young, p.7

[63] Barnett, p.89

[64] Burk and Cairncross, p.41

[65] See Burk and Cairncross, pp.41-7, and Dell, pp.219-222

[66] quoted in Burk and Cairncross, p.37

[67] quoted in Burk and Cairncross, p.38

[68] Healey, p.427

[69] See Dell. pp.220-222

[70] quoted in Burk and Cairncross, p.43

[71] See Burk and Cairncross, p.45, for details of the loan

[72] quoted in Harmon, pp.144-145

[73] Callaghan, p.419

[74] See Burk, et.al., 1989, for a discussion of the conspiracy theory.

[75] Interview with Lord Donoughue, (12/10/00)

[76] Callaghan, p.420. Some of those close to Crosland also felt that the Treasury officials were not negotiating with sufficient strength in the IMF discussions later that year. Message from Lord Lipsey, (June, 2001)

[77] Dell, pp.219-220

[78] Ibid.

[79] Interview with Sir Nick Monck

[80] Callaghan, pp.419-420

[81] Ibid. p.420

[82] Barnett, p.89

[83] See Burk and Cairncross, pp.47-52, Holmes, pp.88-91

[84] Healey, p.428

[85] Pliatzky, p.149

[86] Burk and Cairncross, pp.47-8. See Barnett, pp.89-96, for a detailed discussion of the debate over the expenditure cuts in July 1976.

[87] Crosland, pp.341-342

[88] Anthony Crosland Papers, BLPES, Notebook, August 1976

[89] This led to a conflict between Tony Crosland and Jim Callaghan. Callaghan asked what Crosland was prepared to give up from the Foreign Office budget in order to protect the transport budget. Crosland said that he would do the same as Callaghan himself would have done when Foreign Secretary – nothing. Callaghan retorted that at least as Foreign Secretary, he would have supported the Chancellor. See Jefferys, p.204, and Barnett, p.93

[90] See Benn, T., *Against the Tide: Diaries 1973-6*, (Arrow, London, 1989), 2/7/76, pp.588-590

[91] Burk and Cairncross, pp.48-50

[92] Barnett, p.89

[93] Ibid. p.90

[94] Ibid. pp.90-92

[95] Ibid.

[96] Ibid. p.95

[97] Ibid.

[98] Pliatzky, p.149

[99] Dell, pp.229-230

[100] Hansard, House of Commons Debates, (22/07/76), Col.2019

[101] Brittan, S., and Lilley, P., *The Delusion of Incomes Policy*, (Temple Smith, London, 1977), p.89

[102] Dell, p.230

[103] Holmes, pp.90-91

[104] Ibid., p.90

[105] Interview with Martin Holmes, (23/03/00)

[106] Pliatzky, p.150

[107] Dell, p.231

[108] Ibid.

[109] Ibid., pp.229-230

[110] Keegan and Pennant-Rea, p.164

111 Burk and Cairncross, p.52
112 Fay and Young, p.19
113 See Burk and Cairncross, p.53, and Morgan, pp.532-533
114 Burk and Cairncross, p.53
115 See Burk and Cairncross, pp.53-54; Callaghan, pp.422-423; Healey, p.428; and Holmes, p.91
116 Callaghan, p.422
117 Burk and Cairncross, pp.54-55
118 Davies, in Burk, et.al., (1989), p.44
119 Dell, p.235
120 cited in Burk and Cairncross, p.55.   Benn, unpublished diary, (23/09/76)
121 Benn, *Against the Tide*, (29/07/76), pp.615-616
122 Burk and Cairncross, p.55. Morgan, pp.533-534
123 Callaghan, p.428. Margaret Garritsen De Vries states that the IMF was unhappy about Healey's decision and that it added to later difficulties, De Vries, M.G., *The International Monetary Fund 1972-78: Cooperation on Trial*, 3 vols. (Washington D.C., International Monetary Fund, 1985)
124 Healey, 1976 Labour Party Conference, Report, p.319
125 Burk and Cairncross, p.57
126 Benn, *Against the Tide*, (30/09/76), p.616
127 Callaghan, Parliamentary Report, 1976 Labour Party Conference, Report, (28/09/76), pp.185-194
128 Ibid. See also Callaghan, pp.425-427; and Morgan, pp.535-537
129 Smith, D., *The Rise and Fall of Monetarism*, (Penguin, London, 1987), p.65
130 Seldon, A., 'Ideas are not Enough', in Marquand, D., and Seldon, A., (Eds.), *The Ideas That Shaped Postwar Britain*, (Fontana, London, 1996), p.260
131 Thompson, N., *Left in the Wilderness: The Political Economy of British Democratic Socialism*, (Acumen, Chesham, 2002)
132 Marquand, D., *The Unprincipled Society*, (Cape, London, 1988)
133 Letter from Peter Jay, (23/05/00). Jay was Economics Editor of The Times, and along with Sam Brittan, was a leading advocate of monetarism in Britain in the 1970s. See also his *Employment, Inflation and Politics*, (Institute of Economic Affairs, No.46, London, 1975), for a theoretical statement of his views on the causes of inflation and unemployment.
134 Callaghan, p.427
135 Callaghan speech
136 Ibid.
137 This point was emphasised by Lord Lipsey. Interview with Lord Lipsey, (12/10/00)
138 Interview with Lord Morgan, (22/05/00)
139 Correspondence from Lord Callaghan to the author, (06/06/00)
140 Ibid.

[141] Interview with Lord Morgan
[142] Morgan, p.537
[143] quoted in Morgan, p.537
[144] Dell, p.237
[145] Ludlam, S., 'The Gnomes of Washington: Four Myths of the 1976 IMF Crisis', *Political Studies*, XL, (1992), pp.713-727: pp.724-726
[146] Burk and Cairncross, pp.57-58

CHAPTER 5

POLITICS AND ECONOMIC POLICY: OCTOBER 1976 – JANUARY 1977

Introduction

In the last two chapters, I described events from the election of the Labour Government in March 1974 through to the 1976 Labour Party Conference. In September 1976, the Government decided to approach the IMF. Despite the introduction of various measures to reduce the public sector borrowing requirement and inflation in order to restore market confidence in sterling, the pound continued to fall. The period from October 1976 to January 1977 saw the agreement of the IMF loan and measures to protect sterling. This chapter has two main aims. The first is to complete the narrative begun in the last two chapters. Secondly, it contributes original material on some aspects of this narrative: in particular, the process of Cabinet negotiations, on which I have been able to conduct a wide range of interviews. Specifically, three sets of negotiations occurred. From October, Jim Callaghan sought to obtain the support of President Gerald Ford and Chancellor Helmut Schmidt. The IMF team arrived in early November, beginning a lengthy bargaining process with the Government. Finally, the Cabinet itself divided, and did not reach agreement until early December. I begin by examining events in October, which sheds some light on the thoughts of Jim Callaghan and Denis Healey.

October 1976

After the dramatic events of the Labour Party Conference at the end of September, things appeared to settle down in October.

In fact, October could be viewed as a 'phoney-phase'. Although there was a feeling of impending crisis, little of a decisive nature occurred.[1]

Healey raised the interest rate to a record level of 15% on October 7.[2]   According to the Treasury, there were two immediate economic problems.   The first was the stagnant guilt-edged market, which had been weak since early summer. The second problem was the continual fall in the value of sterling.   By October 6, Healey had been convinced by his officials of the need to raise interest rates.   However, Callaghan initially refused.   In response, Healey threatened to resign. Returning to his office at 11 Downing Street, Healey talked things over with Edmund Dell; described by Healey as, "the only member of the Cabinet on whom I could count."[3]   During the meeting between Healey and Dell, Callaghan's Principal Private Secretary, Kenneth Stowe, appeared and said that having tested the Chancellor's resolve, the Prime Minister would support him. The following day, Healey announced his decision to raise the minimum lending rate by 2% to 15%, and to increase the ratio of sterling deposits by 2%. According to Tony Benn, "these (were) crisis measures of tremendous moment."[4]   Stephen Fay and Hugo Young add that, "to men such as Crosland, Lever and Benn, the 15 per cent interest rate did not save the pound, it was a blow to hopes for growth and jobs."[5] However, the Economic Strategy Committee accepted this decision with little criticism. Kathleen Burk and Alec Cairncross argue that this was so for a combination of two reasons: Cabinet does not normally decide the interest rate, and Healey now had the backing of the Prime Minister.[6]

Given Healey's objectives, the measures taken on October 7 were largely successful. The pound remained steady for just over two weeks and there was also a rush to purchase guilts. Indeed, the guilt-edged market was to remain healthy, and the only remaining problem from this point was therefore the pound itself. The pound came under renewed pressure from October 24, when a Sunday Times article claimed that the terms with the IMF had already been agreed. In the article, written by the Economics Editor, Malcolm Crawford, it was argued that the IMF wanted to devalue the pound from around $1.64 as it then was to $1.50.[7] This caused a further run on the pound until it reached a low of $1.535 on October 28, despite rebuttals from the IMF and from William Simon, the US Treasury Secretary. Although Crawford defended his view, later arguing that it was based on leaked documents from the IMF, the alleged policy has been categorically denied by Alan Whittome, the Head of the IMF delegation to London, who says that, "no one was talking about $1.50."[8] The incident shows the fragility of sterling at this time. The markets appeared to be willing to accept any 'news' that the authorities wished to reduce further the value of the pound.

Callaghan's refusal to support Healey on October 6 raised questions over the attitude of the Prime Minister. Edmund Dell writes that, "this incident must have created considerable doubt in Healey's mind as to how far he could rely on the Prime Minister's support."[9] Callaghan appeared to have serious doubts over the course of action favoured by Healey and the Treasury. At 15%, the minimum lending rate was higher than it had ever been. According to Burk and Cairncross, Callaghan, "feared that it would jeopardise further economic growth, with rising unemployment as a consequence."[10] Callaghan, at least at this early stage, appeared to have some concerns over Treasury policy. According to Bernard Donoughue, then Head of the Policy Unit, Callaghan took control of economic policy.[11] However, this is a rather ambiguous comment. As Burk and Cairncross write: "it is unclear just what this might mean: on most major decisions the Chancellor needs the agreement of the Prime Minister in any case, and even if, strictly speaking, he did not, any prudent Chancellor would obtain it."[12] Donoughue therefore misses the full significance of this event. Instead, it can be argued that Callaghan was still unconvinced of the need to approach the IMF and was starting to intervene in economic policy in order to find an alternative solution, or at least to minimise the demands that the IMF were likely to make on the British Government. This can be detected in his attempts to obtain the support of Gerald Ford and Helmut Schmidt, and I return to this below.

Callaghan caused further concern on October 25, when he appeared on the BBC television programme *Panorama*.[13] Callaghan talked openly of the need to reduce the sterling deposits. Callaghan was to become fixated with the issue of sterling deposits, which he blamed for the instability of the pound both in 1967, as Chancellor of the Exchequer, when he was forced to devalue, and again in 1976. This was basically the desire of a large number of countries to hold their currency reserves in sterling. As this issue was not to be concluded until January 1977, I will discuss it in more detail in the final section of this chapter. Callaghan also raised the issue of Britain's military commitments in Germany and Cyprus and the possible threat of withdrawal. According to Fay and Young, "the broadcast caused consternation in the Treasury. Until it was made, no one there understood the depth of Callaghan's commitment to a course so different from the one they were pursuing."[14] Although this may have been the case with Treasury officials, it appears that Healey had approved of the approach taken by Callaghan. Tony Benn writes in his diary that Healey had informed him on October 28, that he had given his approval to these comments prior to the *Panorama* interview.[15]

Callaghan, the Americans and the Germans

Callaghan, then, was trying to reduce the conditions that the IMF would be likely to place on any loan. One crucial method of trying to achieve this was by obtaining the support of Gerald Ford and Helmut Schmidt. For purposes of clarity I intend to discuss separately Ford and Schmidt, and begin with Ford.

On September 30, while the Labour Party Conference was still taking place, Callaghan telephoned Ford.[16] He told him of the economic situation and asked for his assistance. Specifically, Callaghan wanted two things. First, he wanted Ford to put pressure on the US financial authorities, which were urging the IMF to take a tough line against Britain. Callaghan also asked for help with the sterling balances, as he had already convinced himself that the instability of the pound was due to the existence of large reserves held by the governments of other countries. Ford replied by complementing Callaghan on his conference speech. This appears to have surprised Callaghan, as he did not expect to hear that his speech was already headline news in America. Callaghan believed that Ford was offering his support for the British Government. However, Ford also expressed some concern over the likelihood of import controls. Callaghan responded by mentioning both the issue of the troops and the issue of import controls, as he was to do on October 25 in his *Panorama* interview, adding that this was the leading alternative strategy if the IMF loan was not forthcoming. Callaghan clearly intended to be alarmist, in the hope of moving Ford to act. Ford commented: "we would have reservations, and hopefully, Jim, you could avoid the trade limitation."[17]

At this juncture Callaghan also got the support of George Meany, the President of the AFL/CIO trades union organisation. In a letter to Ford, Meaney urged the US Government to, "devise and initiate concrete measures in the form of whatever guarantees, loans, or other programs of aid that may be required to overcome this emergency and to restore confidence in the future of the British economy, so that the United Kingdom may resume its proper role as a great asset to the universal cause of human progress and freedom."[18]

Callaghan believed that he had the support of Ford. In his memoirs, Callaghan writes: "I never had cause to doubt Gerald Ford's word or his good faith."[19] He accounted for this by the commitment which both had to the Anglo-American alliance, which transcended their party differences. Callaghan may or may not have been right in this judgement. However, it was to become clear that Ford was unable to help, or at least not to the extent that Callaghan had wished. This was so for two reasons. The first was that Ford was fighting a difficult Presidential election campaign, which he was to lose on November 2, the day after the IMF team arrived in London to begin the negotiations. From November until mid-January when the new President, Jimmy Carter, would be sworn in, Ford was a lame-duck President. Hence, he was in a position of weakness for the entire period of the IMF negotiations, as Callaghan notes: "his influence quite naturally waned, at a time when we most needed his help."[20]

The second reason why Ford was unable to help was that the US authorities were deeply divided.[21] Callaghan was to have frequent telephone conversations with Ford, who appeared to offer his support. Ford's Secretary of State, Henry Kissinger, was also known to be in sympathy with the British Government. However, the finance officials were hostile to the Labour Government and were known to be pushing the IMF to obtain the strictest terms that it could. William Simon (Treasury Secretary), Ed Yeo (Under-Secretary of the Treasury) and Arthur Burns (Chairman of the Federal Reserve) were all critical of the British Government. There was, therefore, a conflict of opinion between Ford and Kissinger on the one hand and the finance officials on the other. The Treasury and the Federal Reserve traditionally enjoyed a semi-independent status. Moreover, the defeat of the Ford Administration on November 2 added to their sense of independent authority since they could effectively ignore Ford and Kissinger during the height of the IMF Crisis.[22]

These internal divisions were to be most clearly demonstrated in mid-November when Harold Lever, the Chancellor of the Duchy of Lancaster, visited Washington. The mission was a tight secret in London. Only Callaghan, Lever and Healey were aware of it. Other ministers found out at the Economic Strategy Committee on November 17, after Lever had visited Washington. In a letter to Ford, Callaghan asked if he would receive Lever in Washington to discuss the unfolding crisis. According to Callaghan, Ford "at once agreed to my request to receive Harold Lever."[23] The Treasury and the Federal Reserve were unhappy about this decision. They believed that the British Government was trying to avoid taking the IMF loan. Yeo says that, "for a while it looked as though we were going to get our tail kicked... At this stage we regarded the sterling balances as a Trojan horse, because an agreement about them would have made the Fund irrelevant."[24]

Lever arrived in Washington on November 14. That day he held meetings with Simon and Burns. According to Sir William Ryrie, the UK Executive Director of the IMF, who attended the meeting held between Lever and Simon, the latter "was like a brick wall."[25] Later Lever warned Burns: "be careful, Arthur, if you push too hard you'll get your cuts but they'll include major defence cuts...We're going to come to terms with the IMF, but they must be sensible terms."[26]

Lever then met Henry Kissinger the following day. William Ryrie again attended the meeting. According to Ryrie, the discussion did not go well. Kissinger told Lever that he was bound to fail in his mission, that he lacked the support of the British Cabinet and that he failed to understand the nature of the crisis. When Lever told him that the British economy was not in a bad condition, Kissinger replied by asking: "how come you got this crisis then?"[27] Lever appeared to make more progress when he raised the issues of import protection and military responsibilities. Kissinger then offered help.

The following morning, Lever met Gerald Ford. Lever told the President of the British Government's intention to reach agreement with the IMF and of the wish to obtain agreement on the sterling deposits. Lever then pressed for a kind of parallel agreement, so that the British could announce simultaneously the IMF and sterling agreements. Although Ford did not clearly state his support for simultaneity, his response was sufficiently vague to lead Lever to think that there had been agreement on this point. Lever was pleased with the apparent agreement and contacted Callaghan via the British Embassy. When news of this got out, the US Government was quick to respond; saying that no such agreement had been reached. Robert Hormats, the economic adviser to the National Security Council, Helmut Sonnenfeldt, Kissinger's Deputy, and Kissinger himself told Lever that no such agreement had been reached. Lever was angered by this, but was placated by Kissinger, who pledged to continue to support the British in Washington.

Lever returned to London, while arguments raged in Washington. As Fay and Young noted, "hostilities in Washington continued after Lever's departure. The US Treasury was incensed by the agreement in principle and aghast at any possibility of ambiguity on timing. The White House was locked in discussions with the Treasury, with Kissinger intervening."[28] At the end of the week, a position had been reached. The British Government was informed that the US had agreed in principle to the sterling deposits scheme, but only after the IMF terms had been finalised in London.

What then was the significance of all of this? The answer to this question depends upon how one interprets Callaghan's aims. In a recent interview, Shirley Williams has argued that Callaghan was convinced from an early stage of the need to reach agreement with the IMF and consequently of the need to cut public expenditure.[29] If this was so, then it may be argued that Callaghan was keen to send Lever to Washington in order to convert him to the case for IMF agreement. As will be seen below, Lever was one of the leading members of the Cabinet arguing against public expenditure cuts as being unnecessarily deflationary. Lever had expressed his support for the position advanced by Tony Crosland. Callaghan was keen to reach agreement with the IMF without ministerial resignations, and therefore, sent Lever to Washington. Callaghan hoped that Lever would realise the strength of American opinion against the alternative strategies being advanced in the British Cabinet. Once Lever appreciated this fact he would switch his support to Healey.

However, it is possible to argue against this on two grounds. Firstly, this interpretation misunderstands the relationship between Callaghan and Lever. It appears that Callaghan respected Lever's opinions.[30] Lever had been close to Harold Wilson, and was also close to Callaghan. As Chancellor of the Duchy of Lancaster he had no departmental responsibilities, and could therefore be used in whatever capacity the Prime Minister wished. Moreover, Lever had an expert knowledge of the finance markets. It is more likely, therefore, that Callaghan sent Lever to Washington in the hope that he could exert some influence over the Americans. This is reinforced by a second consideration. It has already been noted that Callaghan was undecided as to the best way to proceed in October. This appears to have been the case in the first half of November as well. Callaghan's concerns were largely political, in that he wanted to maintain the Cabinet, Parliamentary Party and Social Contract with the trades unions, and therefore sought to soften the demands of the IMF.[31]

Edmund Dell has written that the visit to America was a failure.[32] Given that Callaghan had tried to obtain the support of the Americans, he had failed. The US refused to support an agreement on the sterling balances and had not promised to soften the position of the IMF. However, this is too critical. Callaghan had obtained the first clear statement of support on the sterling balances given by the Americans. Furthermore, he had obtained stronger support from both Ford and Kissinger, although in the end this was to count for little against the intransigence of the Treasury and Federal Reserve.[33]

Having discussed relations with the US at some length, I now intend to examine the role of Germany. On September 30, the same day that he rang Ford, Callaghan also discussed the situation with Helmut Schmidt.[34] On October 9, Schmidt visited London on invitation from Callaghan following his success in the German elections. Callaghan discussed the economic situation. The demands that the IMF were likely to make were neither politically nor economically desirable. They would threaten the unity of the Cabinet and the basis of the Social Contract, and may actually lead to a change of Government. Moreover, the measures would be strongly deflationary. Schmidt appeared to have had much sympathy with Callaghan. Schmidt believed that the British economy still faced several structural problems and is likely to have urged the need for further cuts in public expenditure. Schmidt's attitude was that Callaghan was the "last best hope" of changing course.[35] Callaghan asked for help with the sterling balances. Again Schmidt seemed willing to help, and criticised the Americans for running a large deficit.

Schmidt kept in constant touch with Callaghan for the whole of the crisis period by telephone. In addition, he sent Karl Otto Pohl, State Secretary in the Finance Department, on visits to London and Washington. According to Pohl, Schmidt took a key role in the sterling crisis: "Callaghan called Schmidt nearly every evening and asked him to support Britain in negotiations with the IMF."[36] On November 5, Schmidt told Callaghan, during a telephone call, that he had now drawn up plans to help. Callaghan described this as, "an unexpected offer that was to be of tremendous reassurance during the difficult weeks that followed... Schmidt said he felt Germany must be ready to act when required, in order to make the British Government feel a little more secure."[37] It appears that Schmidt was offering to provide assistance for the sterling deposits. Sir John Hunt, the Cabinet Secretary, was sent by Callaghan to Bonn to discuss the possible plan. In the end, Schmidt was unable to help with the sterling plan until the IMF agreement had been reached. This was so for two reasons.[38]

The first was that Schmidt had made commitments he was unable to meet. Karl Otto Pohl has said that, "Schmidt always made promises of that kind at this time, committing the reserves of the Bundersbank to people like Callaghan...but he was not empowered to do that."[39] This was because of the role of the German central bank. The 1957 Bundersbank Law made the central bank the 'protector of the currency' under paragraph three, and not subject to Government control under paragraph twelve. It was therefore the Bundersbank that had the power to make such decisions, and it was unlikely that it would do so prior to agreement with the IMF.

The second factor was the role of the United States. By the end of October, news had reached Washington that Schmidt was prepared to do a deal with Callaghan on the sterling balances. The news was met with some alarm by the US financial authorities, and William Simon flew immediately to Bonn. Simon discovered that Schmidt was being advised not to reach such an agreement, and added his voice to these calls. In the end, Schmidt was persuaded that if this action were taken unilaterally by the West German Government, he would be undermining the role of the IMF. Callaghan was therefore unsuccessful in persuading Schmidt on the sterling balances. He did, however, have more success on getting Schmidt to help in tempering the demands of the IMF. Schmidt consistently urged the German Executive Director of the IMF, Herr Pieske, to argue for restraint. In addition, the German banks were significant in granting a further loan to the British. Hence, as Burk and Cairncross conclude: "it can be argued that in the end Schmidt helped to deliver what Callaghan wanted."[40]

Negotiating with the IMF

Treasury officials had been visiting Washington since August.[41] Given that it looked increasingly likely that Britain would apply to the IMF, it was desirable to obtain an understanding of what the IMF would demand. After Healey had formally declared Britain's application on September 29, these visits became necessary. During October, the Treasury discussed the National Income Forecast. However, the Treasury ministers and officials could not agree. The other significant development in October was the formulation of the Public Expenditure White Paper (PEWP).[42]

The PEWP was largely the responsibility of Joel Barnett, as Chief Secretary to the Treasury. Barnett had to reduce public expenditure following earlier decisions to cut the PSBR. In a series of meetings over the course of October and early November, Barnett sought to reach agreements on specific areas of expenditure. This usually took the form of bilateral meetings with spending ministers, but also included Cabinet discussion on October 26 and November 4. Eventually, Cabinet agreed to cuts on November 11. However, as Barnett writes, the whole exercise was largely academic since there would have to be a fresh round of discussions after the terms had been agreed with the IMF.[43]   Barnett shows how the public expenditure forecast was difficult to complete.   The largest single area of government expenditure was social security, but Cabinet would not accept cuts in this area.   Moreover, local government expenditure still bore little relationship to its revenue from central government, despite the introduction of cash limits earlier in the year.   Finally, in several areas, the total was likely to increase.   Many areas of central government expenditure were linked to prices, pensions were related to earnings and housing subsidies to interest rates.   All of this made public expenditure cuts more difficult.

The six-man IMF team arrived in London on November 1.[44] The team was led by Alan Whittome, who had previously been Deputy Chief Cashier at the Bank of England.   His deputy was the Australian, David Finch.   The team also included a Greek, a New Zealander, and more significantly a German and an American.   Sir William Ryrie also attended the visit, but not as a member of the team.   The visit was kept secret, with the team assuming false names and refusing to hold a press conference. The usual procedure was to study the figures and allow the applicant to formulate its own policies.   Once these were agreed, the IMF would grant the loan.   All this should have taken about two weeks, but the IMF delegation was not to leave until mid-December.   The first meeting between Healey and Whittome took place on November 4, and the Chancellor said that the figures were not yet ready.   This was significant.   As Edmund Dell writes: "it is a problem for a visiting team, however expert, to determine in a matter of weeks what measures are necessary."[45]   The IMF team needed advice and information, and, despite a full month of preparation, this was not forthcoming.

The IMF team regarded this as deliberate obstructionism. The Treasury was aware of the normal procedures for agreeing a loan, but was not prepared to engage in them.   They prepared no detailed figures, nor policy proposals.   Fay and Young say that this, "was the first of many obstructions which hampered the team.   In the early days of their visit, they had to spend hours waiting in their hotel rooms wondering, with some reason, if doors were being closed deliberately and the British were consciously delaying."[46]   Negotiations began only slowly.

Relatively junior members of the Treasury were present at the earlier meetings, and even at the first full meeting between Treasury ministers and officials and the IMF delegation on November 10, much of the work was conducted by an under-secretary, Geoffrey Littler. Formal negotiations did not begin until November 19. The Treasury was also anxious to show that it was not under the control of the IMF, and may actually have delayed presenting the figures.[47] The 'conspiracy theory', which had surfaced earlier in the year, began to be discussed again, and the Treasury was keen to demonstrate its independence from the IMF.

In fact, the main reason why the figures were not yet ready was that the Treasury was itself divided.[48] It is worth spending some time looking at this, since it demonstrates the nature of economic thinking in the Treasury at that time. The account is based on published material and interviews conducted in the course of my research. At the top of the Treasury were a number of ministers and senior civil servants. In addition to Healey there was Joel Barnett (Chief Secretary), Bob Sheldon (Financial Secretary) and Denzil Davies (Minister of State). On the civil service side were a number of Permanent Secretaries. The First Permanent Secretary was Douglas Wass. In addition, there were a number of Second Permanent Secretaries: Leo Pliatzky (Public Expenditure), Alan Lord (Domestic Economy), Derek Mitchell (Overseas Economy) and Brian Hopkin (Chief Economist). As well as the ministers and civil servants, Nicholas Kaldor acted as an advisor to the Treasury. All of the ministers and civil servants were to have an input into the IMF Crisis since Healey held regular meetings and appeared to listen to all strands of opinion.[49] The Treasury was divided into two broad groups:

Firstly, there was a strong strand of opinion in favour of public expenditure cuts. According to this group, the public sector was too large and was threatening the ability of companies to invest and export. Moreover, the falling pound was hampering investment, since companies were not prepared to invest in a period of uncertainty. Alan Lord and, more notably Derek Mitchell, took this view. The role of Mitchell has already been discussed in the previous chapter. His closeness to the US financial authorities led to charges of conspiracy. I do not intend to discuss this again. Given that the Treasury was divided it seems unlikely that there could have been a conspiracy, and there is no evidence to suggest that Mitchell was part of a conspiracy. The second broad group was sympathetic to the Keynesian tradition. Wass appears to have taken this attitude. In addition, Pliatzky has pointed to the difficulty of cutting public expenditure. Pliatzky was more appreciative of the political consequences of cuts, than were Mitchell and Lord.[50] The divisions appeared at the first full meeting of Treasury ministers and officials. When Healey asked Wass for the Treasury's opinion, the Permanent Secretary replied that he was unable to present a united view. Although it is widely known that these divisions were present in the civil service, it has not been recorded that such divisions reached as far as the Ministers also. In particular, Denzil Davies argued against cuts and emphasised the Keynesian position.[51] Given that the economy was in recession with rising unemployment, further deflation was unnecessary. Davies also argued for the adoption of a scheme whereby the supply of North Sea oil could be sold forward, but this was rejected as it would not obtain support from the IMF.

According to Davies, Healey was initially in favour of IMF agreement, since he believed that the issue was largely one of confidence, and that the IMF was therefore the best way of restoring confidence. However, as time went on, and Healey experienced difficulties in negotiating with the IMF and the hard-line position adopted by America, he became less enthusiastic. There is evidence to support this view. In a later Cabinet meeting he told Tony Benn that he was looking forward to getting rid of the IMF and to announcing what he called 'sod-off' day.[52]

Nicholas Kaldor had a rather obscure role in the Treasury at this time.[53] Kaldor had been a leading economist for a number of years, and had been an advisor to the 1964-70 Wilson Government. In the 1960s he had been an enthusiastic supporter of devaluation as a means of stimulating economic growth. By the 1970s, he had evolved into an enthusiastic supporter of import restraint. It appears that Healey did not take his advice seriously by 1976, but he still had a role in the Treasury. He had free access to all ministers and civil servants, and circulated a number of papers advocating import controls.

By 1976, Kaldor can be regarded as a key figure on the Labour left, advocating the Alternative Economic Strategy (AES), and had frequent meetings with Tony Benn, Peter Shore, Wynne Godley and Francis Cripps.[54] All three of the rival economic paradigms – Keynesianism, economic liberalism and the AES – were therefore represented to a greater or lesser extent in the Treasury.

The Treasury was therefore clearly unable to present a united view. This was so not only in terms of a united policy position, but also in terms of agreement over the economic forecasts. On November 3, Healey informed the Cabinet's economic committee that there was still no agreement over the likely trend in the economy in the immediate future. Therefore, when Healey met Alan Whittome on November 4 and informed him that the figures were not yet ready, it was not meant as a delaying tactic. Instead, in the words of Burk and Cairncross, it was "no more than the simple truth."[55]

The response of the IMF team was to recommend a PSBR target of £6.5-7 billion.[56] The IMF negotiators informed the British Government of this at the first full meeting with the Treasury team November 10. In effect, this would require cuts of over £3 billion for the financial year 1977/8. The IMF team recommended further cuts of £4 billion for the financial year 1978/9, and added that the Treasury should look to find any additional cuts in the current year. Leo Pliatzky has written that, "it was never on the cards that the Treasury Ministers would put such proposals to Cabinet, let alone succeed in getting approval for them."[57] However, Edmund Dell appears to have found little wrong with either the tactics or the policy of the IMF: "this was a negotiation in which the IMF team, confronted by a divided Treasury, was well advised to take the line it did."[58] Given that the Treasury were unable to present clear figures, it was necessary for the IMF team to provide some direction to the negotiations. Moreover, Dell continues, the cuts demanded by the IMF were not unrealistic since the *Times* and the Conservative Party had both recommended immediate cuts of £5 billion.[59]

Arguably, however, Dell's view lacks any real understanding of the political realities of the situation. At this stage, Callaghan intervened. The latest PSBR forecast was £10.5 billion, having been revised down from £11.2 billion. Both Callaghan and

Healey intimated that this was too high and that they would therefore be keen to introduce cuts. But, as Callaghan writes in his memoirs: "I was not willing to go below the £9 billion that the Cabinet had agreed as recently as July."[60] To Callaghan the issue was one of confidence. Given that the PSBR forecast had exceeded the £9 billion figure agreed in July, it was necessary to show that the Government was taking action to maintain the PSBR at this level. Callaghan recalls that, "the IMF took this badly."[61] He therefore arranged for Len Murray, the General Secretary of the TUC, to meet Alan Whittome. Murray argued against the cuts demanded by the IMF since they would threaten the Social Contract. This view was supported by John Methven and Donald MacDougal of the Confederation of British Industry, who also met Whittome. There was obviously a substantial difference of opinion between the IMF and the Government, and negotiations were to continue into early December.

Cabinet Divides

Given that one of the Prime Minister's main objectives was to avoid ministerial resignations, he felt it necessary to allow as full a discussion as possible.[62] He therefore took the highly unusual step of suspending other business and letting Cabinet discuss the issues at considerable length. In addition to published material, I again draw on interviews and correspondence with the leading participants in Cabinet for this section.

The first full discussion of the IMF terms did not take place until the Cabinet of November 23, when the IMF team had already been in London for three weeks. However, the views of the leading contenders were already well known. In many ways the debate was a rerun of the earlier discussions in July, when the Cabinet had agreed to £1 billion cuts plus a £1 billion increase in National Insurance. Tony Crosland was to write in his notebook that Christmas, that much of what he had recorded for July could be repeated.[63] Moreover, the Cabinet had believed, as apparently did Healey at the time, that enough had been done in July. Given this, the Cabinet was initially reluctant to accept the need for further cuts.

A number of discussions took place before the first major Cabinet debate on November 23. At the Economic Strategy (EY) Committee on November 3, Healey set out the general economic situation, saying that there was a need for cuts in order to obtain the IMF loan and restore confidence.[64] He also appears to have argued for reductions of the level of unemployment benefit and the higher rate of income tax. Tony Benn described this as, "hair-raising".[65] With the exception of Edmund Dell, nobody supported the cuts. Benn and Peter Shore advocated import measures. At the next meeting of the EY Committee on November 17, Healey informed his colleagues that they had to agree a PSBR forecast of £9 billion by November 23, in order to negotiate with the IMF delegation.[66] However, he failed to obtain the support of the committee. Roy Hattersley commenting that, "the PSBR seems to becoming a sort of God."[67] At the full Cabinet the following day, Callaghan repeated that the PSBR had to be agreed by November 23, but reassured ministers that final agreement would require their approval.[68]

Callaghan followed this up by arranging a meeting of senior ministers that evening at 10 Downing Street.[69] Those present were Healey, Dell, Crosland, senior Treasury officials and the Prime Minister. Healey began by outlining the economic situation and stressing the need to restore confidence, which would require expenditure cuts in order to obtain the IMF loan. Crosland responded by outlining his position. There was no case for further deflation given that the measures implemented so far were working. Dell criticised Crosland, by arguing that, "he could not know whether what he was saying was true; and, secondly, that even if it were true the disbelief of the market could undermine it, and, indeed, bring down the Government before we reaped the benefit of having at last got everything in place."[70] Moreover, there was a strong justification for market opinion as the balance of payments and inflation were still poor, and many of the figures had proved unreliable and unpredictable, with the latest PSBR figures moving upwards. There was also the added problem of the lack of reserves to finance the debt on the balance of payments. Dell concluded that; "we had to make a choice, to negotiate successfully with the IMF, or to be swept from office."[71] At this stage, Callaghan did not comment. It was still unclear which side he would take.

The Cabinet of November 23 gave the opportunity for the leading contenders to outline their positions.[72] Following discussion of the latest situation in Rhodesia, Cabinet turned to the IMF Crisis. I do not intend to assess the relative merits of the various arguments put forward. Instead, it is important to clarify the various positions and activities of Cabinet ministers at this crucial stage. In addition to the published material, the following discussion is based on extensive interviews with many of the leading participants. Callaghan began by stressing the need for unity, to avoid leaks and to reach a decision on the PSBR forecast. Healey then described the latest discussions with Alan Whittome. The IMF team recognised the importance of the Social Contract. The IMF and the Treasury had agreed that the PSBR was likely to be £10.5 billion for the financial year 1977-78, and the IMF wanted cuts of £1.5 billion for next year and a further £3 billion in the following year in order to achieve a PSBR of £6.5 billion by 1978-79. Healey went on to repeat the arguments he had made in earlier EY Committee meetings and at 10 Downing Street on the evening of November 18.

Tony Crosland then set out his position in full.[73] There was no need for cuts. Unemployment had reached 1.25 million and looked as if it would continue to rise without Government action. Further deflation would produce even higher unemployment and thereby add to the PSBR by reducing revenue and adding to unemployment benefit. Given the current level of unemployment there was sufficient spare capacity for exports. The forecasts were in themselves unreliable, and it would therefore be wrong to base the policy on them. The level of cuts demanded by the IMF were too high, and would be likely to lead to resignations, defeat in the House of Commons and the break-up of the Social Contract, and would thereby undermine confidence further. Crosland then added that if the IMF and the Americans persisted, Britain should threaten import restraint and to pull the Army out of Germany and Cyprus.

Susan Crosland has emphasised the rationale for this: "as the IMF was even more passionately opposed to protectionism than it was attached to monetarism, this threat would be sufficient to persuade the Fund to lend the money without unacceptable conditions."[74] Crosland accepted the need for a small cut – about £500 million – to allow Healey to negotiate with the IMF.

The defence argument was a new one, which Crosland had not made on November 18. It is likely that he had raised it in response to criticism from Dell, among others, that Crosland had failed to take account of the importance of 'confidence'. However, Dell was to be highly critical of this particular argument as well: "the folly of these threats confirmed in my view that Crosland could no longer be trusted... His remarks showed a Crosland who had lost all power of judgement. Indeed, it was difficult to know how seriously to take such proposals. I was certain they would never be implemented."[75]

Although Callaghan had pressed for an agreement of the £9 billion figure at this meeting, it was to end without it. Roy Hattersley supported Crosland, and Michael Foot said that Crosland's intervention was significant and needed to be treated seriously. Benn argued for the Alternative Economic Strategy, including sweeping import quotas. Peter Shore also spoke in favour of import restraint saying: "we are being asked to bite the bullet but in fact we'll blow our political brains out."[76] According to Benn, only Dell and Reg Prentice supported Healey, with Prentice saying that the cuts demanded by the IMF were insufficient, and of the possible need for a coalition government.[77] The meeting, which had been intended to be decisive, had broken up without agreement.

The result was a flurry of activity.[78] Callaghan, concerned over the Cabinet disunity displayed that day, again contacted Ford and Schmidt, and impressed upon them the reluctance of Cabinet to agree to further cuts. Cabinet ministers, particularly Crosland, were so strongly opposed that they may resign. Callaghan says that: "I began to get the impression that in the last resort he (Crosland) would regard the break-up of the Government as the lesser evil. I used this in my conversations with President Ford and the German Chancellor (Schmidt) to make sure that both knew the strength of feeling in Cabinet."[79] Callaghan again felt that he had the support of Schmidt, who contacted Washington, but that the influence of William Simon was decisive in influencing Ford. Healey met Alan Whittome, who then both met with Callaghan. The strength of opposition from within the Cabinet was impressed on Whittome.

Meanwhile, as Dell writes, "the cabals had been forming."[80] Two groups were beginning to emerge at this stage: the Keynesian social democratic revisionists led by Tony Crosland,

and the left led by Tony Benn. It is worth spending some time examining these groups since they have often been misrepresented. The two groups are often perceived as being much more united than they were, and the opinions of particular individuals are also misrepresented.[81]

The first meeting of the social democratic group took place on the evening of November 22 in Tony Crosland's room in the House of Commons.[82] Crosland was absent as he was attending a State function at Buckingham Palace. Those present were Harold Lever, Roy Hattersley, Shirley Williams and David Ennals, with Bill Rodgers coming in half way through. All were united in their view that the measures proposed by Healey were wrong. Lever, Hattersley, and Crosland were opposed to the measures because they believed that they were deflationary and threatened the Social Contract. Williams and Ennals were opposed, according to Susan Crosland, because they "wanted to protect their department's budgets."[83] Rodgers did not feel that Healey had made a sufficiently strong case for the cuts. The 'Crosland group' was therefore only a loose collection of ministers, who each had different motives for opposing the Treasury.[84] I return to the activities of this group below.

The same evening, the left-wing group met in Peter Shore's room in the House of Commons.[85] This group included Shore, Michael Foot, Tony Benn, John Silkin, Stan Orme and Albert Booth. It is widely assumed that this group was united around the Alternative Economic Strategy (AES). I will set out the AES, as outlined by Tony Benn in Cabinet, below. However, it was clear that this group was also divided. Given that Michael Foot had come second in the leadership contest earlier in the year, he should have been regarded as the leader of this group. However, although Foot made clear his concerns over public expenditure cuts to Callaghan, he regarded the unity of Cabinet as the most crucial objective and therefore did not give his full support to the group.[86] Bill Rodgers has rightly drawn the distinction between what Benn was proposing and the position advocated by Shore.[87] Benn was calling for the full implementation of the AES including widespread import quotas, further public ownership, regulation of industry, and capital controls. In contrast, Shore advocated temporary import deposits in order to restore the balance of payments problem.[88]

Bill Rodgers has argued that Shore had the support of Michael Foot, Albert Booth and John Silkin.[89] Shore has said that he did not believe in the AES, and argued against the position advocated by Tony Benn in private.[90] Whereas he supported import measures as a temporary response to the problem, Benn appeared to regard the IMF Crisis as an opportunity to implement the AES. Shore felt that he had the support of the majority of the group. Booth has explained the manoeuvrings of the group at that stage. Booth says that, "Tony Benn was taking the view that you had to win the case for the Alternative Economic Strategy per se because if you didn't you wouldn't be able to reject IMF terms... Peter Shore didn't take that view."[91] To Booth then the difference between Shore and Benn was over tactics. Booth actually supported Benn in trying to obtain support for the AES, rather than Shore who only put forward the case for temporary import deposits. Given that he believed in the AES, Booth felt that it was better to try to obtain all of it rather than merely one part. Booth goes on to argue that had the IMF not provided the loan, the AES would be required, and so it was best to work towards it. Therefore, Booth was closer to Benn, and felt that Stan Orme was of the same opinion. John Silkin, however, was more convinced by Shore's argument.

This raises a further complication. On November 24, Crosland and Hattersley wrote a paper, which was delivered to the Cabinet the next day.[92] In the paper, Crosland and Hattersley argued for import deposits (effectively a tax placed on imported goods). It was hoped that the paper would serve two functions. Firstly, it would show that Crosland had an alternative strategy ready for if the IMF refused the loan. Secondly, they may also have hoped that the import deposits scheme would appeal to the left-wing group. On the same day, presumably at the behest of Hattersley, David Hill approached Francis Morrell (the political assistants of Hattersley and Benn respectively) to ask if the Bennites would support the Crosland group in Cabinet. Morrell replied that the Bennites were not prepared to play that game with the Crosland group, and so there was no united opposition in Cabinet.[93] There was a wide disagreement between Benn and the social democratic centre-right at this stage, and it is difficult to see how a common position could have been reached between Benn and Crosland.

There would appear to have been more opportunity for a deal between Crosland and Shore, given that both now advocated import deposits. However, Shore was unaware of such a proposal and was never consulted.[94] There was still a wide difference between what Shore was strongly committed to, and what Crosland was only tentatively considering. Albert Booth was also unaware of any proposed alliance between the two camps, but would have supported one had he known of such moves.[95] This shows two things. The first was the unusual role played by Benn since he appears to have acted largely independently, without consulting the group which he was supposed to be leading. The other point was that despite coming to adopt similar positions over import measures, there was no serious attempt to build a coalition.

During these activities, the opinion of Callaghan is still far from clear. It is widely accepted that, as Callaghan himself writes in his memoirs, he wished to maintain the unity of Cabinet. However, it is not clear that Callaghan always intended to support Healey. Indeed, Healey was not himself clear that Callaghan would support him, at one stage confiding in Dell that he was anxious about this.[96] Callaghan had two groups to support and advise him. The first was the Central Policy Review Staff (CPRS), which produced a Cabinet paper for discussion on November 10.[97] The CPRS advocated redistribution of current expenditure, but did not advocate cuts. Apart from this, the CPRS played little role. Of more significance was the Policy Unit, led by Bernard Donoughue. The Policy Unit supported a Croslandite strategy, and urged the Prime Minister to adopt this position. Donoughue argued that there was "no economic justification for deflation now," and of the need to avoid both the "suicidal extremism of the Treasury and the protectionist extremism of Mr Benn."[98]

As Kenneth Morgan writes, "the Prime Minister's position was a complicated one. In some measure, he was genuinely uncertain how to proceed and deliberately left all options open in Cabinet discussion as a result."[99] It was difficult for those around him to know what he thought. The Treasury was concerned that the Chancellor did not have the support of the Prime Minister.[100] It looked as if Callaghan would eventually support Crosland in the early stages of the discussions. Bill Rodgers has highlighted the early confidence of the Crosland group that this would occur: "in this we were encouraged not only by the Prime Minister's promise of a full discussion but by a strange message conveyed through Shirley (Williams) that he did not entirely agree with the recommendations the Chancellor was about to make."[101]

Callaghan appeared to have an open mind. This was no doubt in part a deliberate strategy designed to maintain the unity of Cabinet. It may also be that in the early stages of the negotiations he may have had sympathies with the Crosland position.[102] In the end he supported the Chancellor for two reasons. The first was that he became convinced of the intellectual merits of the Treasury position. Callaghan has said that he was not convinced by the arguments of Crosland nor Benn.[103] Secondly, he had searched for support from Helmut Schmidt and Gerald Ford. By the end of November, he had been able to reduce the cuts demanded by the IMF. Shirley Williams has argued that Callaghan realised the strength of the Treasury position, while keeping open the possibility of a more palatable alternative. This is probably correct, but this is not how it appeared to those around him at the time.[104]

Reaching a Decision

Meanwhile, things were rapidly coming to a head. In mid-November, the various factions were as far apart as ever. By December 2, Cabinet had accepted the Treasury position.[105] On November 26, Karl Otto Pohl, of the German Finance Ministry, visited London. He was surprised by the hostile reception he received from Healey. Alan Whittome was also far from pleased to see him. Whittome thought that Pohl had come to London to put pressure on the IMF to back down, but Pohl told him that he was keen to see the British Government accept the loan and to cut public expenditure. This was Pohl's own view, and was in contrast to the belief of Helmut Schmidt.

William Simon stopped off in London on his way to Moscow.[106] In order to avoid the press, he met Ed Yeo in his tailors. Both Simon and Yeo then visited Whittome and encouraged him to maintain his position. Simon contacted Pohl, who was still in London. Pohl was concerned with possible tapping of his telephone, and so met Yeo in the German Embassy. They were all agreed on the need to pressure the

British Government into accepting cuts. This was in contrast to Schmidt. When Pohl returned to Bonn, he was asked by Schmidt to go to Washington to ask the Americans to weaken their demands. When Pohl arrived in Washington he was shown a letter from Schmidt written to the President asking him to weaken the conditions of the IMF loan. Simon, Yeo and Arthur Burns were annoyed with Schmidt for writing the letter. Although Pohl told them of Schmidt's request, he also added that he had not been aware of the letter.

Burk and Cairncross have accurately summarised the tactics of Germany and America at this time: "both the Germans and the Americans – and the IMF – understood that to bring the British to a decision, the key man in Britain whom they had to convince was the Prime Minister, and the only way he was going to be convinced was to be told this himself by the top men. This they proceeded to do."[107] Pohl returned to Bonn and informed Schmidt that his letter was looked on unfavourably and that America wanted the British to agree quickly. On November 29-30, Jim Callaghan and Tony Crosland attended the European Council at The Hague.[108] Callaghan, Schmidt and Crosland had breakfast together on the morning of November 30. Schmidt informed them that he would not give any further assistance to the British. Callaghan now realised that Schmidt was not prepared to go any further. Callaghan writes in his memoirs that although he had already understood this, he was keen to include Crosland in the negotiations with Schmidt so that the Foreign Secretary could understand the opinion of the Germans as well.[109] On the flight back from The Hague, Callaghan informed Crosland for the first time that he now intended to support Healey in Cabinet.

On December 1, Cabinet debated at length the IMF loan.[110] Tony Benn was asked to present his paper. Benn had submitted a paper to Callaghan to be circulated around the Cabinet. Callaghan appears to have been determined to undermine the paper and had passed it to the Policy Unit. Bernard Donoughue had scrutinised the document and had circulated questions to Ministers in order to defeat the paper in Cabinet on December 1. Benn began by arguing that neither Ford nor Schmidt would help, and that the British Government therefore had to introduce measures that would protect the economy by itself. Existing policy had not worked, and deflation should be avoided in order to preserve the Social Contract. Both Len Murray and Jack Jones had put their reputations at risk by supporting the Government, and therefore the Cabinet had an obligation to respect their positions. There was a need for reflation given the current state of the economy. In turn, this required protectionist measures in order to defend domestic industry from cheap imports, and greater state control in order to avoid excess profits. Benn therefore called for import quotas, to be phased in by a period of import deposits. In addition, Benn went on to advocate other measures as part of the AES, including exchange controls, a more extensive role for the TUC in policymaking, free collective bargaining and greater state control of banking and investment through both nationalisation and a more powerful National Enterprise Board.

Benn was then subjected to intense scrutiny as Callaghan and Donoughue had intended.[111] He told Callaghan that it would be possible to obtain the IMF loan on the basis of the AES, which demonstrated that Benn misunderstood the position of the IMF. Shirley Williams asked about the impact of import quotas on trading relations. Again, Benn failed to provide an adequate answer, by replying that quotas would only apply to the manufacturing sector, in which Britain had a surplus. Quotas would therefore fail to resolve the balance of payments deficit. Bill Rodgers asked about the affect of quotas on unemployment. Benn admitted that he did not know, as he had not got access to the Treasury computer. Rodgers notes that, "it became a game that no-one took seriously, as Benn's proposals were stripped bare of credibility."[112] As the cross-questioning went on, Peter Shore responded by accusing Cabinet colleagues of teasing Benn, but Benn himself did not accept that this was so.[113] In fact, he did not appear to understand the extent to which his case was undermined.[114] Ken Morgan argues that, "Benn in his diary does not seem to appreciate how cataclysmically he had been routed, and his case substantially collapsed from that time on."[115] Cabinet, then, had effectively rejected the AES on December 1.

The second paper was presented by Peter Shore. In contrast to Tony Benn, he repeated his argument that import controls were needed as a short-term measure to cure the current account deficit. He did not intend to cut imports, merely to maintain them at the current level. Cabinet colleagues were more sympathetic to Shore's case than they had been towards Benn. Shore argued that both the European Economic Community (EEC) and the General Agreement on Tariffs and Trade (GATT) allowed for temporary import measures in order to protect the currency and the reserves. Finland and Italy already had similar measures, and Germany, Japan and America would be likely to accept temporary measures. The IMF would not turn the Government down. Shore was therefore advocating import restraint on pragmatic grounds, and differed substantially from Benn on this point.[116]

Again, Shore was subjected to cross-questioning. He advocated tax increases to resolve the public sector deficit, but Healey responded that tax increases would have a deflationary impact. Shore was also forced to accept that import controls would have a deflationary impact, and would be likely to result in as much unemployment as the expenditure cuts advocated by Healey.[117] Shore also realised the need to repay the June stand-by by December 9. However, he argued instead that a further three-month extension be requested, and finally that the current account be closed for a year. Although Shore was received more positively than Benn, he failed to win over Cabinet support. In particular, Shore's concession on the effect on unemployment of the import deposits was fatal, given that they had been designed to avoid additional unemployment. Moreover, Shore's measures for closing the current account and extending the period of the June stand-by seemed unrealistic given the attitude of the IMF, the Americans and the Germans.[118]

The next speaker was Tony Crosland, who began by asserting that his paper was much more convincing than either Benn or Shore. Crosland outlined the case he had presented on November 23, and was then cross-examined.[119] By talking about Britain's military role, the Government would force the IMF to provide the loan without cuts. Crosland now accepted the need for cutting £1 billion off the PSBR. But instead of achieving this through cuts in public expenditure, it could now be achieved through a combination of the sale of BP shares, import deposits and by announcing the cuts made in July. There was therefore no need for further cuts now. It was, however, clear from the response of Cabinet colleagues that this strategy also had little support. Some of those ministers who had previously remained silent, joined in the cross-examination of Crosland.   In particular, Roy Mason spoke of Healey's strength of character, and of the need to rally around him. John Morris argued that the issue of confidence was central, and only the IMF could help to achieve this. Fred Peart warned of the risk of retaliation if import quotas or deposits were introduced. Healey and Dell again spoke against Crosland's strategy, with Healey pointing out that the July cuts had already been accounted for in the IMF's figures.   There was a clear shift towards the Chancellor of the Exchequer in Cabinet on December 1, and Callaghan was able to reject the strategies of Benn and Shore in his summing-up.

Events were now coming quickly to a head.   Before the Cabinet, Callaghan met Jack Jones and Len Murray.[120] The three were going to meet together, but had to meet separately due to prior engagements. Murray and Jones both expressed concern with expenditure cuts and the likely rise in unemployment that would result. However, they realised that a Labour government was preferable to a Conservative administration led by Margaret Thatcher. Callaghan was keen to protect welfare expenditure; Thatcher would seek to cut it. They would therefore support Callaghan. A similar result was reached in a meeting that evening between Callaghan and the Government whips led by Michael Cocks.[121] Callaghan was informed that although the left were extremely unhappy, they would not vote against the Government in a confidence motion. They would, however, vote against individual cuts, and so it was best to avoid any measures that would require legislation.

The most significant meeting that evening was between Callaghan and Crosland.[122] Crosland went to Callaghan's room in the House of Commons to tell him that although he thought that the measures were wrong, he would support them in order to avoid resignations. Two factors were important in changing Crosland's mind. The first was that Callaghan was coming to support Healey. It would therefore be wrong to oppose the Prime Minister and Chancellor. There was a good chance that news of this would get out given that Cabinet discussions had already been widely leaked. If news got out, it would lead to the collapse of the pound. Although he did not agree, he would now support the Prime Minister in Cabinet the following morning.

The second factor was the disintegration of his support in Cabinet. The group met on the evening of December 1. Bill Rodgers had already switched support to Healey on the grounds that Crosland's proposed threat of withdrawing the troops from Germany and Cyprus was unrealistic. Rodgers told the group on the evening of November 30 that he was sceptical, arguing that "if this was the alternative to Healey's proposal, our bluff would be called. In Britain's own interest there could be no question of abandoning our NATO obligations and if we threatened to do so it would be a further blow to confidence. I was sorry, but if this was all there was on offer they could no longer count on me."[123] Rodgers felt that the threat was very serious since it would be made in the midst of the Cold War, and would lead to a fundamental loss of confidence. Moreover, it would actually require additional expenditure, as the troops would have to be demobilised. It would, therefore, add to public expenditure.[124]

David Ennals and Shirley Williams had both received reassurances from Callaghan that their department budgets would not be cut. Williams was also opposed to import deposits since they were both damaging to the Third World and would undermine Britain's relations with the EEC.[125] Similarly, Harold Lever was opposed to the import deposit proposal. Lever was said to be hostile when he met Crosland. Import deposits were objectionable to a free-trader and would have a deflationary impact. Moreover, Healey had promised tax cuts the following spring. Lever had welcomed this, and pledged his support to Healey.[126] The meeting was therefore disappointing for Crosland. Only Roy Hattersley remained. Crosland admitted defeat, and told Hattersley to do the same. Therefore, Crosland informed Callaghan of his decision. Callaghan recorded that, "he said this very coolly but I knew it had cost him a lot."[127]

The decisive Cabinet was held the following day.[128] Healey began by reiterating the case he had already made. There was a need to obtain IMF support to restore confidence and to repay the June stand-by. The latest forecast for the PSBR was £10.2 billion, which had to be reduced since it would be highly deflationary. He admitted that there were alternative forecasts, particularly from the National Institute of Economic and Social Research of £9 billion, but the IMF would not accept it as a valid forecast. The main issue was one of confidence, and smaller cuts than he proposed would not work even if the IMF were prepared to accept a smaller figure. He had not put the Crosland strategy to the IMF delegation, but they would not accept it. He therefore proposed to raise £500 million from the sale of Burmah oil shares and to reduce the PSBR by a further £1 billion for 1977/8, and an additional £1.5 billion reduction in 1978/9, thus reducing the PSBR to £8.7 billion by 1978/9. This would increase unemployment by 140 thousand over the two years, but some of this could be offset by selective measures.

Callaghan then announced his decision to support Healey to Cabinet for the first time. According to Benn, Callaghan began by saying that he was still not sure what to do.[129] However, he had been informed by Helmut Schmidt and Gerald Ford that no further help would be given without having first reached agreement with the IMF. He therefore wanted agreement, and was still confident of getting support on sterling balances and import deposits.

At first, this appeared to have little impact on the debate. Michael Foot spoke next, and explained that he was very unhappy about the unemployment effects of the policy. However the next speaker was Crosland, who repeated his statement to Callaghan from the previous evening: that although the policy was wrong it was necessary to back the Prime Minister in order to avoid the defeat of the Government. The left-wing ministers were very angry about this with Shore asking if it was right to support a policy having said that it was wrong[130], and another later commenting that, "he collapsed like a pack of cards."[131]

Other ministers then spoke. David Ennals was opposed to cuts in excess of £500 million, and said that there was a need to protect benefits. He was criticised by Callaghan who pointed to record increases in benefits, and of the priority given to employment schemes. Albert Booth stressed the benefit of job protection schemes. Harold Lever and Shirley Williams accepted the package, but also stressed the need for tax cuts the following spring. Stan Orme was highly critical of the package: "I can't credit a Labour Cabinet discussing these things... It is not on."[132] Fred Mulley supported the reduction of the PSBR, but also favoured tax increases in order to avoid large expenditure cuts. Eric Varley, Reg Prentice, Elwyn Jones, Bill

Rodgers, John Morris and Merlyn Rees all supported Healey, with Prentice suggesting that the cuts did not go far enough. Roy Hattersley followed Crosland in giving his reluctant support. Bruce Millan had a similar attitude and expressed his wish to see the introduction of import deposits and to avoid benefit cuts. Peter Shore was opposed, as was Tony Benn who compared the situation to 1931 when the Labour Government had split. By the end of the debate at 1.15pm, it was clear that there was now a majority in favour of the measures proposed by Healey. Callaghan summed up by saying that Cabinet had given approval for Healey to negotiate on the basis of £1.5 billion cuts in 1977/8, with Cabinet having final approval. Hence, Cabinet had agreed to what it had rejected on November 23.[133]

Towards the Final Agreement

Cabinet had given its consent to cuts of £1.5 billion in the PSBR for the following financial year. Two things now had to be agreed. The first was to reach agreement with the IMF over both the level of cuts and the terms of the loan. The other was to reach agreement in Cabinet over where the cuts should fall. Both of these were resolved between December 1 and 15.

The possibility of Cabinet agreement in early December was almost completely destroyed by the actions of the Managing Director of the IMF, Johannes Witteveen.[134] Cabinet on December 1 was delayed by half an hour, and Benn speculated that this was due to a row between Callaghan and Healey.[135] There was a row, but it was between Callaghan and Witteveen. Events at this point are shrouded in secrecy, with Callaghan completely omitting the incident from his diary.[136] Moreover, the Cabinet Secretary, Sir John Hunt, did not know of the visit either.[137] Healey believes that Witteveen had visited London to stiffen the resolve of the head of the IMF delegation, Alan Whittome.[138] Witteveen apparently regarded Whittome as a rather weak character. Healey's interpretation was shared by William Ryrie, the British Executive Director at the IMF.[139] In contrast, Margaret Garritsen De Vries argues that Witteveen made the visit at the behest of Whittome, other IMF staff and the US Treasury. However, the other Directors did not know and were later to be very critical of the move.[140] Whittome had returned to Washington, as he had done every weekend while in

London, and explained the situation to Witteveen. The Managing Director then visited London and dictated terms to Callaghan. Witteveen refused to discuss the terms, as he did not wish to appear to be negotiating. According to the rules of the IMF, the visiting delegation conducted negotiations free from the interference of the Managing Director. Therefore, according to Ryrie, Witteveen only had one meeting with the British Government. This is contradicted by Fay and Young, who argue that after an acrimonious meeting between Callaghan and Witteveen, the two met again in the afternoon, at which stage they agreed to £2.5 billion cuts over two years.[141]

The meeting was certainly acrimonious. Callaghan and Witteveen clashed over public expenditure. Witteveen admitted that unemployment would increase as a result of the expenditure cuts requested by the IMF, and Callaghan was close to sending Witteveen back to Washington. However, it is not clear whether Callaghan and Witteveen had reached an agreement. Witteveen asked for a £2 billion cut in public expenditure. Both Callaghan and Healey argued that this was unacceptable, but the Prime Minister allowed for cuts of £1 billion for the first time. In this sense then, the meeting did mark a breakthrough.[142]

It was still not clear that the IMF would accept the position reached by Cabinet on December 2: namely £1 billion cuts plus £500 million from the sale of shares. Healey records that he got Whittome to accept cuts of only £1 billion for 1977-8 for the first time on December 3. However, Witteveen then rang Healey and asked for a further £1 billion of cuts. Healey responded by telling Whittome that Witteveen should "go take a running leap." Healey threatened to call a General Election on the issue of the IMF versus the Government. The delegation returned to Washington for the weekend. Healey had not in fact been authorised to say this.[143] Callaghan notes: "I had not given the Chancellor any authority to threaten a general election but I was quite happy that he should have done so."[144]

In fact, Healey's threat had worked in bringing about an agreement. Burk and Cairncross write that, "his brutal negotiating manner had at least made it clear that a line was drawn in the dirt."[145] The following day, Saturday December 4, Callaghan arrived at Chequers and received an urgent telephone call. The IMF team wanted to reach an agreement the following week. The breakthrough had been made by the substitution of a two-year programme, for the original position of immediate cuts. The IMF were prepared to accept the practical difficulties of achieving all the cuts in the financial year 1977/8, and were therefore prepared to accept cuts over two years. If economic recovery was faster than expected, then the Government would find additional cuts for 1978/9.[146]

When Cabinet reconvened on December 6, to begin the process of expenditure cuts, Healey was able to inform them that the IMF had agreed to PSBR targets of £8.7 billion in 1977/8 including the sale of the BP shares, and £8.6 billion in 1978/9. The reversal of the IMF's position was sudden. This is probably explained by the actions of William Simon and Ed Yeo. It has already been noted that these two wanted tough conditions. They had been pushing the IMF since November. However, it was clear that the British Government was not prepared to go any further. Although it is unlikely that they were concerned about the survival of the British Labour Government, they realised that the very survival of the IMF depended on a successful outcome. It is therefore likely that Witteveen's interventions on December 1 and 3 were made at the behest of Simon and Yeo, and Witteveen may have been decisive in getting Simon and Yeo to agree to the deal by impressing upon them the opposition of Callaghan and Healey to further cuts.

Cabinet met on December 6 to decide where cuts should fall.[147] There were two problems here. The first was that in his summing-up at the end of the decisive Cabinet on December 2, Callaghan had only referred to the financial year 1977/8. Joel Barnett, who as Chief Secretary to the Treasury, had to negotiate the cuts, therefore had to get further agreement for the financial year 1978/9. Barnett managed to achieve this in the Cabinet on December 6. The second problem was that, as already mentioned, there were difficulties in introducing cuts in large areas of public expenditure. Healey had initially argued for cuts in social security, adding that recent rises had exceeded increases in pay and there was a justifiable grievance among the low paid. This raises a question over the extent to which Healey had come to support the supply-side theory, with its emphasis on incentives. I intend to discuss this in the Chapter 7. However, the significance at this stage is that the cuts to the social security budget were rejected in the Cabinet on December 6. There was sufficient opposition from within the Cabinet to make Callaghan reject it. In contrast, many welfare payments were indexed linked, and would require legislation to alter this. The Cabinet majority felt that although there was a case for reducing further increases both to preserve the Social Contract and to free resources for employment measures, but felt that legislation would be opposed by the left in Parliament. Cuts in local authority expenditure were also ruled out because there was no way of ensuring that local councils would introduce cuts. The IMF were therefore reluctant to accept cuts in this area.

On December 6, Barnett managed to get defence cuts totalling £100 million and £200 million for 1977/8 and 1978/9 respectively. Overseas aid, which had escaped cuts in July, was reduced by £50 million in each of the two years. Roy Hattersley agreed to the scrapping of all remaining food subsidies and Peter Shore accepted cuts in the budgets of water authorities. The meeting was, however, largely indecisive, and it was clear that cuts were going to be difficult. At the next Cabinet on the following morning, further cuts were agreed. In particular the Regional Employment Premium (REP) was abolished, except in Northern Ireland. The REP had been introduced by the Labour Government in the 1960s, largely at the behest of Nicholas Kaldor as a means of reducing unemployment in the poorer regions. By the 1970s, however, there had been a general drift towards selective measures. It was widely agreed that the REP should be abolished in favour of selective measures.

Callaghan admits that he found the process difficult: "for ministers such occasions, which all Cabinets go through during their lifetime, are like teeth-extractions, with the Chancellor and the Chief Secretary to the Treasury as the dentists. My role was to encourage the victim to believe that it would not hurt as much as he had thought, and to stop the drill when the pain was too great."[148] At 1pm, Cabinet had still not agreed. Callaghan appeared to lose his temper and gave instructions that a further meeting would be held that evening. If Cabinet could not agree, the terms would be dictated. It is not clear whether Callaghan had genuinely lost his temper, or if he had done it deliberately to force the issue.[149] Either way the intervention worked. At the second meeting that day, Callaghan was able to achieve a settlement. Healey had nearly destroyed any possibility of any agreement by requesting a further £200 million cuts for 1977/8. This was necessary because of a further weakening of sterling following recent Cabinet leaks, and to finance selective employment measures. However, it was agreed that the additional £200 million would be financed by tax increases. The final package would therefore include measures other than expenditure cuts.

Cabinet reconvened on Tuesday December 14, to discuss the Letter of Intent.[150] The agreement between the Government and the IMF would take the form of a letter detailing the measures agreed and setting targets for such things as the PSBR and the money supply. The details of the Letter of Intent were debated between the Treasury and the IMF delegation on December 11-12. Callaghan had adopted what he termed a three-legged stool approach involving expenditure cuts, the introduction of import deposits and measures to stabilise the sterling balances. In Cabinet on December 14, the details of the Letter of Intent were set out. There would be no agreement on the sterling balances until the Letter had been approved. Moreover, the IMF had rejected the import deposits. Callaghan admitted that he was disappointed on this and that he felt "anti-American."[151] There were further protests from the left, with Benn saying that it was "pure Thatcherism."[152]

The following day, December 15, the Letter of Intent was read to Parliament.[153] The mood was largely negative, but without the expected criticism from the left. Healey was able to get through the debate with very little difficulty, due mainly to an ineffective performance from the Shadow Chancellor of the Exchequer, Geoffrey Howe. Barnett notes that, "any other Shadow Chancellor would have destroyed him."[154] Healey was then subjected to cross-questioning in the House, with a number of left-wing MPs asking about the consequences for unemployment.[155] The press was largely critical, with tabloid headlines such as "Britain's Shame."[156] The more serious press was, however, more balanced in its judgement, emphasising that the Government had successfully negotiated with the IMF.[157] On December 16, a meeting of the Parliamentary Labour Party was held[158], which Healey opened by saying that there had been a united Cabinet.[159] Benn remained silent, but noted in his diary that this was a "bloody lie."[160] Callaghan summed up more fairly by pointing to the lengthy process of

Cabinet discussions in which every minister had had an input. The meeting was acrimonious, with several left-wing MPs criticising Government policy, particularly with regards to unemployment. However, the Government was able to win the vote in the House of Commons easily on December 21. The final result was 219-51, with the Conservatives abstaining.[161]

The Letter of Intent set out the terms of agreement. The Government stated that its existing policies had worked in bringing down inflation and the PSBR, but that they had not yet been reduced to acceptable levels. It would therefore continue with the Social Contract in order to reduce wage increases and with the industrial strategy to improve economic efficiency and trade. Public expenditure cuts, in addition to those introduced in July 1976, were announced. In total this would result in £1 billion cuts in 1977/8 and £1.5 billion in 1978/9. In addition, there would be £500 million revenue from the sale of BP shares and £200 million expenditure on new schemes to alleviate the unemployment effects of the cuts. This would achieve a PSBR target of £8.7 billion in 1977/8. The PSBR would be 1% higher than in 1975/6, but would be 1% lower by 1978/9. The Government also announced plans to reduce public borrowing by a further £500 million in 1978/9, but did not say how this was to be achieved. Significantly, in terms of the accusations that the Government had introduced monetarism, there were targets for Domestic Credit Expansion: from £9 billion in 1976/7 to £7.7 billion in 1977/8 and £6 billion in 1978/9. The means of achieving this would be to use special deposits, forcing banks to hold a percentage of their assets. This final point had generated controversy since Bernard Donoughue, Head of the Policy Unit, had accused the Treasury of slipping in higher targets than had been agreed.

International opinion was favourable. William Simon issued a statement saying that the programme outlined in the Letter of Intent was, "a responsible and sustained approach which represents a sound and realistic strategy for the United Kingdom rather than a one year transitory effort."[162] Such a positive statement from Simon probably added to the fears of the Cabinet sceptics, but the TUC responded with what Callaghan called a, "markedly understanding public statement."[163] The pound immediately rose to $1.71 by December 29. Indeed, the recovery in 1977 was so rapid that it probably took everybody, particularly those like Roy Hattersley who had argued that there was no economic rationale behind the fall in the value of the pound, by surprise.[164] Hence, as Paul Browning notes: "there are reasonable grounds for wondering whether there was in fact any real crisis at all."[165]

The Public Expenditure White Paper was agreed in Cabinet on January 20, 1977.[166] Joel Barnett had been expecting trouble, but was surprised by the ease with which the Paper was passed. Callaghan simply said that as there was nothing new to discuss, Cabinet should simply move on to the next item. Since nobody objected, the Paper was agreed. Expenditure cuts were introduced in all Departments, with the exception of Social Security, and the local authorities were exempted for reasons already outlined. Defence cuts had been opposed by the military service chiefs, but without any success. Most of the cuts came from capital expenditure, including a six-month postponement on all new building programmes. There were few cuts from the current account. Instead, the rest of the cuts came from tax and pricing reforms. As mentioned above, the Regional Employment Premium was abolished, and, in addition, excise duties on tobacco and alcohol were increased by 10%, gas prices increased by 8%, cuts introduced in the budget of British Rail, the Atomic Energy Authority and Post Office Telecommunications, telephone charges increased and the BP shares were sold on the open market. The Government had therefore avoided substantial cuts in current expenditure, and was criticised for this by the House of Commons Expenditure Committee: "the Government is thus itself acting like those industrialists it criticises for failing to invest. Indeed, even worse, it appears to be cutting capital expenditure and selling off productive assets...in order to sustain current expenditure, the classic action of an ailing industrial country."[167]

The Sterling Balances

So what about Callaghan's plan to end the reserve status of sterling? It is necessary to look at this in order to complete the narrative of events, but I do not intend to examine it in much detail, as it is not particularly relevant to the debate over the shift in political economy.

Callaghan had always wished to see the winding down of the reserve status of sterling. He had come to the conclusion that the reserve status had been the cause of instability in sterling when he had been the Chancellor of the Exchequer in the 1960s, and was also convinced that this was the cause of the current crisis as he had stated on the *Panorama* interview on October 25. Harold Lever was particularly influential in persuading Callaghan of the need to act on the sterling balances.[168] The Americans, however, thought that the British Government was trying to get an agreement on this in order to avoid having to cut public expenditure. They therefore refused to negotiate the sterling balances until the IMF agreement had been completed. When it was apparent that the British Government had accepted the need to reach agreement with the IMF in Cabinet on December 1-2, the US financial authorities began to formulate plans for the sterling balances.[169]

In early November, the Bank of England produced a three-page memorandum on the sterling balances.[170] The memorandum pointed to the difference between the official and private balances. The official balances were those held by Governments and central banks, and had been volatile in 1976: falling from £4,020 million in March, to £2,639 million by December. In contrast, the private balances – those held by commercial banks, companies and private individuals – had remained steady.[171] The memorandum formed the basis of future discussion. The Bundersbank had been positive on the issue of the sterling balances; arguing that although it was not sufficient to restore confidence, it would help to stabilise the pound.[172] Following Harold Lever's visit to Washington in mid-November, the Americans began to formulate plans for the sterling balances. By early December, there were at least three plans. Paul Volcker, the President of the Federal Reserve Bank of New York, and the Bank of International Settlements had both produced plans which were more generous than the third plan formulated by the US Treasury, under the direction of William Simon and Ed Yeo.[173] Just as the US Treasury was taking a hard line with the British Government over the IMF terms, so they were only prepared to offer limited assistance on the sterling balances.

The differences between the British, the Americans and the Germans over the sterling balances came to a head in mid-

December. As early as October 27, the Bundersbank had formulated a plan for the sterling reserves. In contrast, Yeo had refused to negotiate until December 9, when he made a telephone call to Derek Mitchell, the head of the overseas economy section of the British Treasury.[174] Three days later, Mitchell met Yeo and Simon, who argued that nothing could be done as they were to leave office on January 20, when the Carter administration would be sworn in. They were also concerned that a deal would set a dangerous precedent by giving help to one country. Arthur Burns, Governor of the Federal Reserve, was even more strongly opposed to any deal.[175] Mitchell had proposed a $5 billion credit facility, but America was not prepared to go above $2 billion. Meanwhile, Helmut Schmidt was keen to help the British on this issue, as Karl Otto Pohl told Mitchell on December 14. Dr Emminger, Deputy Governor of the Bundersbank, was sent to Washington to argue that a deal should be reached before the end of the year, but Burns simply rejected this.[176]

Meanwhile, the international community still had to agree to the granting of the IMF loan.[177] Britain had applied for a loan of $3.9 billion, approximately SDR 3,360 million (IMF Special Drawing Rights). This was by far the largest amount ever requested from the IMF, and it could only afford SDR500 million. The remainder would have to be funded by central banks and Switzerland. There was therefore a need for the IMF to obtain approval for the loan from its creditors. This was done through Working Party 3 of the Organisation of Economic Cooperation and Development (OECD) and the Group of Ten. Working Party 3 met on December 21, and the Group of Ten the following day. The IMF eventually agreed on January 3, 1977.[178] Finally, the sterling balances were agreed on January 10.[179] A facility of $3 billion would be provided by the Bank of International Settlements and the Group of Ten, but this would apply to the official balances only. The final agreement, which was announced to the House of Commons by Healey the following day[180], was therefore closer to the original British position set out in the memorandum in early December.

The significance of this issue is controversial. In particular, Edmund Dell has argued that the issue was an irrelevance.[181] The problems experienced in 1976 were caused by Government mismanagement of the economy. Once the IMF agreement had been completed, confidence would be restored and there was no need for a deal on the sterling balances. Dell goes on to state that, "an agreement of this kind was totally unnecessary once the government was seen to be conducting a responsible economic policy."[182] George Zis has added that the agreement was unnecessary and showed that the Government was unable to change its policy. Zis believes that the British Government could have attempted to have obtained support from the EEC to finance its external debts. Hence Zis argues: "to the extent that there was a problem, the government could have sought a European solution. But it proved unable to exploit the crisis to chart a new policy direction."[183]

It is, however, possible to construct a more favourable interpretation. Callaghan called the agreement, "eminently satisfactory – just what I had hoped for."[184] This is going too far since the agreement covered only the official balances. There is however, evidence that the agreement worked. The private balances increased substantially after the IMF agreement: from £2,761 million in March 1976 to £4,852 million by June 1979. This was a cause for concern since it increased the prospect of creating instability. In contrast, the official holdings remained steady: from £1,218 million in December 1976 to £1,702 million by June 1979.[185] This demonstrates that the 1977 agreement had the affect of stabilising the official reserves. Had the agreement also included private holdings, as the British Government had hoped, then the reserve status of sterling would have been reduced. Given that it had been the official holdings that had caused instability in the exchange rate in 1976, the agreement was crucial in restoring stability from January 1977. Hence, as Ken Morgan writes: "since the balances had been part of the problem, it seems unreasonable not to see them as part of the solution."[186]

Summary

Between October and December 1976, the British Government had negotiated successfully the IMF loan. The negotiations had been arduous. First, the IMF had made substantial public expenditure cuts a prerequisite for any loan. In this they had been pushed by the US. It took several weeks for the British Government to reach agreement with the IMF. Moreover, the

Cabinet had to be won over. Callaghan therefore sought to mobilise international support and to allow Cabinet discussion to exhaust itself. Only when the Crosland, Shore and Benn alternatives had been rejected, and when Ford and Schmidt refused to help any further, did Callaghan force the issue. Cabinet agreed to cuts on December 1 and 2. The rest of December was spent finalising the agreement. The IMF loan and support for the sterling balances were agreed in early January. The following two chapters will discuss the extent to which the IMF Crisis led to the introduction of economic liberalism.

[1] Burk, K., and Cairncross, A., *Goodbye, Great Britain: The 1976 IMF Crisis*, (Yale University Press, New Haven, 1992), p.59

[2] Ibid., pp.61-62; Healey, D., *The Time Of My Life*, (Penguin, London, 1990, 2nd Edition), pp.430-443; and Dell, E., *A Hard Pounding: Politics and Economic Crisis 1974-76*, (Oxford University Press, Oxford, 1991), pp.238-239

[3] Healey, p.431

[4] Benn, T., *Against the Tide: Diaries 1973-76*, (Arrow, London, 1990), p.620

[5] Fay, S. and Young, H., *The Day the Pound Nearly Died*, (Sunday Times, London, 1978), p.20

[6] Burk and Cairncross, p.61

[7] Ibid., p.68

[8] Quoted in Burk and Cairncross, p.68

[9] Dell, p.238

[10] Burk and Cairncross, p.62

[11] Donoughue, B., *Prime Minister: The Conduct of Policy Under Harold Wilson and James Callaghan*, (Cape, London, 1987), p.97

[12] Burk and Cairncross, p.62

[13] Ibid. p.68

[14] Fay, and Young, p.25

[15] Benn, p.632

[16] Burk and Cairncross, p.62; Callaghan, J., *Time and Chance*, (Collins, London, 1987), pp.429-430

[17] Quoted in Callaghan, p.430

[18] Quoted in Callaghan, p.429

[19] Callaghan, p.430

[20] Ibid.

[21] See Burk and Cairncross, p.64

[22] Burk and Cairncross, pp.75-83; and Morgan, K.O., *Callaghan: A Life*, (Oxford University Press, Oxford, 1997), pp.544 for a discussion of Lever's visit

[23] Callaghan, p.433

[24] Quoted in Burk and Cairncross, p.77

[25] Quoted in Burk and Cairncross, p.78

[26] Ibid.

[27] Ibid.

[28] Fay and Young, p.31. They add that Kissinger was to support Lever. Kissinger said that Lever "did have an impact because I agreed with him, and eventually Ford did too." Fay and Young, p.29

[29] Interview with Lady Williams (21/11/00)

[30] Morgan, p.499

[31] Healey also argues that it was a means of bypassing the Treasury, p.430

[32] Dell. pp.255-256

[33] Morgan, p.545

[34] Burk and Cairncross, pp.64-65; Callaghan, pp.431-432

[35] Burk and Cairncross, p.64
[36] Quoted in Burk and Cairncross, p.67
[37] Callaghan, p.432
[38] Burk and Cairncross, pp.66-67
[39] Quoted in Burk and Cairncross, p.66
[40] Burk and Cairncross, p.67
[41] Ibid. p.60
[42] Ibid. pp.60-61; Barnett, J., *Inside The Treasury*, (Andre Deutsch, London, 1982), pp97-103
[43] Ibid.
[44] Burk and Cairncross, pp.68-70
[45] Dell, p.248
[46] Fay and Young, p.26
[47] Burk and Cairncross, p.71
[48] Ibid. pp.71-73. See also Healey, p.430
[49] Interview with Denzil Davies MP, (23/01/01)
[50] Pliatzky, L., *Getting and Spending*, (Blackwell, Oxford, 1982), pp.155-156
[51] Interview with Denzil Davies MP
[52] Healey, p.433
[53] Healey, pp.390-391
[54] See, for example, Benn, (22/11/76), p.651
[55] Burk and Cairncross, p.73
[56] The IMF had believed since the 1950s that balance of payments problems were caused by inflationary pressures. In turn, inflationary pressures were built up by growth in public sector borrowing or wage settlements beyond the scope of economic growth. Bernstein, K., *The International Monetary Fund and Deficit Countries: The Case of Britain 1974-77*, (Unpublished PhD thesis, Stanford University, USA, 1983), pp.462-476
[57] Pliatzky, p.153
[58] Dell, p.429
[59] Ibid.
[60] Callaghan, p.433
[61] Ibid.
[62] Ibid.; Burk and Cairncross, p.83
[63] Crosland, C.A.R., *Xmas '76*, notebook, Anthony Crosland Papers, 16/8, BLPES, London
[64] Burk and Cairncross, p.71
[65] Benn, p.637
[66] Burk and Cairncross, p.85
[67] Quoted in Benn, p.646
[68] Burk and Cairncross, p.85; Callaghan, p.434
[69] Burk and Cairncross, p.85; Dell, pp.256-258
[70] Dell, p.257
[71] Ibid. p.258

[72] Burk and Cairncross, pp.86-87; Morgan, p.546; and Benn, pp.653-655

[73] In addition to the references above, see Jefferys, K., *Anthony Crosland: A New Biography*, (Cohen, London, 1999); and Crosland, S., *Tony Crosland*, (Coronet, London, 1982, 2nd Edition), pp.377-378

[74] Susan Crosland, p.378

[75] Dell, p.261

[76] Quoted in Benn, p.654

[77] Benn, pp.654-655

[78] Burk and Cairncross, pp.87-88

[79] Callaghan, p.437

[80] Dell, p.258

[81] So, for example, Morgan places Fred Mulley in the Croslandite group, but this is not stated in other accounts, Morgan, p.545. Of all the accounts, only Bill Rodgers deals fairly with the case presented by Peter Shore; Rodgers, W., *Fourth Among Equals*, (Politicos, London, 2000), p.166

[82] Burk and Cairncross, pp.85-86; Jefferys, p.209; Susan Crosland, pp.376-377; Hattersley, R., *Who Goes Home*, (Warner, London, 1995, 2nd Edition), p.173. Interview with Lord Hattersley (31/10/00)

[83] Susan Crosland, p.377

[84] Rodgers, pp.164-165. Interview with Lord Rodgers (19/03/01)

[85] Burk and Cairncross, p.86

[86] Callaghan, p.438

[87] Rodgers, p.166

[88] Interview with Lord Shore (30/01/01)

[89] Interview with Lord Rodgers

[90] Interview with Lord Shore

[91] Interview with Albert Booth (02/05/01)

[92] Burk and Cairncross, pp.88-90; Jefferys, p.210

[93] Burk and Cairncross, p.88

[94] Interview with Lord Shore

[95] Interview with Albert Booth

[96] Dell, p.251

[97] See Benn, pp.640-642

[98] Quoted in Morgan, pp.546-547

[99] Morgan, p.546

[100] Pliatzky, pp.156-157. Interview with Denzil Davies, MP.

[101] Rodgers, p.164

[102] This is the view of Dell. See esp. pp.251-252

[103] Callaghan, p.435

[104] Interview with Lady Williams

[105] Burk and Cairncross, p.90

[106] Ibid. pp.90-92

[107] Ibid. p.91

[108] Ibid. p.92

[109] Callaghan, p.438

[110] Burk and Cairncross, pp.96-99; Benn, pp.661-669; Morgan, pp.548-549; Jefferys, p.211; Dell, pp.268-269

[111] Morgan, pp.547-548

[112] Rodgers, p.166

[113] Burk and Cairncross, p.97

[114] Healey said that Benn "wants to withdraw into the citadel, but only so long as we can slip out to borrow the money to buy the bows and arrows we'll need to shoot at the besieging armies." Quoted in Fay and Young, p.39

[115] Morgan, p.548

[116] Interviews with Lord Shore and Albert Booth

[117] Healey, p.431

[118] Dell, p.266

[119] Benn, p.667-668

[120] Callaghan, pp.438-439

[121] Ibid. p.439

[122] Ibid.; Jefferys, p.211; and Susan Crosland, pp.381-382

[123] Rodgers, p.165

[124] Interview with Lord Rodgers

[125] Interview with Lady Williams

[126] Susan Crosland, p.381; Jefferys, p.211

[127] Callaghan, p.439

[128] Burk and Cairncross, pp.101-102; Benn pp.670-679; Morgan, p.549; Jefferys, pp.211-212; Dell, pp.269-271

[129] Benn, p.671

[130] Ibid. p.676

[131] Quoted in Fay and Young, p.40

[132] Quoted in Benn, p.676

[133] Burk and Cairncross, p.102. Dell is particularly critical of Callaghan for allowing the Cabinet debate to drag on, when it should have been cut short. The Cabinet Secretary, Sir John Hunt (now Lord Hunt of Tanworth) was more supportive of the approach of Callaghan. See Dell, E. and Hunt of Tanworth, 'The Failings of Cabinet Government in the mid to Late 1970s', Contemporary Record, 8/3, Winter 1994, pp.453-472. Interview with Lord Hunt, (21/01/02)

[134] Burk and Cairncross, pp.92-96; and Morgan, pp.547-548

[135] Benn, p.661

[136] Morgan, p.547

[137] Interview with Lord Hunt

[138] Healey, p.431. However, Dell believes that Witteveen had been sent by Ford himself. But there appears to be little evidence to support this view. Dell, p.268

[139] Burk and Cairncross, p.93

[140] See De Vries, M.G., The International Monetary Fund 1972-8: Cooperation on Trial, (International Monetary Fund, Washington, 1985), Vol.1, p.471

[141] Fay and Young, p.38

[142] Burk and Cairncross, p.96
[143] Healey, p.432; and Burk and Cairncross pp.102-103
[144] Callaghan, p.441
[145] Burk and Cairncross, p.103
[146] Ibid. pp103-104; and Callaghan p.441
[147] Burk and Cairncross, p.104; Barnett, pp.105-106; and Pliatzky, pp.157-158
[148] Callaghan, p.442
[149] see Barnett, p.106; Benn, pp.683-686; and Burk and Cairncross, pp.106-108
[150] Benn, pp.687-688
[151] Ibid. p.687
[152] Ibid. p.688
[153] Burk and Cairncross, p.108. The Letter of Intent is recorded in Hansard (House of Commons Debates, Vol.922, 15/12/1976, 1525-1537)
[154] Barnett, p.110
[155] Hansard (House of Commons Debates, Vol.922, 15/12/1976, 1537-1558)
[156] The *Sun*, (16/12/1976)
[157] See the *Financial Times*, (16/12/1976)
[158] Information from Alan Howarth
[159] Burk and Cairncross, p.109
[160] Benn, p.689
[161] Burk and Cairncross, p.110
[162] Quoted in Burk and Cairncross, p.109
[163] Callaghan, p.443
[164] Interview with Lord Hattersley
[165] Browning, P., *The Treasury and Economic Policy: 1964-1985*, (Longman, London, 1986), p.95
[166] Barnett, pp.110-111. See the Public Expenditure White Paper (Feb. 1977, Cmnd.6373)
[167] Quoted in Pliatzky, p.157
[168] Correspondence from Samuel Brittan, March 2002. See also Fay and Young, p.22
[169] Burk and Cairncross, p.111
[170] Ibid. p.113
[171] Ibid. p.114
[172] ibid. pp.112-113
[173] Ibid. pp.115-117
[174] Ibid. pp.117-118
[175] Ibid.
[176] Ibid. p.118
[177] Ibid. pp.119-122
[178] Ibid. pp.122-123
[179] Ibid. pp.123-124
[180] Ibid. p.124

[181] Dell, E., *The Chancellors*, (HarperCollins, London, 1997), pp.437-438

[182] Ibid. p.438

[183] Zis, G., 'The International Status of Sterling', in Artis, M., and Cobham, D., (Eds.), *Labour's Economic Policies: 1974-79*, (Manchester University Press, Manchester, 1991), pp.104-120; p.112

[184] Callaghan, p.446

[185] Zis, p.108

[186] Morgan, p.556

CHAPTER 6

ECONOMIC ANALYSIS

Introduction

In the last four chapters, I have examined the development of British economic policy. I began by looking at the period between 1945 and 1974, and argued that there was something that can be termed a 'Keynesian consensus'. I then examined the development of the Labour Party's economic policy between 1970-74 while in opposition. On coming to power, we have seen how the apparent agreement of the Alternative Economic Strategy was quickly reversed after the General Elections of 1974. I then focused on the events of March 1976 to January 1977. The purpose of this and the next chapter is to analyse the developments of 1974-76. I wish to focus on the issue of the alleged shift in political economy, away from Keynesianism towards economic liberalism. The central question is therefore: did the Labour Government mark a shift in economic thinking?

Although this appears to be a straightforward question, it is in fact very difficult to answer. A study such as this raises several complex problems. The first concerns the relationship between ideas and policy. To what extent do ideas affect policymaking? Do politicians have a role in economic policy, or do they merely respond to structural forces? The second problem follows on from the first: namely how do economic theories relate to specific policy tools and techniques. The chapter therefore begins with a discussion of public policy analysis.

Another difficulty involved in the discussion of economic paradigms is the nature of the paradigms themselves. This chapter therefore discusses economic paradigms. There are three such paradigms. The first is Keynesian economics, which had been dominant in the postwar period. This was challenged from the Left by the Alternative Economic Strategy (AES) and from the right by economic liberalism. I therefore begin by comparing the AES with Keynesian economics in order to identify what was at stake in the left challenge to Keynesianism. I then go on to discuss economic liberalism, a complex set of theories which formed the economic challenge to postwar social democracy from the right.

Public Policy Analysis

I begin with a discussion of public policy analysis. This will require an abstract discussion of a number of theories presented by several public policy analysts. Unfortunately, therefore, it involves a distraction away from the analysis of the IMF Crisis. However, this is necessary in order to make a more accurate assessment of what changed as a result of the IMF Crisis. Two particular issues need to be discussed at this stage. The first is the nature of economic policy paradigms, which needs to be understood clearly when looking at Keynesianism, the AES and economic liberalism. The second is the nature of paradigm shift, which needs to be clarified if we are to ask what changed as a result of the IMF Crisis. This section does not, therefore, intend to discuss public policy in any detail but rather to use public policy analysis to clarify the discussion on the IMF Crisis.

An important contribution is that of Peter Hall's work on policy paradigms. Hall attempts to show how ideas and state institutions interact to produce policy change. A key concept here is 'policy learning'. The concept of 'learning' was first developed by Hugh Heclo in the 1970s to mean a deliberate adaptation of policy in response to evidence that policy was not working as intended.[1] According to Heclo, policy learning has two characteristics. The first is that policy evolves in a rational manner so that the most effective means of achieving better economic performance - lower unemployment, lower inflation, higher growth and a favourable balance of external payments - are used by governments. Secondly, Heclo argued that the key actors in policymaking are state bureaucrats. In a comparative study of social policy in Britain and Sweden, Heclo argues that, "forced to choose one group from among all the separate political factors as most consistently important...the bureaucracies of Britain and Sweden loom predominant in the policies studied."[2] Hall accepts the notion of policy learning, although he seeks to revise it, as I will show below. Hall describes policy learning as "a deliberate attempt to adjust the goals or techniques of policy in response to past experiences and new information. Learning is indicated when policy changes as a result of such a process."[3] Hence, policy learning is the key to explaining policy change.

Hall further characterises economic policy by saying that there are three broad levels of policy change: first, second and third order change.[4] First order consists of the specific settings of policy. This occurs in a continual and incremental way. A good example here would have to be the continual adjustment of interest rates in response to changing economic conditions. According to Hall, first order change is a largely technical measure and is conducted by the Bank of England and the Treasury officials. There is little scope for wider debate, nor even for ministerial input. First order change therefore complies with the notion of policy learning developed by Heclo.

Second order change refers to the level of strategic policy techniques. This occurs less often than first order change, since it is limited to those situations in which existing policy techniques do not appear to offer a means of achieving existing policy goals. An example of second order change was the introduction of cash limits in 1975, as discussed in the earlier chapter, in order to reduce the growth in public expenditure. This can be seen as second order change in that it goes beyond the scope of first order measures since it changes the strategic techniques used to meet certain specified objectives of policy. Again, Hall argues that state bureaucrats were central to the implementation of these reforms, so that Heclo's notion of policy learning still holds.

The most important level of policy is third order. This refers to the overarching policy goals themselves. Here, Hall draws on the work of Thomas Kuhn who argued that 'normal' scientific practice takes place within the framework of the dominant paradigm.[5] So, for example, physicists operated under the paradigmatic framework established by Newtonian principles until it was replaced by the theories of Einsteinian physics. According to Hall, social science operates under a similar structure. Indeed, Hall argues that Kuhn's views, "seem to have even more validity in the sphere of social science."[6] This is because theories in social science are harder to validate on empirical grounds. Evidence is often contestable and inconclusive, and it is harder to conduct controlled experiments. Kuhn's approach emphasises the existence of stable parameters or paradigms under which the actors in a particular field operate. The paradigm both shapes the understanding of what is being studied and how individuals will respond to events. Policymakers can neither control directly, nor observe, all behaviour in the marketplace and therefore require a simplified theoretical model of how the market works. The paradigm in economic policy is therefore the framework in which policymakers understand how an economy works and the likely consequences of policy decisions.

The paradigm provides a theoretical construction of the operation of the economy. In this sense, first and second order policy is 'normal' policymaking.[7] Policy is conducted on rational grounds but only in the sense that it is based on the existing conceptualisation of how the economy works. Since an understanding of how the market operates is mediated through the construction of a theoretical framework it is possible to argue that policymakers operate within a paradigmatic discourse. A paradigmatic discourse is defined by Charles Anderson: "the deliberation of public policy takes place within a realm of discourse...policies are made within some system of ideas and standards which is comprehensible and plausible to the actors involved."[8] Third order change concerns the shift from one paradigm to another. In this sense, the shift from Keynesianism to monetarism can be regarded as third order change or paradigm shift.[9] Both Keynesianism and monetarism are, according to Hall, theoretical constructions of how an economy operates and prescribe radically different policy tools and techniques.[10]

Policy paradigms therefore relate to the role of ideas in policymaking. Deborah Stone argues that, "our understanding of real situations is always mediated by ideas; those ideas in turn are created, changed and fought over in politics."[11] Ideas-based approaches stress the role of ideas, and that these ideas create stable parameters within which policy is conducted. A similar approach to Hall's is the advocacy coalition framework developed by Paul Sabatier.[12] Sabatier describes the advocacy coalition as a system of actors working within a policy subsystem who share a set of beliefs over desirable policy outcomes. The policy subsystem tends to be stable over a long period of time due to the existence of a set of relatively stable parameters such as constitutional structures, social norms and the distribution of resources. A number of external events such as changes in socio-economic conditions, public opinion, governing party and the policy decisions of other subsystems, act to change the internal dynamics of the subsystem.

A tension exists within ideas-based approaches. The advocacy coalition framework, developed by Sabatier, stresses the importance of beliefs in the operation of policy subsystems. Groups of actors operate within a subsystem which, "share a set of normative and causal beliefs."[13] At the centre of the policy subsystem are deep-core beliefs, which cover political values such as liberty and equality. Sabatier argues that, "the familiar Left/Right scale...operates at this level."[14] These beliefs provide stable parameters, and changes in deep-core beliefs of actors are infrequent. Beliefs change little over time.

However, Hall's approach differs from that of Sabatier over the understanding of the policy paradigm. Whereas Sabatier argues that the paradigm, or set of relatively stable parameters, is based on core beliefs, Hall appears to suggest that the paradigm takes the form of a discourse. Here, Hall's analysis is rather unclear. A more useful approach is that of Marteen Hajer who argues that discourse is the key to explaining policy paradigms.[15] Hajer argues that, "people are not seen as holding stable values but as having vague, contradictory and unstable 'value positions'. New discourses may alter existing cognitive commitments and thus influence the values and beliefs of actors."[16] Rather than values shaping the actions of the advocacy coalitions, those values are themselves shaped by a realm of discourse, which provide a way of understanding both what is possible and desirable.

A clear choice therefore has to be made in describing what is meant by an economic policy paradigm. I wish to argue that a paradigm concerns both beliefs and discourse. Actors are motivated primarily by their values. However, in order to make these values operational they require a discourse, in this case an economic theory, to understand how these values can be achieved. The following statement by Wynne Godley and Francis Cripps, two of the leading theorists in the development of the Alternative Economic Strategy, illustrates the point: "it has become pretty obvious that the governments of many countries, whatever their moral and political priorities have no valid scientific rationale for their policies."[17] The use of the term 'scientific' is a little misleading in this context since it can be debated whether or not an economic theory provides a 'scientific' basis for policy. Certainly it is only scientific in the context of 'abnormal' policymaking defined above. However, it is certainly correct that an economic theory provides a comprehensive rationale for the achievement of given moral and political priorities. The adoption and rejection of an economic policy paradigm is therefore bound up in political beliefs. Policymakers do not choose freely from a set of alternative economic models in some kind of value free way. The approach of Sabatier is therefore more accurate, I believe, than that of Hajer. Indeed, it is perhaps possible to talk of a 'fourth order' level of change which consists of political values.

I wish to argue that economic theories are both political and strategic. Often economists will act in such a way that economic theories appear to be technical. In many cases this is so. Economic theories, at both a macro and a micro level, are often highly abstract and specific and have little relation to political economy. However, even certain apparently technical theories have wider political implications. At the level of policy paradigms, by which I mean Keynesianism, the AES and economic liberalism in this particular study, the political and strategic nature of the theory is most explicit. Economic theories are political in two ways. Firstly, the advocates of such theories are themselves political in the sense that they hold to certain value positions that their theories seek to establish. This is clearly the case when considering such thinkers as Hayek and those who formulated the AES. Secondly, economic theories are political in the sense that they will be taken up by politicians who wish to achieve a certain form in economic and social life, as was clearly the case with Margaret Thatcher and Tony Benn to give two prominent examples. The economic theories discussed here are therefore concerned with certain political goals. As Andrew Gamble has commented, the theories are strategic since the AES and economic liberalism were "major attempts to map out new political courses to overcome Britain's decline and to transform British institutions and British society,"[18] just as Keynesianism had been in the immediate postwar period.

What then is the nature of paradigm shift? Third order change has three characteristics. Firstly, it is non-rational and controversial. Since paradigm shift occurs in periods of deep uncertainty, and given the nature of social scientific theories, advice will become controversial. Under these circumstances, judgements are made on political, rather than scientific grounds. The ability of particular interests to promote a coherent and appealing case is therefore important, and the likely outcome will depend on the capacity of interests to achieve this. A similar point is made by D. Colander and A.W. Coats.[19] Colander and Coats therefore refer to the non-rational nature of the spread of ideas: "at one point in time a set of ideas might be considered outlandish but subsequently become accepted as orthodoxy; or part of conventional wisdom... However, rather than an evolutionary process, this may simply reflect changes in fashion."[20] Colander and Coats go on to present three models, which may be used to explain how ideas spread.[21] The first is called the 'infectious disease' model. Just as an infectious disease spreads when carriers come into contact with non-carriers, so ideas can spread by contact between those who promote certain ideas and those who do not. However, Colander and Coats reject this model since it fails to account for barriers to the spread of ideas.

There is therefore a need to explain how these barriers can be overcome. The second model is termed the 'marketplace for ideas'. In any market there is an interaction of supply and demand. In this instance there is a supply of theories from economists, and a demand for theories by the government. As ideas spread they are distorted in the way described above. The way in which ideas are promoted and the likely success of an idea depends on the particular historical context in which they occur. Given the absence of perfect competition, the successful idea, i.e. the one that is implemented by government, will not necessarily be the 'best' one, i.e. the most theoretically sound. Instead, factors such as the resources available to those who promote certain ideas, the ideological nature of the governing party and so on all contribute to the likely success of an idea. The third model presented by Colander and Coats is the information theory model. Here ideas can be seen in terms of information theory. The theory states that information moves through several distinct stages. These are dispatch, transmission and reception. As information moves between these stages it becomes distorted. In the same way, economic theories follow the same course. They are dispatched by economists, transmitted by institutions and received in revised form by citizens.

The second important feature of paradigm shift, following on from the first point, is that issues of 'authority' will be crucial. Advocates will compete in order to show that their position has authority and to try to discredit others.[22] Sabatier argues a similar point. Information becomes distorted as evidence is sought to support the beliefs of the coalition, and evidence that undermines the values of the coalition is 'filtered' by the coalition. However, evidence can build up against the coalition to the point at which it is eventually undermined. A coalition can use evidence to undermine the position of a rival coalition.[23] Authority here implies both a technical and a political meaning. It is technical in the sense that it appears to offer a solution to existing economic problems which the current paradigm has failed to resolve. It is political in the sense that it is concerned directly with strategic policy goals. Hence, Hall argues that it is not possible to conceive of policy learning at third order level in the way that Heclo has done.

Finally, paradigm shift is closely associated with policy failure. A growing number of anomalies will emerge, which the existing paradigm both failed to predict and fails to offer possible solutions to.[24] As a result the paradigm is stretched to deal with such anomalies. However, this undermines the coherence of the paradigm, for example through the use of previously unacceptable techniques. Moreover, the new paradigm will emerge as a likely explanation of and solution to these anomalies and policy failures.

An important conclusion follows. Paradigm shift can take a long time to complete. The shift from Keynesianism to monetarism occurred over the course of the 1970s, and can be seen to have six stages.[25] Starting from a position of paradigm stability, a number of anomalies in the form of real world events occurred, which the paradigm did not predict or did not have solutions to. This in turn leads to experimentation with a number of new policy techniques, which stretched the meaning of the paradigm and undermined its coherence. Further policy anomalies lead to the discrediting of those in authority who had held to the paradigm. In this sense, authority refers to politicians, civil servants, academics, journalists and others who advanced a Keynesian position. As their authority breaks down, advocates of alternative paradigms emerge to contest the policy agenda. Finally, a new paradigm is institutionalised by the governing party.

The above analysis is of significance in relation to this chapter since it provides us with a means of understanding how policy tools and techniques fit together with economic theories. The discussion of public policy analysis points to the need for greater contextualisation. An accurate understanding of first and second order change requires a detailed analysis of the conduct of policy in this period. Similarly, the successful adoption of new ideas depends, as Colander and Coats have pointed out, on the wider context in which those ideas are promoted. Moreover, a valid interpretation of third order change requires an understanding of the values and intentions of the relevant actors, for reasons outlined in Chapter One. This chapter discusses the three economic theories – Keynesianism, the AES and economic liberalism – and the extent to which they had become popular by 1976.

Keynesianism and the AES

There were two broad economic theories which were fashionable in the Labour Party, and on the left more generally, in the 1970s; these were Keynesianism and the Alternative Economic Strategy (AES), both of which have been discussed in earlier chapters but which require some further comment. I begin by looking at Keynesianism. Keynes had challenged the orthodox economic theory that free markets were self-stabilising, arguing instead that inefficiencies in the market mechanisms resulted in disequilibria. The cost of high unemployment was the result of the inefficiencies of free markets. Public sector intervention was therefore justified and necessary in order to reduce unemployment by stimulating aggregate demand. In the immediate postwar period, both the Conservative and Labour parties accepted a broadly Keynesian framework, together with a welfare state and wider public ownership in what has become known as the postwar consensus (See Chapter 2). Between 1945 and the early 1970s, a number of policies were implemented to stimulate aggregate demand and business organisations and trades unions were incorporated into economic policymaking. The clearest statement of Keynesian economic thought in the postwar period were by Conservative Party revisionists who promoted a more 'One Nation' approach, and by Labour Party revisionists who campaigned for greater equality in a mixed economy.[26]

The second paradigm was that of the AES, which was developed by new-left theorists in the early 1970s. An intellectual basis for the AES was provided by Stuart Holland in his book *The Socialist Challenge*.[27] The thesis can be seen as a response by a resurgent Labour Party left wing against the revisionist thesis of the 1950s. Revisionists, such as Crosland, had argued that ownership of the means of production no longer mattered since the power of the state and of the trades unions had increased in the postwar economy. Moreover, there had been a separation of ownership (in the form of shareholding) from control (in the form of management).[28] Against this, Holland argued that there had been an increase in the number of transantional corporations and the growth of meso-economic power (large-scale corporations which could resist both microeconomic activity by holding a large market share and macroeconomic policy which was based on a competitive market economy). Large-scale corporations could therefore make large profits and faced no competitive pressure to reinvest. At the same time as making excess profits therefore, which added to inflationary pressures, corporations were inefficient and undermined British economic performance.

A number of policy reforms were proposed under the AES. It was necessary to increase the role of the state over the meso-economy through compulsory planning agreements, pricing policies, centrally planned investment and further public ownership. This all adds up to a rejection of the Keynesian economic strategy followed by both Labour and Conservative governments since 1945, which had accepted large-scale private ownership albeit permeated by demand-management policies and a larger public sector than had had operated before World War Two. It also represented a more assertive stance by the left.

In addition to the theory developed by Stuart Holland in *The Socialist Challenge*, and elsewhere[29], the AES contained a second strand. This was the work of the Cambridge Economic Policy Group, including Wynne Godley and Francis Cripps.[30] The central argument of the 'New Cambridge' school, as it became known, was that there was a need to restore the balance of payments surplus. Past attempts to reflate the domestic economy had resulted in full employment in the short-term, but this was quickly reversed by a subsequent balance of payments crisis. The balance of payments surplus could only be maintained by the introduction of protectionist measures such as import quotas. This, therefore, was the intellectual underpinning of Benn's advocacy of import measures in Cabinet.[31] In addition, the New Cambridge theorists argued that there was a need to restore industrial efficiency, largely through compulsory planning agreements, and the need to reduce the public sector borrowing requirement, which had a 'crowding-out' effect on international trade and investment.

The full implications of the 'crowding-out' argument are discussed below. The crucial point here is that the 'left-wing' Cambridge thesis advocated what was to be a central aspect of economic liberalism. Given that New Cambridge had strong links with the Labour Party, it is possible to argue that this school was influential in policymaking at this time. Hence, as Paul Mosley argues: "the New Cambridge School's influence was...the Trojan horse through which monetarism made its entrance into the policy-making circle in Britain."[32] This is a controversial claim, and one that, I believe, it is possible to reject. It is possible to reject this argument by looking at the influences on Healey at this time, to which I return later.

The historical development of Keynesianism and the AES has already been discussed in earlier chapters. However, it is necessary here to make further comparisons between the two in order to understand the theoretical development and intellectual origins of the AES, and what the points of contention were between Keynesianism and the AES. Given that the AES was largely a response to the dominant position of Keynesianism both within the Labour Party and within British economic policymaking more generally, it is best to contrast the two directly. This point has been made by Noel Thompson: "any explication of the Alternative Economic Strategy must begin with its critique of Keynesian social democracy. For in many respects, the former defined its position with reference to the latter's failings and consciously...set out to replace it as the dominant political economy of democratic socialism."[33] It is therefore for purposes of clarity that I wish to use the seven categories used to define Keynesianism in Chapter Two: namely, the state, macroeconomic objectives, fiscal policy, monetary policy, direct intervention, industrial relations and the international economy.

First, the Keynesians and the AES left shared a similar perspective of the state. Both Keynesianism and the AES accepted a legitimate role for the state in economic activity. Keynes had first legitimised state intervention in the economy in the 1930s by pointing out that markets did not clear to a point of equilibrium at which there would be a full employment of resources. This was so because of inefficiencies in the market and due to the presence of insufficient demand. The government should according to Keynes intervene in the market in order to create full employment. This view was accepted by postwar governments of both left and right, and was significant in social democratic theories of state intervention. The AES largely accepted this, but argued that the conditions of state intervention had changed. This was largely due to a transformation in the international economy, which required a change of policy at a national level, to which I return below. The key point was that such policy changes would re-allow the continuation of state intervention in the way that Keynes had argued. The agreement over the legitimacy and desirability of state intervention in the economy between Keynesianism and the AES contrasts with the free market policies of economic liberalism.

However, the apparent agreement between Keynesianism and the AES belies a fundamental tension on a particular aspect of the 'state' between the two. A principle commitment of the AES was to 'democratisation'. This was true of all strands of AES thought, ranging from left-Keynesianism to those on the radical left, and embraced industrial democracy, aspects of worker control and public ownership, as well as the reform of state institutions. It was not that the social democrats had been opposed to such reforms, particularly the reform of state institutions, but rather that they lacked the political will or the means to achieve their objectives. However, the lack of democratic involvement in the welfare state had undermined public faith in welfare institutions and strengthened the relative position of capitalism. Many on the AES left argued that the welfare state served the interests of capital in that the middle classes had benefited from welfare institutions disproportionately, and that governments chose to cut welfare expenditure at times of economic crisis. Only democratisation could alter this balance of power in favour of the workers.

Turning to macroeconomic objectives and the role of policy techniques, we can again see that there is much overlap in the approaches of Keynesianism and the AES. Keynes had justified the intervention of the state in the market in order to stimulate demand and to achieve full employment. This could be achieved by the use of fiscal policy, and particularly deficit financing, with monetary policy playing a subsidiary role in the fine-tuning of the economy. This was broadly the position of the AES, which stated that such policies and policy objectives were desirable, but were only attainable within the framework of a protected domestic economy. This argument was presented most clearly by the Cambridge Economic Policy group. The 'New Cambridge' model was essentially 'left-Keynesian', a position associated with Nicholas Kaldor, an early advocate of devaluation who had come to favour protection following the failure of the British economy to recover following the devaluation of 1967.[34]

There was, however, a certain difference of emphasis here between the Keynesians and the AES left. Advocates of the AES also came to favour the implementation of supply-side measures. The use of demand-management techniques, even after the introduction of import controls, would have a limited impact due to the persistence of inherent weaknesses in domestic production. As will be shown below, economic liberals also advocated measures to effect the supply-side of the economy, but the nature of these measures differed radically from those proposed within the framework of the AES. For supporters of the AES the democratisation of the economy was related closely to the level of productivity. Democratisation would improve the flow of knowledge from workers to managers and would increase the commitment of the worker to their work. Hence, Geoff Hodgson, a leading theorist within the

AES left, wrote that the AES was primarily concerned with "the 'supply-side' of the economy. In other words it aims at the transformation of the social relations of production both to humanise and democratise work and to increase output and productivity."[35]

There was also broad agreement between the Keynesians and the advocates of the AES over the role of trades unions. Although the increased role of the trades unions in economic management after 1945 had not been a part of Keynes's theory, it was not inimical to it. The trades unions, government and employers organisations had co-operated in the conduct of economic policy, particularly after the formation of the National Economic Development Council with its smaller sectoral committees. In theory the AES was committed to maintaining, if not adding to, the role of the trades unions. Indeed, the AES commitment to 'democratisation' would mean a more direct and explicit role in corporate decision-making. However, there was a tension in the thinking of the AES left on this point since the commitment to the pursuit of greater equality of outcome was potentially in conflict with the increased power of the trades unions, since it was commonplace for the trades unions to seek to maintain wage differentials. The response of the AES left was to argue that material factors would be less important to workers when they had more autonomy over their working lives.[36]

Thus we see a broad-based agreement between the Keynesians and the AES theorists over the role of the state in the economy, the pursuit of macroeconomic objectives, the use of fiscal and monetary policy and over trades union activity. However, the AES commitment to 'democratisation' meant that it was far more interventionist in the market than Keynesianism had been. The main difference was to be found in the approach to the international economy. Keynesianism was committed to an open, international economy. However, the AES asserted that Keynesian policies at a national level were no longer possible in the changed international economy of the 1970s. The international economy was now marked by a number of large firms which controlled markets and because of their international activity could effectively by-pass national control. This was mirrored by the growth of international finance markets. The objective of the AES was to restore national control over the domestic economy, a point made by Cripps, "the Alternative Economic Strategy (sought) to counterpose national self-government against the anarchic pressures of a global market system."[37] In terms of policy, this meant import controls, either in the form or tariffs or quotas, and controls on capital flows. For some, it also meant control of the banking sector by means of public ownership, or a state investment bank.

According to Andrew Gamble, the AES was a form of national political economy.[38] National political economy had its origins in the Nineteenth Century, and is largely a response to liberal political economy. Liberal political economy sees the economy as being composed largely of markets. Instead, national political economy is concerned with the nation as an economic actor, as Gamble writes: "what marks national political economy so clearly is its tendency to treat the nation as a single strategic commercial and industrial enterprise competing with other similar enterprises in the world economy."[39] Two examples of a national political economy are the 'social imperialism' associated with Joseph Chamberlain's campaign for tariff reform in the first decade of the last century and the fascism of Oswald Mosley in the 1930s. Both were concerned with the protection of the domestic economy. Therefore, although motivated by radically different political values, the AES can be seen as a manifestation of national political economy, for as Gamble goes on to say, "the main condition for the implementation of the alternative economic strategy, as its proponents see it, is the substantial severing of the ties that bind the British economy to the world economy...From the labour left's standpoint a social democracy can only be created if the British state regains control over the national economy."[40] This was in stark contrast to the Keynesian strategy of maintaining an essentially open economy, and thus marked the main fault line on the left in British politics in the 1970s.[41]

Economic Liberalism

The 1970s witnessed the emergence of a second broad critique of Keynesian political economy, this time from the right in the form of economic liberalism. Economic liberalism was part of a wider philosophical critique of social democracy: the 'New

Right'.[42] The New Right consisted of neo-conservatives and neo-liberals, and sought to restate traditional political values in order to challenge the policies of the postwar consensus. My concern here is with economic liberalism, which was that aspect of the New Right which sought to critique the role of government intervention in the economy. Economic liberalism can be defined as broad movement against the existing mixed economy and in favour of a free market with minimal state intervention. Peter Hall refers to 'monetarism' as a policy paradigm.[43] That is, a fully developed theory of the economy rivalling the Keynesian paradigm. The Keynesian and monetarist paradigms differ significantly over how the economy operated and the likely affects of the implementation of different policy tools and techniques. In short, monetarism, according to Hall, equates to economic liberalism. However, as I will show in this section, monetarism was not the same thing as economic liberalism, although I will argue that it was an integral part of it. Economic liberalism contains several elements. I will therefore summarise the main themes in each theory and relate them to liberal economic thinking more generally. Economic liberalism became fashionable in the 1970s as Keynesianism faced the problems of the collapse of Bretton Woods, the OPEC Crisis and so on, but had in fact been gradually emerging in the postwar period. The leading figure in the rise of economic liberalism had been Hayek, and so I begin with a brief discussion of his work.

Hayek[44]

Friedrich von Hayek had been a long-standing critic of all forms of government intervention and all but a minimum level of welfare protection. He was a firm advocate of free market policies. However, this was not because he believed that a free market was a perfect model of economic activity, unlike the classical liberals, since he accepted that markets had imperfections, but he did believe them to be the best option available. This was so for two reasons. The first was that he objected to the basing of policies on rationalist principles. Markets had not been invented by a deliberate act by individuals or by governments, but had in fact emerged spontaneously. This was important since it did not mean that markets were based on rationalist principles. Such principles cannot be based on objectivist foundations since they ultimately depend on subjectivist moral reasoning. Any measure based on such subjectivist foundations reflects the moral predilections of their originator, and in a morally pluralist society cannot reflect any general interest, only the interests of those who promote such a policy. It is therefore not possible to formulate principles of social or distributive justice. Such an argument has also been presented by Samuel Brittan in his work on public expenditure.[45] Given that it is not possible to establish general principles on which to distribute public expenditure, there will be a competition among particular interests for the distribution of resources. Public expenditure will therefore be directed to those who campaign the most effectively. Similarly, the public choice school argues that since the state does not act in the general interest, it seeks the allocation of resources in order to fulfil its own interests.[46] Only the market is capable of acting in the true public interest since it was created spontaneously and is not based on abstract principles.

The second reason why Hayek favoured free markets is that he was based in the 'Austrian school' of economic thought.[47] The Austrian school accepted the imperfection of the market, since economic activity took place between consumers with imperfect knowledge and companies with differing market shares. However, the Austrian school accepted the imperfect market model as the best that could be achieved, since the interaction of supply and demand was based on the free flow of knowledge, or information. The market allowed for alterations in consumer tastes and information automatically by allowing the level of prices to alter. The price mechanism is a means of demonstrating changing consumer tastes. Such knowledge, or information, for Hayek is largely subjective, or tacit, and is not therefore amenable to objective and explicit rationalisation. This point is explained by Norman Barry: "in a complex society knowledge (or information) is dispersed among millions of actors, each one of whom can only be acquainted only with that knowledge which affects him personally. The idea that social and economic knowledge (of production costs, consumer tastes, prices and so on) can be centralised in the mind of one person, or even in one institution, is an epistemological absurdity for Hayek."[48] Only the market therefore can allow the efficient spread of such information for Hayek, which in turn is essential for the preservation of human freedom.

The assertion that markets occurred spontaneously and that human knowledge is not subject to rationalist principles is a strong argument in favour of free markets, especially when combined with the more overtly political arguments from the neo-liberals concerning the nature of rights and justice and forms the basis of a wholesale rejection of the mixed economy.[49] Indeed, as Norman Barry makes clear, the operation of the free market is so efficient that, "for liberal political economy, it is clear that dislocations and break-downs in the market system can only occur through impediments to the exchange process."[50]   There are specifically two impediments that economic liberals tend to emphasise. The first is the state. State intervention is wrong because it is not possible to plan the economy in a given way due to the nature of human knowledge, as outlined above. Moreover, given the absence of any objective basis for the allocation and distribution of resources, the state will be faced by competing demands from sectional interests. Ultimately, this will destroy the legitimacy of political institutions and the efficiency of the free market. The second impediment concerns the role of the trades unions, which distort the pricing mechanism of the labour market, undermine the free supply of labour and coerces employers into accepting certain rates of pay, conditions of work and under a closed shop arrangement as operated in Britain in the 1970s ensure that the trades union has a monopoly on the representation of a workforce.   The drift of postwar policy was towards intervention.   The economic liberals therefore demanded nothing less than the rejection of postwar orthodoxy. I now wish to discuss further three particular elements of economic liberalism that have a direct bearing on the discussion of the IMF Crisis: monetarism, crowding-out theories and supply-side theories.

Monetarism

Monetarism begins by stressing the role of monetary policy in the economy, which Keynes had largely overlooked. According to Milton Friedman, the leading monetarist theorist, there were several reasons for this reassertion of monetary policy.[51] Keynes had failed to diagnose correctly the cause of the 1930s slump, which according to Friedman had been due to the mismanagement of monetary policy by the US Federal Reserve. Moreover, in contrast to the Keynesian prediction of a postwar slump, there had in fact been an upturn. The main problem in the postwar international economy had been inflation, and so central banks had returned to an orthodox monetary policy.

Monetarism re-emphasised the monetary equation, or quantity theory, first developed by Irving Fisher at the end of the Nineteenth Century:[52]

$$MV=PT$$

MV represents the stock of money in the economy multiplied by the velocity of its circulation. PT represents the average price level multiplied by the total number of monetary transactions. MV represents the total expenditure and PT the total income in the economy. Since income and expenditure are a flow, the two must be equal. The number of transactions equates roughly to the total output (Q) in the economy[53], so that it can be expressed as the national income:

$$MV=PQ$$

Fisher had argued that V and Q were constant so that a change in the money supply fed directly into higher prices. In contrast, Keynes argued that V was unstable, so that there was no such direct relationship between alterations in the money supply without a corresponding rise in inflation. Arguing against this, Friedman said that V was likely to correlate positively with M so that an increase in M would affect an increase in V, or vice versa.[54] Since nominal national product could not increase, a change in the money supply would cause a rise in inflation.[55] This argument has a clear implication for public policy since the type of deficit spending championed by Keynes as a method of reducing unemployment could not work, since a rise in the public sector borrowing requirement (PSBR), through the sale of bonds and bills, would add to inflation.[56]

The wider political implications of monetarism are open to debate. Although monetarism is often seen as an integral part of the economic liberal agenda, it has been reinterpreted.

Dennis Kavanagh argues that: "in principle, monetarist ideas are politically neutral between left and right."[57] This argument has been elaborated by Kenneth Hoover and Raymond Plant.[58] An increase in the money supply adds to inflation. Therefore, a government which seeks to increase aggregate demand by raising the PSBR will raise inflationary pressures. The traditional social democratic response in postwar Britain was to reflate the economy by means of deficit expenditure along the lines suggested by Keynesians. However, instead of causing higher employment, according to the monetarists, it led to higher inflation. According to Hoover and Plant, monetarism only makes a case for the avoidance of deficit financing. It is neutral as to the issue of public expenditure. Accepting the monetarist argument on the money supply still leaves open the question of what the level of public expenditure should be. It would still be possible to have a high level of public expenditure so long as it was financed through taxation, since this would not add to the inflationary pressures in the economy. Although it may be fair to claim, from a reading of his more overtly political texts[59], that Friedman himself would have preferred lower public expenditure; there is nothing within the quantity theory to suggest that this is the only policy option available to government. Rather than seeing monetarism as a political theory, it is best to regard it as a technical theory that is neutral on the issue of public expenditure. This is an important argument since if it can be demonstrated that the Labour Government embarked on a monetarist policy in 1976, it does not necessarily follow that it had moved to the right.

The argument is a persuasive one, and there is evidence to suggest that Friedman was concerned only with deficit financing in his earlier works.[60] Moreover, Samuel Brittan, one of the leading monetarist commentators in Britain has argued the same point.[61] There are, however, three reasons why monetarism as it developed in the 1970s should, I believe, be regarded as part of the broader economic liberal thesis. The first concerns the monetarist approach to unemployment. Again this attained its most developed form in the writing of Friedman.[62] According to Friedman there is a long-term or 'natural' rate of unemployment. The case that monetarism is politically neutral rests mainly on a discussion of the quantity theory. I wish to argue that this is incorrect; the significance of monetarist doctrine lay more in the 'natural rate' of unemployment model. This is represented in Figure 6.1 below (U_N). In the short-term there may be possible trade-offs between inflation and unemployment as argued by the Keynesian economist, A.W. Phillips. As the government stimulates aggregate demand in order to reduce unemployment from U_N to U_L (point F on the Phillips curve), inflation increases to B. However, according to Friedman, workers respond to the real wage rate. At first they may be prepared to accept higher prices as their nominal wage increases. Eventually, workers realise that their real wage rate has remained constant and so demand higher wages. The resulting increase in unemployment as employers seek to reduce costs pushes the unemployment level back to the natural rate (G). A further attempt to reduce unemployment by means of government stimulation of aggregate demand leads to the third Phillips curve.

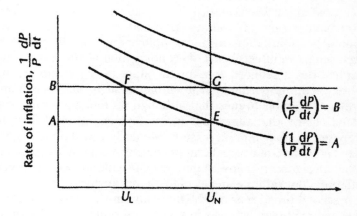

Unemployment

Figure 6.1 The 'Natural Rate of Unemployment' Model[63]

Hence, Friedman argues that: "the way unemployment can be kept below the 'natural rate' is by an ever accelerating inflation."[64] In short, Friedman rejects the Keynesian approach to reducing unemployment. As Andrew Gamble argues, the "monetarists' belief in sound money was much more than just a technical case for how best to reduce inflation in a time of recession. Monetarists believed that the full employment objective of postwar stabilisation policy was fundamentally misconceived."[65] This is not to argue that Friedman rejects all means of reducing unemployment. However, the only way of achieving a permanent reduction in unemployment is to act on the supply-side of the economy, particularly in the labour market where it would be necessary to remove barriers to the free operation of the market such as minimum wage legislation and trades union bargaining.[66] Therefore, Friedman defines the natural rate as: "that rate of employment which is consistent with the existing real conditions in the labour market. It can be lowered by removing obstacles in the labour market, by reducing friction. It can be raised by introducing additional obstacles."[67]   Friedman argued that the natural rate had increased in postwar America due, in part, to the increase in the level and scope of welfare payments.[68]   The monetarist approach to inflation and unemployment can therefore be regarded as an integral part of economic liberalism in two ways: it advocates a reduced role for the state in the economy, and relegates the importance of unemployment in macroeconomic strategy. Gamble argues that although no monetarist has ever stated clearly that they want unemployment to rise, they are prepared to allow it to increase.[69] Similarly David Smith argues that, "monetarism was not...an uncontroversial tool of economic policy designed to allow stable growth without accompanying inflation. But rather a means of justifying austerity."[70]

A second broad reason why monetarism was an integral part of economic liberalism was in its general philosophical attitude towards the market. Neo-liberals dislike government intervention in the economy for several reasons. According to Tim Congdon, a leading monetarist writer in Britain in the 1970s, monetarism was also committed to free markets.[71] Money is important since it acts as a medium of exchange. It allows for the free exchange of knowledge in the sense of allowing people to maximise their utility by observing prices in uncoerced market activity.   Stable prices are therefore important in facilitating freedom of exchange. Congdon regards the minimal role of the state advocated by the monetarists as fundamental to economic freedom: "the government's powers in the economic sphere should be restricted. The monetary rule is perhaps the most effective barrier to political discretion."[72]

The final reason for regarding monetarism as a constituent part of economic liberalism was its implicit assumption of perfect markets in the quantity theory. An increase in the stock of money (M) will cause an increase in inflation (P) according to the theory. However, this is only the case if output (Q) cannot increase. The only way in which it can be argued that Q cannot increase is by assuming the existence of free markets, which clear to the point of equilibria. If this argument is not accepted it allows for the re-entry of Keynesian economics.   On Keynesian grounds, a rise in the money supply by either deficit expenditure or adjustment in the interest rate can result in a rise in output rather than prices since the economy is operating at less than full employment. It has already been shown that the monetarists had a free-market approach to unemployment, but it is therefore also true that the monetarist approach to inflation assumed the operation of free markets.[73]

Supply side theory

Supply side theory comprises two elements. The first is a concern with taxation, while the second is concerned with the labour market. Both, however, emphasise the importance of incentives and are concerned explicitly with the reduction of state intervention. The supply-side approach to taxation is most clearly elaborated by Arthur Laffer.[74] According to Laffer, there is a strong relationship between taxation and incentives. As tax rates increase there is a disincentive to work, and so total tax yield declines as people work less. Equally, tax yield will increase with rising tax rates up until the point at which people begin to feel that there is a disincentive to further work. There is therefore a "tax rate structure which maximises government tax receipts."[75] This is represented by point o in Figure 6.2 where T represents the tax yield and t the tax rate. Although there is a definite point at which tax revenue is maximised on the model, this point will in fact vary with cultural and historical circumstance.[76] Two points follow from this. The first is that tax rates have to be introduced with the consent of taxpayers. Secondly, it is likely that lower tax rates will increase economic output, so that tax cuts for higher earners will benefit the poor through the 'trickle-down' effect.

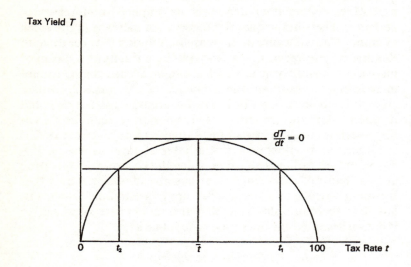

Figure 6.2 The 'Laffer Curve'[77]

The second element of supply side theory concerns the labour market.   The basic assertion is that British economic performance, which had been lagging behind that of major competitors throughout the postwar period, a fact which had become increasingly apparent since the 1960s, was largely due to the persistence of supply-side problems.   In this sense, economic liberalism and the AES were in agreement since both regarded Keynesian demand management as ineffective. However, it was over the exact nature of the supply-side difficulties, and therefore remedies, where the AES and economic liberalism differed. For the AES the problem was the alienation of the worker, and the remedy was therefore to be found in a radical extension of public ownership and industrial democracy. In contrast, the economic liberals emphasised the barriers to the operation of the free labour market. It was necessary to restore individual incentives and to remove the collectivist and coercive barriers within the labour market. In terms of policy, this came to mean two things above all others. Firstly, the reduction in the power of trades unions in order to restore a true market price for labour and the reduction in workers rights in order to make them more responsive to changes in market rates. Secondly, the reduction of both the scope and the level of welfare benefits in order to make employment more attractive financially. Increasingly, a moral argument was added to this by neo-conservatives that benefit payments should be reduced as this created a culture of welfare dependency and reduced individual responsibility.

Crowding-out theory

The crowding-out theory has already been introduced in the above discussion of the AES. However, the main proponents of the crowding-out thesis were the economic liberals. Crowding-out theory has two distinct elements. The first refers to a 'physical' crowding-out.[78] As the public sector grows it takes resources, essentially in the form of labour, away from the private sector. This had occurred in Britain since the early 1960s, but had coincided with a rise in unemployment and relative economic decline as the British economy was out-competed by other leading nations. According to Walter Eltis this was because the public sector had taken resources away from the wealth-creating private sector.[79] In order to restore economic growth, the government should cut taxes, which would result in lower labour costs and increase incentives to invest and to work. Moreover, there was a need to reduce the level of public expenditure directly as this was consuming the wealth created by the private sector. Crowding out theory, as developed by Bacon and Eltis, was far more explicit on the need to reduce both government debt and government spending as a proportion of GDP than monetarism had been. The second notion is that of 'financial' crowding-out.[80] By financing its budget by borrowing from the private sources, the government would take away resources from the private sector. An investor would normally choose to invest in the public sector because there is a greater security of return. However, the public sector does not create wealth and therefore takes resources away from the wealth-creating private sector. The crowding-out effect of deficit financing is therefore in addition to the inflationary effects emphasised by the monetarists and became part of the broader monetarist thesis.

As it is demonstrated in the next chapter the conduct of policy was influenced strongly by the physical crowding-out thesis, it is necessary to state at this stage that the Bacon and Eltis thesis was widely criticised at the time and has since been rejected. The thesis attempts to demonstrate a causal relationship between the growth of the public sector and the decline of the economy. Instead, no such causal relationship could be demonstrated since the increase in the size of the public sector could equally have been a response to economic decline. This point is significant since it shows that even economic theories that are later shown to be false can have an immediate impact on policy.[81]

The Spread of Economic Ideas Prior to 1976

The theoretical aspects of the spread of economic ideas have already been discussed in terms of the process of paradigm shift. The following discussion therefore concerns the institutional aspects of the spread of new economic ideas in the 1970s. Here, primary importance can be attached to think-tanks.[82] Crudely, the role of the think-tank is to promote certain ideas or theories in an attempt to persuade government to implement them in the form of concrete policies. There were three neo-liberal think-tanks: the Institute of Economic Affairs, the Centre for Policy Studies and the Adam Smith Institute.

The Institute of Economic Affairs (IEA) was established in the immediate postwar period by liberals who were opposed to the growth of collectivism.[83] The chief intellectual force behind the IEA was Friedrich von Hayek, who had argued in *The Road to Serfdom*[84] that the emergence of the mixed economy and the welfare state threatened individual liberty. Hayek had a significant influence on a number of like-minded negative libertarians such as Antony Fisher, who established the IEA in

1955.[85] From 1955, two figures were to have a significant impact on the IEA: Ralph Harris and Arthur Seldon. From the mid-1950s through to the mid-1970s, the IEA produced a number of reports on microeconomic issues, but rather than seeking to convert specific policymakers, they sought to change the wider agenda. It can be said that in general terms the IEA had little impact until the late 1960s. Although the Conservative Party, under Edward Heath from 1965, did not accept the arguments presented by the IEA, the Institute did have an impact on right-wing MPs such as Enoch Powell, Keith Joseph, Angus Maude and Geoffrey Howe. From 1969, with the publication of a paper entitled 'Money in Boom and Slump' by Alan Walters[86], the IEA promoted monetarist theories. This included the publication of a number of papers by Milton Friedman.[87] The position of the IEA therefore changed substantially from one of obscurity in the 1950s to an influential position by the 1970s. This point has been emphasised in a recent study by Andrew Denham and Mark Garnett: "the influence of the IEA increased steadily during the late 1960s and early 1970s among both politicians and political commentators."[88]

The second important think-tank was the Centre for Policy Studies (CPS).[89] This was established in 1974 by Keith Joseph. Joseph was convinced of the need to establish the CPS by his colleague Alfred Sherman. According to Sherman and Joseph, there was a need for a new institution for three reasons. The first was the need to formulate new policies following the defeat of the Conservative Party in the 1974 General Election. The second was the need for an institution which would serve the Conservative Party given the traditional independent role assumed by the IEA.[90] Edward Heath reluctantly accepted the need for the new body. However, it became clear that the main supporters of the CPS were opposed to the leadership of Edward Heath. By the time of the public announcement of the creation of the CPS in January 1975, there were already moves to force Heath out. Following the success of Margaret Thatcher in the leadership contest, the CPS had an important role in the Conservative Party's internal policymaking process. The new leadership were sceptical of the Conservative Party Research Department, which still contained a large number of Heathites. The third justification of the CPS was therefore to circumvent the Research Department. The views of the CPS were widely publicised from 1975 with the publication of a number of speeches by Keith Joseph. In particular, Joseph promoted the idea of the 'social market': that free market economics was closely related to values of negative liberty and responsibility.[91]

The third think-tank was the Adam Smith Institute (ASI).[92] Although the ASI was to have an impact on public policy in the 1980s, it is not important for this discussion since it was not founded until 1977.

Three points need to be emphasised. The first is that think-tanks were closely related to other sources of pressure. The relationship between the CPS and the Conservative Party is an obvious one, and the Conservative Party was advocating an economic liberal stance in Parliament during the debates over the IMF agreement and the earlier public expenditure cuts.[93] The IEA and the CPS formed close links with a number of university departments, thus ensuring that economic liberal ideas, which were evolving in the universities, reached a wider audience. Moreover, there were close links between the serious press and the think-tanks. In particular, Samuel Brittan and Peter Jay, who had been promoting monetarist arguments in their newspaper columns, also wrote for think-tanks. The Bacon and Eltis thesis on 'crowding-out' had been featured regularly in the *Times* since 1974.

The second point is that the think-tanks allowed for the spread of ideas from America to Britain. The clearest example of this was Milton Friedman. Friedman had published early monetarist tracts in the early-1960s, and had first given a statement of the full theory in the United States in 1968.[94] The IEA then published several pieces by Friedman in Britain from 1970 onwards. Without the IEA, it is difficult to see how Friedman's ideas could have spread as widely and as quickly as they did. The final point is therefore that economic liberalism had spread to a wide audience in Britain by the time of the IMF Crisis. It is therefore possible to see if these ideas affected policy outcomes in 1976.

[1] Heclo, H., *Modern Social Politics in Britain and Sweden*, (Yale University Press, New Haven, 1974), pp.304-322

[2] Ibid., p.301

[3] Hall, P., 'Policy Paradigms, Social Learning and The State: the case of economic policymaking in Britain', *Comparative Politics*, 25, April 1993, pp.275-296 p.278

[4] Ibid., pp.278-279

[5] Kuhn, T., *The Structure of Scientific Revolutions*, (University of Chicago, Chicago, 1970)

[6] Hall, P., "Policy Paradigms, Experts and the State: The Case of Macroeconomic Policy-making in Britain" in Brooks, S., and Gagnon, A., (Eds.) *Social Scientists, Policy and the State*, (Praeger, New York, 1990), pp.53-78; p.61

[7] Hall (1993), p.279

[8] Quoted in Hall (1993), p.279

[9] Hall uses the term 'monetarism' to refer to the new paradigm, but I take issue with this later in the chapter

[10] Hall (1993), pp.279-281

[11] Stone, D., 'Causal Stories and the Formation of Policy Agendas', *Political Science Quarterly*, 104/2, Summer 1989, pp.281-300; p.283

[12] Sabatier, P.A., and Jenkins-Smith, H.C., (Eds.), *Policy Change and Learning: An Advocacy Coalition Approach*, (Westview, Boulder, 1993); Sabatier, P.A., 'Toward Better Theories of the Policy Process', *PS: Political Science and Politics*, 24/2, June 1991, pp.147-156; and Sabatier, P.A., 'The Advocacy Coalition Framework: revisions and relevance for Europe', *Journal of European Public Policy*, 5/1, March 1998, pp.98-130

[13] Sabatier (1998) p.103

[14] Ibid.

[15] Hajer, M., *The Politics of Environmental Discourse: Ecological Modernisation and the Policy Process*, (Oxford University Press, Oxford, 1995)

[16] Ibid., p.71

[17] Godley, W., and Cripps, F., *Macroeconomics*, (Fontana, London, 1983), p.13

[18] Gamble, A., *Britain in Decline: Economic Policy, Political Strategy and the British State*, (Macmillan, London, 1981) p.184

[19] Coats, A.W., and Colander, D., 'An Introduction to the Spread of Economic Ideas', in Colander, D., and Coats, A.W., (Eds.), *The Spread of Economic Ideas*, (Cambridge University Press, New York, 1989)

[20] Ibid., p.10

[21] Ibid. pp.11-15

[22] Hall (1990) p.68

[23] Sabatier (1998) pp.104-105

[24] Hall (1990) p.68

[25] Ibid.

[26] An example of the former is Hogg, Q., *The Case for Conservatism* and the latter Crosland, C.A.R., *The Future of Socialism*, (Schocken, London, 1963, 2nd Edition)

[27] Holland, S., *The Socialist Challenge*, (Quartet, London, 1974)

[28] See Crosland, *The Future of Socialism*, part one

[29] Holland's work is given excellent treatment by, Wickham-Jones, M., *Economic Strategy and the Labour Party: Politics and Policy-making 1970-83*, (Macmillan, Basingstoke, 1996),

[30] For a discussion of the Cambridge Economic Policy Group and its relationship to other versions of the AES see Sharples, A., 'Alternative Economic Strategies: Labour Movement Responses to the Crisis', *Socialist Economic Review*, 1, 1981, pp.71-91

[31] The connection was Benn's economic adviser, Francis Cripps

[32] Mosley, P., *The Making of Economic Policy: Theory and Evidence from Britain and the United States Since 1945*, (Harvester Wheatsheaf, Brighton, 1984), p.155. A similar view is presented by Tomlinson, J., *British Macroeconomic Policy Since 1940*, (Croom Helm, Beckenham, 1985), pp.189-206

[33] Thompson, N., *Left In the Wilderness: The Political Economy of British Democratic Socialism Since 1979*, (Acumen, Chesham, 1979), p.29

[34] Other left-Keynesians included Joan Robinson and to a lesser extent Robert Nield

[35] Hodgson, G., *Labour at the Crossroads: The Political and Economic Challenge to the Labour Party in the 1980s*, (Martin Robertson, London, 1981), p.209

[36] A similar tension existed within Keynesianism since it was pointed out that under conditions of full employment there would be inflationary pressures as trades unions would demand higher wages without the fear of unemployment. Hence the importance of incomes policies for Keynesians.

[37] Cripps, F., 'The British Case – can the left win', *New Left Review*, 129, 1981, pp.93-97, p.93

[38] Gamble. A., *Britain in Decline: Economic Policy, Political Strategy and the British State* (Macmillan, London, 1981), pp.165-197

[39] Ibid., p.170

[40] Ibid., p.184

[41] In their defence, the advocates of the AES argued that it was socialist to protect the domestic economy in order to defend the gains made by the working classes under welfare capitalism and that the poorer countries would benefit from increased trade with a stronger British economy that protection would bring. I must admit that I find these arguments unconvincing. The argument that the AES was part of a national political economy tradition does not exclude the influence of other ideas. I still think that Holland in particular was influenced

strongly by neo-Marxist ideas, a view also expressed in Wickham-Jones, *Economic Strategy and the Labour Party*.
[42] The New Right like the Labour left held that the postwar consensus was a 'social democratic' compromise. I have argued in Chapter Two that this is incorrect, at least in my opinion, because the postwar consensus was one between a social democratic Labour Party and a 'One Nation' Conservative Party.
[43] Hall (1993) p.284
[44] My discussion is based on Barry, N., *Hayek's Social and Economic Philosophy* (Macmillan, London, 1979) and Barry, N., *The New Right* (Croom Helm, Beckenham, 1987)
[45] Brittan, S., *The Economic Consequences of Democracy*, (Temple Smith, London, 1977)
[46] For a discussion of the public choice school see Hoover, K., and Plant, R., *Conservative Capitalism in Britain and the United States: A Critical Appraisal*, (Routledge, London, 1989), pp.60-70
[47] Other leading members of the Austrian School included Carl Menger and Ludwig von Mises.
[48] Barry (1987) p.30
[49] For a discussion and powerful critique of Hayek's political philosophical position see Plant, R., *Modern Political Thought*, (Blackwell, Oxford, 1991)
[50] Barry (1987) p.40
[51] Friedman, M., 'The Role of Monetary Policy', *The American Economic Review*, LVIII, March 1968, pp.3-15; and Friedman, M., 'The Counter-revolution in Monetary Theory', Wincott Memorial Lecture, 1970 and IEA Occasional Paper, No.33, republished in Friedman, M., *Monetarist Economics* (Blackwell, Oxford, 1991), pp.1-19; pp.8-10
[52] Friedman, M., 'Counter-revolution...', pp.2-4
[53] There is some debate here since T does not quite equate to Q. I am grateful to Sir Samuel Brittan for this point
[54] Friedman 'Counter-revolution...', p.10
[55] Friedman assumes a perfectly competitive market. This has clear political ramifications to which I return later
[56] Friedman 'Counter-revolution...', p.12
[57] Kavanagh, D., *Thatcherism and British Politics: The End of Consensus?*, (Oxford University Press, Oxford, 1987), p.79
[58] Hoover and Plant, pp.26-28
[59] See for example, Friedman, M., and Friedman, R., *Free to Choose*, (Pelican, London, 1980, 2nd Edition)
[60] Friedman 'Counter-revolution...', p.16
[61] Brittan, S., *How To End the Monetarist Controversy*, Hobart Paper 90, (Institute of Economic Affairs, London, 1981), p.31 and Brittan, S., *The Role and Limits of Government: Essays in Political Economy*, (Temple Smith, Middlesex, 1983), p.85

[62] Friedman, M., 'Unemployment Versus Inflation? An Evaluation of the Phillips Curve', IEA Occasional Paper, 44, 1975. Republished in Friedman (1991), pp.63-85; and Friedman, M., 'Inflation and Unemployment: The New Dimension in Politics', 1976, Alfred Nobel Memorial Lecture (1976), republished in Friedman (1991), pp.87-111

[63] From Friedman 'Inflation and Unemployment...', p.94

[64] Friedman, 'Unemployment Versus Inflation...', p.74

[65] Gamble, A., *The Free Economy and the Strong State: The Politics of Thatcherism*, (Macmillan, Basingstoke, 1988), p.41

[66] Friedman, 'Unemployment Versus Inflation...', p.74

[67] Ibid.

[68] Friedman, M., 'The Future of Capitalism', Federation of Swedish Industries, Stockholm, 1977, republished in Friedman, M., *Tax Limitation, Inflation and the Role of* Government, (Fisher Institute, Dallas, 1978), pp1-13

[69] Gamble (1988) p.41

[70] Smith, D., *The Rise and Fall of Monetarism*, (Penguin, London, 1997), p.66. This point is tacitly accepted by Brittan (1981) p.103

[71] Congdon, T., *Monetarism: An Essay in Definition*, (Centre for Policy Studies, London, 1978), pp.75-83

[72] Ibid., p.83

[73] Again, I am grateful to Samuel Brittan on this point. He accepts that this matter is largely empirical, not theoretical, but that there is sufficient evidence to say that Friedman is correct. For a more critical interpretation of the empirical work of the monetarists see Desai, M., *Testing Monetarism*, (Pinter, London, 1981)

[74] Canto, V., Joines, D., and Laffer, A., 'Tax Rates, Factor Employment, Market Production and Welfare', in Canto, V., Joines, D., and Laffer, A., (Eds.), *Foundations of Supply-side Economics: Theory and Evidence*, (Academic Press, New York, 1983), pp.1-24

[75] Ibid., p.23

[76] Wanniski, J., 'Taxes, Revenues and the "Laffer Curve"', *Public Interest, 50, 1979*, pp.3-16

[77] From Shaw, G. K., *Keynesian Economics: The Permanent Revolution*, (Edward Elgar, Aldershot, 1988), p.136

[78] Bacon, R., and Eltis, W., *Britain's Economic Problem: Too Few Producers*, (Macmillan, Basingstoke, 1978, 2nd Edition)

[79] Eltis, W., 'The Need to Cut Public Expenditure and Taxation', in Minford, P., Rose, H., Eltis, W., Perlman, P., and Burton, J., *Is Monetarism Enough? Essays in Refining and Reinforcing the Monetary Cure for Inflation*, (Institute of Economic Affairs, London, 1980), pp.61-86

[80] This idea first emerged in US economic policy-making. For an early British perspective see Congdon, T., 'Monetarism and the Budget Deficit', Speech, 14/9/76. Reprinted in Congdon, T., *Reflections on*

Monetarism: Britain's Vain Search for a Successful Economic Strategy, (Elgar, Aldershot, 1992)

[81] See Hadjimatheou, G. and Skouras, A., 'Britain's Economic Problem: the growth of the non-market sector', *Economic Journal*, 89, June 1979, pp.392-401; Bosanquet, N., 'Has Manufacturing Been "Crowded Out"?', *Socialist Commentary*, January 1977, pp.4-5.

[82] Denham, A., and Garnett, M., *British Think-tanks and the Climate of Opinion*, (UCL, London, 1998); Cockett, R., *Thinking the Unthinkable: Think-tanks and the Economic Counter-revolution 1931-1983*, (HarperCollins, London, 1994); and Britton, A., *Macroeconomic Policy in Britain 1974-87*, (Cambridge University Press, Cambridge, 1991)

[83] Denham and Garnett, ibid., pp.83-115

[84] Hayek, F.A., *The Road to Serfdom*, (Routledge, London, 1944)

[85] By negative liberalism, I mean that wing of philosophical liberalism which sees freedom as freedom from external constraint

[86] Walters, A., *Money in Boom and Slump: An Empirical Inquiry into British Experience Since the 1880s*, Hobart Paper 44, (Institute of Economic Affairs, London, 1971)

[87] These include 'The Counter-revolution ...', 'Unemployment Versus Inflation...', and 'Inflation and Unemployment...'

[88] Denham and Garnett, p.100

[89] Ibid., pp.117-150

[90] Ibid., p.118

[91] Ibid., pp.127-136

[92] Ibid., pp.151-173

[93] See the contributions from Conservative MPs during the debate over the Letter of Intent in the House of Commons, (Hansard, House of Commons Debates, 922, 1976, 1537-1558)

[94] Friedman, 'The Role of Monetary Policy'

CHAPTER 7

DISCUSSION

Introduction

In the last chapter, I set out the central features of the three paradigms in economic thought in the 1970s: Keynesianism, the Alternative Economic Strategy and economic liberalism. The purpose of this chapter is to relate these ideas to the conduct of economic policy by the Labour Government during 1976. I begin by examining the changes in policy tools and techniques introduced in this period. This is followed by an examination of the Cabinet debates and the views of Callaghan and Healey in order to identify the major influences on the thinking of ministers at this time. Such an analysis will involve the use of the three paradigms outlined in the previous chapter.

Fiscal and Monetary Policy

Before examining any possible shift in economic thought in 1976, it is first necessary to see what, if any, changes there were in policy tools and techniques. Here, I wish to draw heavily on the argument presented by Steve Ludlam.[1] According to Ludlam, many of the policy changes associated with the IMF agreement were actually introduced before December 1976. In particular, Ludlam identifies four policy reforms that were introduced before December 1976: what Ludlam calls the "four myths of the 1976 IMF Crisis."[2]

The first is public expenditure cuts.[3] For many within the Labour movement, the central importance of the IMF Crisis was that expenditure cuts were introduced by the Government in response to the demands of the IMF.[4] Indeed, the Government may actually have encouraged this view in order to hide the fact that it had been cutting expenditure since early 1975. The Government was initially elected in 1974 with a manifesto commitment to increase public expenditure both for improved public services and for higher levels of investment in private industry. As I have shown in the narrative chapters, public expenditure was increased in the first budgetary measures. However, the first cuts were introduced in the April 1975 budget. In total, there were to be £1.1 billion cuts for 1976-77. Paul Ormerod writes that, "the received wisdom is that once again a Labour Government was blown off course; resulting in measures of austerity imposed upon the Government by external pressure of the International Monetary Fund at the end of July 1976. But, in fact, the strategy of a reduction in the share of the public sector in total output was already in existence by then."[5]

The picture presented by Ormerod appears to be correct when we recap on the events following the budget of April 1975. Over the summer of 1975, Healey continued to stress the need for further cuts. In August 1975, Crosland made the 'party is over' speech stressing the need for local authorities to cut expenditure and warning of the need for greater central government control over council spending. The debate over the 1976 Public Expenditure White Paper began in Cabinet in November 1975. Despite the announcement of £4.6 billion cuts in the White Paper, a further £1 billion cuts and £1 billion increase in the employers' National Insurance contribution was announced in July 1976. All of this was therefore agreed before the IMF negotiations began in early-November 1976, which amounted to a further £1 billion cuts for 1977-78 and £1.5 billion for 1978-79. Ludlam argues that the Government had introduced real cuts in public expenditure before agreement with the IMF was reached in December 1976. This was done in order to reduce the rate of inflation and to free resources for the private sector. As will be shown in the next section, both of these aims were advocated by the economic liberals.

It is first necessary to examine Ludlam's claim that the real level of public expenditure was cut. Ludlam argues that, "planned cuts announced from 1975 onwards sought to reduce the rate of growth in public spending, rather than produce absolute overall reductions, although the plan to reduce not just the rate of growth of spending but also reduce the rate of growth of GDP was a clear breach of social democratic orthodoxy. This did not, however, mean that spending programmes were protected, they were not."[6] There are three distinct terms here. The first is absolute levels, referring to the total amount spent on each programme. The second is planned future spending referring to the addition or reduction in the spending totals of future financial years. The third refers to real levels of spending, or the level of spending adjusted for inflation. The Government sought to reduce the third, as could be expected at a time of high inflation. Public spending was growing, according to the Government, too quickly. It is not therefore entirely clear why a reduction in the real level of spending, implying a reduction in the levels of planned future spending below 1974-75 projections, should necessarily be seen as a breach in social democratic orthodoxy since the social democrats had always stressed the importance of economic growth in order to redistribute the fiscal dividends of that growth. There are, however, further issues relating to the Labour Government's attitude towards public expenditure to which I return towards the end of the Chapter. Finally, a reduction in the second and third forms of calculation does not equate to a reduction in overall cuts. There is still a question over the timing of cuts in the absolute level of public expenditure.

Peter Jackson argues that the Government had a clearly stated aim to reduce the growth in public expenditure.[7] This objective was first emphasised in the Public Expenditure White Paper of January 1975. Spending had increased from £16,012 million in 1971 to £44,465 million by 1976.[8] It was feared that the standard marginal rate of income tax would rise to 50% and the PSBR would become so large that to finance it would be damaging to the economy.[9] Between the Public Expenditure White Paper of January 1975 and July 1976, public expenditure cuts were introduced in order to reduce the rate of increase. The single exception to this was social services, where absolute cuts were introduced in January 1976.[10]

The cuts in the autumn of 1976, as part of the IMF agreement, were of a different kind. Earlier cuts had not, with the exception of the social services programme, reduced absolute levels of public expenditure. Moreover, earlier reductions had been justified in terms of the effects on the domestic economy. That is to say that high rates of direct taxation acted as a disincentive, finance of debt interest undermined economic activity in the private sector and so forth. Although similar arguments were presented by Healey in the Cabinet and other ministerial meetings in November-December 1976, it was clear that the main justification for the cuts on this occasion was the need to satisfy international opinion. Moreover, the cuts announced in the Letter of Intent on December 15, were cuts in the absolute level. This point is emphasised by Peter Jackson: "cuts were being made in real service levels. It was no longer an exercise in cutting the fairy gold of some planning total."[11] Taking the figures published in the National Income and Expenditure Surveys for 1978 and 1979, it is possible to show that the absolute levels of expenditure were cut as part of the IMF package. Total expenditure fell from £42,516 million in 1976, to £41,193 million in 1977. Hence, the Government had moved beyond cutting planned expenditure, to cuts in the overall level by the end of 1976.[12]

Figures show that the Government was successful in meeting its objectives, set out in the Public Expenditure White Paper in January 1975, to reduce the total level of public expenditure as a proportion of GDP. In 1970, public expenditure consumed 41.7% of GDP. In 1974, this had increased to 44.9%. Altogether it further increased to 45.6% in 1975; it was then reduced year on year to 42.8% by 1979.[13] However, this is different from saying that there were cuts in public spending totals.[14]

It should also be re-emphasised that the Cabinet approval for public expenditure cuts took several long and difficult meetings to obtain. The opposition of the groups led by Tony Crosland and Tony Benn respectively is well known and has been described at length in the previous chapters. It has also been noted that both Jim Callaghan and Denis Healey were sceptical of the position taken by the IMF. Although Healey was more prepared to implement cuts in public expenditure than any other member of the Cabinet with the exception of Reg Prentice and Edmund Dell who both felt that the cuts did not go far enough, on both economic and confidence grounds, he was not prepared to accept the IMF demands in full. The original position of the IMF was to demand £5 billion cuts for the financial year 1977-78. Eventually, this was negotiated down to £2.5 billion over two years. The details of this were set out above. The crucial point here is that despite the theoretical differences between the leading participants in the Cabinet debate, no senior minister was as willing to cut public expenditure, to the extent demanded by the IMF. With the exceptions of Prentice and Dell, the other Cabinet ministers can all be regarded as trying to reach an accommodation between the maintenance of public expenditure to fulfil social policy objectives, and the need to reach agreement with the IMF in order to restore international confidence.

Closely related to budgetary decisions was the introduction of cash limits. Ludlam refers to this as the second 'myth' of the IMF Crisis because it is argued that cash limits were introduced at the behest of the IMF.[15] Again, this is an error since cash limits were introduced by the Labour Government in July 1975. One impact of cash limits was to have the unintended consequence of causing underspending in many government departments. Cash limits were introduced to replace the existing framework of public expenditure decisions. The earlier system was effectively inflation-proof, with the consequence that public expenditure often exceeded the planned levels. Cash limits would set a nominal figure on public expenditure, which would not be increased after it had been agreed. By 1976, 80% of public expenditure was covered by cash limits. It was becoming clear to Treasury officials such as Leo Pliatzky, the Head of the public expenditure section, that Departments were underspending due to the fear of using all of its allocated funds. In 1976-77, the underspend was £2.2 billion, for 1977-78 slightly over £2 billion, and for 1978-79 was £2.5 billion.[16] The introduction of cash limits was therefore significant in reducing public expenditure for they had, as Steve Ludlam writes, "a negative impact on spending far greater than those public spending reductions that can properly be called IMF cuts."[17] Moreover, the use of cash limits was assisted by the introduction of a procedural rule by Harold Wilson in late 1975 to the effect that Treasury ministers could not be overruled on public expenditure matters in Cabinet committees.

Although the significance of cash limits in further helping to stabilise public expenditure should not be underemphasised, its primary significance was in the form of the unintended outcome of consistent underspending by Government departments. It had been introduced to halt the spiralling of costs, which had become a common feature in capital projects. The aim was therefore to encourage departments to control expenditure more tightly so that overall the budget would stabilise. It was not intended that departments should cancel capital projects, thus causing substantial underspend. Yet this was the outcome. It is therefore clear that cash limits were only a significant change in policy techniques due to the unintended consequences of underspending.[18]

Ludlam also refers to a third 'myth' over the introduction of money supply targets.[19] Although this is of direct relevance to the argument that monetarism was introduced in 1976, to which I return below, it is important to state at this stage that the introduction of money supply targets preceded the Letter of Intent. A reference had been made to monetary targets in the budget of April 1976, and a forecast for growth in M3 had been announced as part of the July measures. Further reference had been made in the Letter of Intent. However, two points need to be emphasised here. The first is that money supply targets were introduced, in part, due to international pressure in earlier sterling crises, particularly the July 1976 crisis. The second is that they were introduced for largely cosmetic reasons. Healey argues that, "in order to satisfy the markets, I began to publish the monetary forecasts we had always made in private and then described them as targets."[20] The implication is that Healey did not have much confidence in monetary targets nor did he attach much weight to them, but he introduced them to obtain international confidence. Where they were used it was largely in combination with other measures. This pragmatic stance was criticised by leading monetarist writers such as Alan Walters: "since 1970...there has been virtually no fundamental change in the principles that have guided policy discussion in Britain. The most obvious and far reaching development - the adoption of monetary targets - is largely cosmetic and probably for foreign consumption."[21] It has also been argued that the IMF Crisis marked the abandonment of the commitment to full employment[22], which had been supported by both parties since 1945. Ludlam refers to this as the fourth 'myth' of the IMF Crisis since this decision had in fact been taken before 1976.[23] This takes us in to the realm of ideas, and so I do no intend to discuss it any further at this point.

What then was the significance of the 1976 IMF Crisis? According to Ludlam, the actual agreement in the form of the

Letter of Intent was largely symbolic.[24] It did not result in a new approach to fiscal and monetary policy because public expenditure cuts, cash limits and monetary targets had already been introduced before December 1976, and the decision to abandon the historic commitment to full employment had already been taken. All of this amounts to a shift in the overarching policy paradigm. The Letter of Intent was therefore of symbolic importance since "it was the public acceptance by the government that it had abandoned the full employment commitment and the postwar consensus."[25] Although I have shown that the cuts announced as part of the agreement went beyond the earlier cuts in that they amounted to reductions in total expenditure rather than merely in the growth of expenditure, Ludlam has correctly shown that monetary targets and cash limits were introduced prior to December 1976. The IMF agreement can therefore be said to have had two consequences. The first is that absolute levels of public expenditure were cut. The second was the symbolic importance emphasised by Ludlam. Ludlam's analysis has a bearing on the shifting economic thought of this period, to which I now turn.

The Cabinet Debates in Retrospect

In Chapter Four, I discussed the July measures, which included £1 billion cuts. Chapter Five traced in more detail the discussions over the cuts involved in the IMF package announced on December 17. A discussion of the Cabinet debates demonstrates the importance of economic ideas to those involved.

Turning first to the radical left position, which took the form of the Alternative Economic Strategy. The AES was developed in opposition between 1970-74 and formed the basis of the 1974 General Election manifestos.[26] This was largely because the left had obtained control of the policymaking committees within the Labour Party. In contrast, the right of the Party did not get involved in detailed policymaking at this time. Therefore, although the manifesto made several commitments on public ownership, planning agreements, banking regulations and industrial democracy, it was never accepted by the leadership, which remained right-wing. Indeed, Harold Wilson watered down the manifesto commitments in 1974. The history of the

Labour Government between 1974-1976 can therefore be seen as a shift away from the manifesto position, or to put it another way as a shift away from the AES.

Nevertheless, the AES remained important to certain government ministers, most notably Tony Benn. Benn himself had been a Keynesian revisionist in the 1950s, but had moved away from that position over the course of the 1964-70 Labour Government and even more so between 1970-74. Benn attempted to implement policies in line with the AES as Secretary of State for Industry, and then as Secretary of State for Energy from June 1975. In his advocacy of the AES, Benn was supported by a number of other Cabinet ministers. These include Albert Booth and, to a lesser extent, John Silkin and Stan Orme from within the Cabinet. Benn also had a number of outside advisers including Francis Cripps and Wynne Godley, who had been the chief intellectual inspiration behind the New Cambridge thesis[27], Nicholas Kaldor who had moved away from a Keynesian to a protectionist position and Frances Morrell.

Although Michael Foot and Peter Shore were, broadly speaking, close to Benn, it is not entirely clear that they supported the AES. In the case of Foot, there was a tension between outright support for the Benn strategy and the need to remain loyal to Callaghan, which Foot regarded as important in his role as Deputy Leader. Foot therefore remained committed to the Benn group when they met in the run-up to the Cabinet on December 1. However, he did not push the AES as strongly as he could have done. In the case of Peter Shore, it is widely argued that he advocated the AES position in Cabinet and that there was no difference between the Benn and Shore positions. At most it was accepted that Shore proposed a more moderate import protection scheme. However, as I have argued in an earlier chapter, there were substantial differences between Benn and Shore. Benn advocated comprehensive import quotas, whereas Shore only favoured import deposits. In fact, Shore rejected the theoretical assumptions and wider policy prescriptions of the AES. Rather than calling for the introduction of long-term import controls as part of a wider strategy as favoured by Benn, Shore only favoured temporary measures to assist the balance of payments situation. The Shore position can therefore be seen as a rejection of the AES. Instead, it would be better to see it as a form of 'Keynesianism-plus'. Shore had earlier been a critic of the Keynesian framework advocated by Labour Party revisionists in the 1950s, but had subsequently come to accept it.[28] However, the main problem, according to Shore, was now the influx of cheap imports and there was a need for a combination of demand-management policies in the domestic economy plus import deposits. In this sense, Shore demonstrates the nature of thinking on the Labour Left. First, there was a growing divide between the 'Old Left' of the Party, of which he and Foot were representative, and an emerging, more radical, New Left, which championed the AES.[29] Secondly, that on the fringe of the AES were a group of 'left-Keynesians' of which Shore was again representative, along with Kaldor and the Cambridge Economic Policy Group[30], and was distinct from the radical left who regarded the AES as the means of achieving a thoroughgoing socialist transformation.

To recap, Benn first proposed the AES in the Economic Strategy Committee of Cabinet on July 2. But it was not until November that Benn put the full case to Cabinet after meeting with the other left-wing ministers. The decisive Cabinet debate over the AES was on December 1. Benn argued that there was a need for import quotas in order to protect domestic industry. This needed to be coupled with compulsory planning agreements, nationalisation of the leading clearing banks and so on.[31] For Benn, the Crisis should be seen more as an opportunity to implement the AES.[32] At the same Cabinet, on December 1, Shore put forward his proposal for temporary import deposits, to close the balance of payments account and to defer payment of the loan for a further three to six months. However, both the Benn and the Shore proposals were defeated in Cabinet that day.

Why, then, were the Benn and Shore proposals defeated? In the case of Benn, there was a combination of power realities and intellectual weaknesses, which led to the defeat of the AES. Benn was emerging as the 'unofficial' leader of the left. However, the left had only a handful of ministers in Cabinet in 1976. These were Benn, Foot, Shore, Stan Orme, John Silkin and Albert Booth. Although Shore was often seen as a figure on the left at this time, this view can be regarded as incorrect for reasons already discussed. Despite this Shore had the support of Silkin and perhaps Orme.[33] Foot, as I have already mentioned, remained somewhat aloof from the other left-wingers in Cabinet. This left only Booth as a firm supporter of Benn in Cabinet.[34] Moreover, unlike Shore who could have moved over to Crosland, there was too great a gulf between Benn and Crosland so that Frances Morrell rejected the offer of a coalition between the two groups when David Hill approached her on November 24. The Benn position also suffered from a number of intellectual weaknesses. Benn could not give any information on the likely employment effects of import quotas. In contrast, Healey was able to show that they would be deflationary. Moreover, Benn thought that the IMF would have accepted the AES, which was far removed from the position taken by the IMF. Cabinet ministers felt that the Benn position could not be taken seriously, and it was ruled out by Callaghan.[35]

In a similar way the Shore position was defeated by a combination of power realities and intellectual weaknesses. Although Shore could have carried some of the junior ministers with him, he was unable to do so. Firstly, the Bennites were opposed to any deal with the Croslandites. Secondly, Shore was reluctant to give support to Crosland for personal reasons. The two had disagreed vehemently over the issue of membership of the European Economic Community in 1975, something which still rancoured with them.[36] Moreover, the two had a personal rivalry, which made it difficult for them to cooperate. Hence, despite the fact that Shore and Crosland came to accept similar positions in their final Cabinet papers, the likelihood of a possible deal was only slight. Shore also faced tough cross-questioning in Cabinet on December 1. Shore was forced to concede that the deposits scheme would be deflationary, and failed to convince colleagues that the Government could obtain international support for the scheme.

The Keynesian position was advocated most forcefully in Cabinet by Tony Crosland.[37] Crosland had been a leading revisionist in the 1950s, arguing that the Labour Party should accept equality as the core value, rather than ownership. Crosland further argued that Keynesian economics was the most effective means of achieving equality. For Crosland, therefore, Keynesianism was both an economic analysis and a necessary means of obtaining core values.[38] Any move away from Keynesianism was therefore a move away from egalitarian socialism. The rise in public expenditure from the early 1970s had become a problem since it had increased much more quickly than economic growth. There was, Crosland admitted, a need to control public expenditure. Crosland was not therefore opposed to cuts in public expenditure in all cases. Instead, he opposed the cuts in December 1976 because they were introduced in order to win international confidence and because they cut into absolute levels of expenditure.

Crosland had voiced his lack of support for the cuts introduced in the Public Expenditure White Paper in January 1976, and again in July. By the autumn of 1976 he had become convinced that the Government was pursuing the wrong strategy. He therefore voiced his opposition to the IMF cuts in mid-November.   On November 18, Crosland met with Callaghan, Healey and Dell at 10 Downing Street.[39]   He presented the argument he was to make in Cabinet over the course of the next few weeks. He was opposed to the cuts since there was no economic case, and presented a Keynesian response to the Crisis. Under pressure from various sources he was to adapt his argument in an attempt to show that it was possible to negotiate with the IMF. Crosland argued that the Government should threaten to withdraw the troops from West Germany and Cyprus, withdraw from the EEC, and finally to introduce import deposits. Crosland initially had the support of the social democratic wing of the Cabinet including Harold Lever, Shirley Williams, Roy Hattersley and Bill Rodgers. The argument was presented to Cabinet on December 1, but Crosland withdrew his paper the following day.

Why, then, did Crosland back down? Again, the answer can be given in terms of a combination of power realities and intellectual weaknesses. Support for Crosland was at its highest in mid-November. After that it declined as the Crosland group fell apart. Bill Rodgers felt that the threat to wind-down Britain's military commitments was unrealistic and dangerous.[40]   Harold Lever, a convinced free-trader, did not have a problem with the military issue, and indeed may well have suggested it.[41]   However, he was opposed to the import deposits scheme. Shirley Williams feared the negative effect the measures would have on Britain's relations with the EEC and the Third World.[42]   Only Roy Hattersley was left to support the Crosland position.[43]   Moreover, as I mentioned above, Crosland was unable to reach an agreement with the Bennites, or even with Shore. Even on the issue of import deposits there remained a divide between the broad measures favoured by Shore and the selective measures which Crosland had only began to consider on November 25. It should also be pointed out that personality matters and Crosland, who had an arrogant and abrasive personality, was unable to win the loyalty of those to whom he was close politically at this time. Finally, Crosland had been unable to win over the support of the Prime Minister. Callaghan informed Crosland that he was prepared to back Healey in Cabinet for the first time, on November 30. To Crosland, it was necessary to maintain Cabinet unity and to stay in Government. He therefore reluctantly agreed to support Callaghan in Cabinet on December 2.

Although it is possible to defend the Crosland position as intellectually superior to the Benn and Shore positions[44], there were some weaknesses in the argument. The first was that Crosland had to accept that the import deposits scheme would be mildly deflationary. However, this was not a serious weakness since Crosland had accounted for it and his case did not rely as heavily on import measures as did the Benn and Shore proposals. A more serious weakness was the threat to withdraw troops. Although this can be defended in economic terms since it would reduce both the balance of payments and the PSBR, it was felt by his colleagues to have been politically naive, as it was likely to reduce confidence still further. One final point is that Crosland argued that the July cuts had not been accounted for and should therefore be included in the IMF cuts in order to reduce the amount of future cuts. Healey pointed out that the July cuts had already been accounted for by the IMF.[45] Although this appears to be a minor point, it did have the effect of reducing the confidence of the other social democratic ministers in Crosland, as he appeared somewhat out of touch. It also shows the reality that the Treasury maintained its dominance over economic policy as it alone had information on the negotiations with the IMF delegation. The decisions taken in Cabinet on December 1-2 to reject the Benn and Shore proposals and the decision of Crosland to support the Prime Minister's policy of accepting the IMF conditions therefore marked an important turning-point, for it amounted to a

significant defeat for the AES and for significant parts of the
Keynesian framework.

Callaghan and the Primacy of Politics

Callaghan's own position is more difficult to summarise. He
had been a Keynesian Chancellor in the 1960s, albeit one who
wished to avoid devaluation.[46] He was now advised by the
Policy Unit under the direction of Bernard Donoughue who took
a firmly Croslandite stance. Donoughue also had a deep
distrust of the Treasury.[47] In addition, Callaghan was advised
by the Central Policy Review Staff, in particular by Kenneth
Berrill. Berrill took a more sympathetic view of the Treasury
position, albeit the rather moderate Treasury view associated
with Douglas Wass and Leo Pliatzky. Finally, Callaghan took
advice from his son-in-law, Peter Jay, who was a leading
monetarist journalist and contributor to the Institute of
Economic Affairs. However, it is not clear what input Jay had
other than that he wrote the section of Callaghan's Labour Party
Conference speech that set out the monetarist position.[48]
Callaghan therefore received widely divergent views on
economic management. Although the sorts of advice that
Callaghan received are well known, it is still not entirely clear
what Callaghan's own views were. I wish to make three
tentative points here.[49]

The first is that Callaghan's primary objectives were political.
Callaghan wanted to maintain the unity of Cabinet and to keep
Labour in power. He therefore allowed Cabinet debate to
continue for some time so that all of the ministers felt that they
had been given full opportunity to discuss the issues and voice
their opinions. Although Dell has argued that Callaghan should
have forced the issue and reached agreement with the IMF
much sooner, it can be argued instead that Callaghan managed
his Cabinet successfully. It must be emphasised that the Labour
Party leadership contest, which took place earlier in the year, is
crucial here. Callaghan won on the third ballot because he
presented himself as a cautious, centrist candidate. His
handling of the Cabinet can be seen in this context. His
subsequent Cabinet reshuffle marked a shift to the right in that
the senior posts were given to the leading social democrats. He
was therefore unlikely to come down on the side of Benn or

even Shore, although he was probably more prepared to give the opportunity to promote their case than Healey or Jenkins would have been. He did, however, face a choice between the positions advocated by Healey and Crosland. This was a serious intellectual and personal dilemma for Callaghan. Callaghan had been a friend of Crosland's for some time, and had been versed in economic theory by associates of Crosland when he had become Shadow Chancellor in 1963. It was reported that Callaghan wanted Crosland to become Chancellor, but had made him Foreign Secretary instead since Healey was to make his budget the day after the leadership contest.[50] On the other hand, Callaghan had been a very cautious Chancellor in the 1960s, and so may well have moved to support Healey without foreign intervention. This is all, in the final analysis, pure speculation since Crosland was to die unexpectedly in February 1977 from a massive stroke. Moreover, Callaghan wished to maintain the Social Contract with the trades unions. Although some of the ministers including Benn and Crosland felt that the IMF agreement would break the Social Contract, Callaghan was able to get the support of the trades union leadership including Len Murray and Jack Jones.

The second point is that Callaghan was more concerned with the international aspects than with the domestic economic situation. This was so in two respects. First, Callaghan sought to obtain the support of the US and German governments in order to help reduce the demands made by the IMF. In the final analysis, it must be concluded that Callaghan was largely unsuccessful. Although Ford and Schmidt placed some pressure on their monetary policy officials and on the IMF, this was of very limited consequence. The second way in which Callaghan was concerned with the international aspects was to obtain support for the sterling reserves. Callaghan, under the influence of Harold Lever, was convinced that the recurrence of economic instability in Britain was not due to the domestic economy, but instead to the place of sterling as a reserve currency. Here Callaghan had more success. He obtained the support of Ford and Schmidt for a safety-net facility, which was introduced in January 1977.

The final point is that Callaghan did not accept the monetarist line. Here, the argument is more controversial. However, given Callaghan's pragmatism it is unlikely that he would have been the sort of politician to be swept away by the rhetoric of any particular economic doctrine. Callaghan's Conference speech was a clear elaboration of the monetarist framework. However, this should not be seen as Callaghan's acceptance of monetarism. Instead, the speech was intended to convince the Labour Party that public expenditure was increasing too quickly, and to win over international opinion. The speech must therefore be interpreted as a mistake, for although it had the political effects that Callaghan had intended, it did appear that the Government had now embraced monetarism. In turn, this was to have political significance much later on when, in facing a Conservative Government presiding over high unemployment, the Labour Party appeared to be somewhat inconsistent when it criticised the Government's use of a monetarist policy.[51]

Healey, Monetarism and Crowding Out

Healey was advised by a Treasury which was clearly divided. Douglas Wass found it difficult to present a united position to the Chancellor. Wass, himself, was a Keynesian and presented his own position to Healey. He did appreciate later that it was becoming more difficult to pursue a Keynesian strategy in an increasingly international economy. The Keynesian position was also favoured by Leo Pliatzky. It was Pliatzky's responsibility to administer the reductions in public expenditure, and he had been chiefly responsible for cash limits. But he felt that those who called for further cuts underestimated the political and practical difficulties involved. He therefore advocated only limited reductions in public expenditure. On the opposite side were Alan Lord and Derek Mitchell who advocated large cuts in order to restore confidence and free resources for the private sector. The other senior ministers in the Treasury were divided. Joel Barnett supported the Chancellor, believing that it would be better to have large reductions in public expenditure in order to restore international confidence. In contrast, Denzil Davies was sceptical of the need for IMF agreement. Healey was initially supported by Edmund Dell and Reg Prentice. Prentice felt that the cuts did not go far enough, while Dell argued against Crosland's economic position saying that cuts were required to restore international confidence and to free resources in the domestic economy.

Healey had become convinced early on in the life of the Government of the need to reduce public expenditure. He first warned Cabinet in early 1975. Moreover, he pushed through cuts in April 1975, January 1976, and July 1976. However, these measures can be seen as an attempt to manage the growth in public expenditure, rather than to cut the total. Indeed, Healey was initially in favour of reflationary measures in response to the OPEC Crisis in order to avert worldwide recession. This was the position taken by the IMF, but was rejected by America and Germany. Healey felt that the July 1976 measures were enough to stop the run on the pound, but by the autumn it was clear that this was not happening. Healey therefore approached the IMF. After initial negotiations with the IMF, Healey asked the Cabinet for £1.5 billion cuts on November 23. This request was rejected. Following protracted negotiations, Healey eventually got approval for the cuts in Cabinet on December 2, and the Letter of Intent was approved on December 15.

There is evidence to suggest that Healey had a change of attitude over the course of these negotiations. Initially, Healey argued in favour of the cuts both to restore international confidence and to free resources for the domestic economy. He initially welcomed the IMF on the basis that they were a successful institution, which shared his economic outlook and was prepared to grant the loan if conditions could be reached. However, he was to become disappointed with the IMF and particularly with the US financial authorities who demanded what Healey thought was politically unrealistic. By early December, relations between Healey and the IMF were openly hostile and, at one point, Healey was close to sending the delegation back to America. Healey then told the Cabinet that he was looking forward to being free from IMF conditions once the economy improved and the loan was repaid.[52] Healey's attitude was no doubt based on the difficulties he experienced in negotiating with the IMF. But it may also point to a difference in economic thinking between Healey and the IMF. The IMF had been a 'Keynesian' institution in the postwar period, and as late as 1974 Witteveen was advancing a Keynesian response to the oil shock. However, largely due to US influence, it was now taking a more economic liberal position.

However, this is not to argue that the Labour Government did not move towards economic liberal ideas, although not in the way that it usually argued. Given that the outcome was a success for Healey, in that he eventually triumphed over Crosland and the left and won over a wary Cabinet, it is possible to consider the outcome of the IMF Crisis and Healey's views together. It is widely argued that the Labour Government introduced monetarism in 1976.[53] Those who maintain this position make one of two distinct points. The first is that the Labour Government accepted a much stronger role for monetary policy, in the form of monetary targets, than had any previous government since the end of the Second World War.[54] The second point is that the Government abandoned the historic commitment to achieve full employment.[55] Usually, the Callaghan speech is emphasised by those who hold this view as clear evidence that the Government had rejected full employment as an objective. For reasons already discussed, it is probably a mistake to interpret the Callaghan speech in this way. An alternative point has been made by Steve Ludlam, who argues that the Government had in fact abandoned its commitment to full employment much earlier than in the Callaghan speech.[56] The Government had introduced deflationary budgets since 1975. Instead, the Callaghan speech should be regarded as the public announcement of the earlier abandonment of the goal of full employment.

I think that several points can be made here. The first is that the Government did shift its policy objectives and techniques. This has been described by Artis and Cobham in the following way: "as we see it, the Labour governments essentially made their way pragmatically to policy settings appropriate for an inflationary era, lowering the premium on full employment and raising that on beating inflation by fiscal and monetary means."[57] Shorthand definitions of Keynesianism and monetarism often state that the former prioritises unemployment and the latter inflation as the primary objective of policy. I think that such a definition is mistaken. Although Keynes placed emphasis on full employment, because he was writing at a time of high unemployment, he was not unconcerned about inflation. The 1944 White Paper therefore stated that full employment should be a goal of government policy, and this should be achieved within the framework of stable prices. The point made by Artis and Cobham is therefore important since, if the Labour Government's policy can be interpreted as seeking to reduce inflation in order to return to conditions of full employment, as I think it can, then it can be said that the policy was conducted within a Keynesian framework.[58]

There is, in fact, much evidence to support such a view. A number of policy statements made by both Callaghan and Healey at this time gave a commitment to full employment, but stressed that this needed to take place within a low inflation economy.[59] Moreover, the Government, while accepting the deflationary nature of the IMF cuts, were keen to reduce the likely consequences on unemployment levels. A number of public schemes were devised by Healey and Booth to limit unemployment. A more accurate way of describing the difference between Keynesian and monetarist frameworks is that the former accepts a role for the government in reducing unemployment, but the latter rejects public sector intervention to reduce unemployment. According to monetarists, the only way of reducing unemployment is to remove impediments to the free operation of the labour market such as minimum wage legislation, trades unions and so forth. This view was rejected by all members of the Cabinet, with the possible exceptions of Edmund Dell and Reg Prentice. Hence, as Burk and Cairncross argue, "it is doubtful whether there were any out-and-out monetarists among them."[60] Instead, the debates in Cabinet were limited to disagreement over the extent to which public expenditure should be cut.

Briefly, there were three other reasons why we can say that policy after 1976 was not monetarist. The first is that the Labour Government took advantage of the economic upturn in 1977 and the underspend which resulted largely from cash limits to increase public expenditure in an attempt to reduce unemployment. Hence, it reverted back to a more orthodox Keynesian position in budgets after 1976.[61] Secondly, the Labour Government used an incomes policy as the main tool for reducing inflation. Such a device was rejected by the monetarists, who regarded inflation as a monetary phenomenon. Hence, the Government held to the Keynesian notion that inflation was caused by excessive wages. Finally, we have already seen that the use of monetary targets was introduced by the Chancellor in 1976 largely for cosmetic reasons. Although it must be stressed that Healey generally regarded monetary policy as more important than had previous Chancellors, this is likely to have been a pragmatic response to an increasingly integrated international economy.[62] In short, therefore, we can argue that the Government did not introduce monetarism in 1976. Instead, the election of the first Thatcher Government and the advent of the Medium Term Financial Strategy marked the true introduction of monetarism.[63]

It should be pointed out that my argument that Healey did not accept monetarism as a basis for policy is not shared by Healey's biographer who argues that the Chancellor was influenced heavily by the economic doctrine of monetarism. Edward Pearce argues that Healey had come to accept a central aspect of monetarist argument that, "the volume of money in the economy seriously mattered," and that this was sufficient to call him a monetarist.[64] There is little evidence that Healey did regard monetary policy as central to the IMF negotiations, except to the extent that monetary targets were seen as an essential means of restoring international confidence and stability. It was the issue of confidence that most distanced him from the position put forward by Crosland, who argued that the bluff of the international financiers should be called. At most, it is possible to call Healey, in Samuel Brittan's phrase, an 'unbelieving monetarist'.[65] However, this particular phraseology has two limitations. First, it reduces monetarism as an economic doctrine to the use of monetary targets. Yet, as I have already argued, monetarism is about much more than this and it appears unlikely that Healey took the money supply nor the 'natural rate' model all that seriously. Secondly, it fails to identify what Healey's influences actually were.

I wish to argue that Healey was influenced by the crowding-out thesis developed by Bacon and Eltis and the available evidence suggests that he was interested in the crowding out thesis. According to Adrian Ham, who had been Healey's adviser up until mid-1976 and continued to meet regularly with him during the IMF Crisis proper, Healey was very interested in the work of Bacon and Eltis.[66] He read the newspaper articles written by them and requested Treasury officials to produce reports on the crowding out thesis. Ham argues that Healey was concerned that he should not become ambushed by events, although this is what eventually happened, and that there was therefore a need for economic theory. He was interested in what economists were saying and was prepared to listen to them. Moreover, he was keen to impress on his colleagues the need for public expenditure cuts and was therefore keen to use economic theories which he felt strengthened his arguments. Once he had reached a decision, Ham states, he would then "use every argument that came to hand and the crowding out thesis was a good one."[67]

There is then sufficient evidence to suggest that Healey was at least aware of and was interested in the crowding out thesis. I wish to argue that Healey was also influenced by the crowding out thesis. Healey said that the Bacon and Eltis thesis was the "most stimulating and comprehensive analysis of our economic predicament which I have yet seen in a newspaper."[68] Healey was to use constantly the resources argument, that the consumption of resources by the public sector took them away from the use by the wealth creating private sector, in Cabinet. He was, despite his frequent assertion that his concern was over the size of the PSBR, more concerned over the level of public spending, and his policy was to cut expenditure throughout 1976. Moreover, this concern to reduce the proportion of GDP consumed by the state went beyond the traditional 'labourist' concern of the manufacturing unions to limit increases in state expenditure in order not to take resources away from the industrial sector by advocating real terms cuts in expenditure. Although Bacon and Eltis dramatised the situation in the press, Ham argues that the major influences were in fact much closer to Healey.[69] Within the Cabinet Edmund Dell had frequently used the resources argument. In particular, he was to criticise Crosland for his use of Keynesian orthodoxy in these debates and pressed upon him and Callaghan the need to take seriously the resources argument at a meeting at 10 Downing Street on November 18 (see Chapter 5). Moreover, within the Treasury the resources argument was being put to Healey directly by Derek Mitchell. Healey's initial concern may well have been with the level of public sector debt, something which may well be due at least in part to the argument put forward by the Cambridge Economic Policy Group that public sector debt had a crowding out effect on exports. However, by the time of the IMF Crisis it is unlikely that the Cambridge Economic Policy

Group was of much significance in Healey's thinking, since he was to reject their more fundamental policy goals such as import controls. By 1976, his concern was with the level of government spending.

Public Expenditure and the Supply Side

Healey, then, was influenced by the crowding out thesis. Given that the crowding out thesis was concerned directly with the level of public expenditure, this had a significant impact on the Labour Party. Roy Hattersley has said that the "Labour Party lost its faith in public expenditure," as a result of the IMF Crisis.[70] This is a controversial claim, yet like most controversial claims it does contain an element of truth. The Labour Government had embarked on a programme of substantial reductions in public expenditure, as detailed above, over the course of 1976. It total this amounted to larger cuts than the Thatcher Government was to achieve within such a limited time period. Yet, on the other hand, the Labour Government was to avoid the substantial cuts originally demanded by the IMF of £5 billion and was to avoid cuts in current expenditure. However, there is, I think, some truth in Hattersley's claim for two reasons. The first is that the Labour Party was to realise, or to put it more accurately to accept, that public expenditure could be inefficient in the sense that it could be wasteful. Arguments that public expenditure had to be targeted at specific groups or problems and that it had to be more carefully audited became more common after 1976. Secondly, many in the Labour Party came to accept that public expenditure was no longer the only method of achieving basic values, and that in some cases there were more effective ways, including markets and charitable activity. Although such arguments did not extend to the left of the Labour Party, it certainly became an issue among those on the right of the Party.[71]

This new approach can also be detected in Healey's argument that there was a need to reduce the level of welfare benefits since they were having a disincentive effect on work and were unpopular among those in low paid occupations. Healey was to put forward these arguments in Cabinet between 2-5 December when Cabinet had to decide where those cuts agreed to in principle on December 1-2 should fall. Healey, in presenting these arguments, incurred the opposition of many of his colleagues and were rejected by Callaghan. Such arguments may have demonstrated the influence of supply-side theory with its emphasis on taxes, benefits and incentives. It is difficult to know, however, whether Healey believed these claims or whether he just made them in order to force a reluctant Cabinet to reach a decision.

Supply-side theory did have a more direct influence in industrial policy. The introduction of the White Paper 'An Approach to Industrial Policy' marked a substantial moderation of the earlier White Paper 'The Regeneration of British Industry' which had been produced by Tony Benn as the AES approach to industrial policy (see Chapter 3). 'An Approach to Industrial Policy' emphasised the importance of competition and supply-side reforms in order to improve domestic productivity. Moreover, Callaghan's conference speech contained several references on the need to improve the supply side of the economy, a fact which was largely overshadowed by the references to monetarist theory. The employment measures introduced at the end of 1976, to offset the deflationary impact of public expenditure cuts, were selective along the lines of supply-side theory. The period marked a rejection of general measures advocated by Keynesianism towards selective measures advocated by the supply-siders, as can be seen in the reduction of pricing controls. The measures implemented at this time mark a shift away from Keynesian industrial policy towards an interventionist supply-side strategy.

[1] Ludlam, S., "The Gnomes of Washington: Four Myths of the 1976 IMF Crisis" *Political Studies*, XL, 1992, pp.713-727
[2] Ibid.
[3] Ibid., pp.716-720
[4] Ibid., p.715
[5] Ormerod, P., 'The Economic Record', in Bosanquet, N., and Townsend, P., (Eds.), *Labour and Equality: A Fabian Study of Labour in Power*, (Heinemann, London, 1980) p.31
[6] Ludlam, p.719
[7] Jackson, P., 'Public Expenditure' in Artis, M., and Cobham, D., *Labour's Economic Policies 1974-79*, pp.73-87; pp.79-82
[8] Economic Trends (CSO, No.281, March 1977)
[9] See Friedman, M., 'The Line We Dare Not Cross: The Fragility of Freedom at 60%', *Encounter*, November 1976
[10] Jackson, p.77
[11] Ibid., p.78
[12] See Mullard, M., *Explanations of Public Expenditure Changes in Britain Since 1968*, (Unpublished PhD Thesis, Southampton University, 1984), p.23. See also Mullard, M., *The Politics of Public Expenditure*, (Routledge, London, 1993, 2nd Edition)
[13] Jackson, p.79
[14] For a more detailed discussion of public expenditure trends at this time, see Mullard (1984) pp.212-297
[15] Ludlam, pp.720-721
[16] Ibid., p.720
[17] Ibid., p.721
[18] See Pliatzky, L., *Getting and Spending: Public Expenditure, Employment and Inflation* (Blackwell, Oxford, 1982), pp.154-157
[19] Ludlam, pp.721-723
[20] Healey, D., *The Time of My Life*, (Penguin, London, 1990, 2nd Edition), p.434
[21] Quoted in Ludlam, p.723
[22] Ludlam, p.715
[23] Ibid., pp.724-726
[24] Correspondence with Steve Ludlam
[25] Ibid.
[26] Wickham-Jones, pp.53-137
[27] Godley, W., and Cripps, F., *Macroeconomics*, (Fontana, Oxford, 1983)
[28] See Crosland, C.A.R., 'Insiders and Controllers', in his *The Conservative Enemy: A Programme of Radical Reform for the 1960s*, (Cape, London, 1962)
[29] See Arblaster, A., 'The Old Left' and Wickham-Jones, M., 'The New Left' in Plant, R., Beech, M. and Hickson, K., (Eds.) *The Struggle for Labour's Soul: Understanding the Political Thought of the Labour Party since 1945* (Routledge, London, 2004)

[30] The role of Cripps as a member of the Cambridge Economic Policy Group and as Benn's adviser was consistent because he was to the left of the former.

[31] Benn, T., *Against the Tide: Diaries 1973-76* , (London, Arrow, 1989), pp.661-669

[32] I mean this quite literally. Benn did not seem to think that there was a crisis at all

[33] Interview with Albert Booth (02/05/01)

[34] Interview with Albert Booth

[35] Benn did not appreciate that this is what had happened

[36] Although it must be pointed out that Crosland was not a pro-European in the sense that Roy Jenkins was. Crosland was criticised by both the pro and anti-Europeans over the issue. Interviews with Peter Shore, Bill Rodgers and information from David Lipsey

[37] Crosland, S., *Tony Crosland*, (Coronet, London, 1982, 2nd edition), pp.374-383; Jefferys, K., *Anthony Crosland: A New Biography*, (Cohen, London, 1999)

[38] This is similar to the distinction between 'means' and 'ends' made by Raymond Plant. It is not possible to change a means (policy) without changing the ends (value) unless there is an alternative means to achieve the same value. See Plant, R., "Blair and Ideology" in Seldon, A., (Ed.), *The Blair Effect*, (Little, Brown and Company, London, 2001), pp.555-568. See Chapter 2.

[39] See Chapter 5

[40] Interview with Lord Rodgers

[41] Ibid.

[42] Interview with Lady Williams

[43] Interview with Lord Hattersley

[44] and perhaps even more than the Treasury position.

[45] Benn, ibid., pp.661-669

[46] The refusal to devalue was based on political and economic grounds. The economic rationale was to avoid international currency instability, along Keynesian lines

[47] Interview with Bernard Donoughue (12/10/2000)

[48] Samuel Brittan suggests talks around the fireside! Interview (28/01/02)

[49] All are tentative, although the first two are more widely accepted than the last

[50] This is the view expressed in the Guardian by Peter Jenkins

[51] It also allowed the Conservative Government to deflect criticism of its policy by showing the apparent similarity with the policy of the previous administration.

[52] What he called "sod-off" day

[53] See Kavanagh, D., *Thatcherism and British Politics: The End of Consensus?*, (Oxford University Press, Oxford, 1987), p.12; Fraser, D., 'The Postwar Consensus: A Debate Not Long Enough?', *Parliamentary Affairs*, April 2000, 53/2, pp.347-362, p.357; Gamble. A., *Britain in*

Decline: Economic Policy, Political Strategy and the British State (Macmillan, London, 1981), p.184; Smith, D., *The Rise and Fall of Monetarism*, (Penguin, London, 1997), p.72; Pearce, E., *Denis Healey*, (Little, Brown and Company, London, 2002)
54 Kavanagh, ibid.
55 See Ludlam, p.715
56 Ibid., pp.724-726
57 Artis, M., and Cobham, D., 'Summary and Appraisal', in Artis, M., and Cobham, D., p.276
58 Artis and Cobham, ibid.
59 See Callaghan (Hansard, House of Commons Debates, 9/6/76, 1457-1472). Callaghan regards this as the definitive public statement of the economic objectives of this government. Letter from James Callaghan
60 Burk, K., and Cairncross, A., *Goodbye, Great Britain: The 1976 IMF Crisis*, (Yale University Press, New Haven, 1992), pp.158-162
61 Artis, M., and Cobham, D., 'The Background' in Artis, M., and Cobham, D., pp.14-15
62 Artis, M., and Cobham, D., 'Summary and Appraisal', p.276
63 This view is argued by Shaw, G. K., *Keynesian Economics: The Permanent Revolution*, (Edward Elgar, Aldershot, 1988), p.5. Bulpitt takes the opposite view, arguing that the MTFS was part of the traditional 'statecraft' of the Conservative Party, to retain central government control of 'high politics' including economic policy. Bulpitt, J., 'The Discipline of the New Democracy: Mrs Thatcher's Domestic Statecraft" *Political Studies*, XXXIV, 1986, pp.19-31. I think that this is incorrect; the MTFS was an innovative measure reflecting the influence of monetarist thinking in the Government.
64 Pearce, E., *Denis Healey*, p.475
65 This term was used by Brittan in his newspaper pieces at the time.
66 Interview with Adrian Ham (15/08/02)
67 Ibid.
68 Bosanquet, N., 'Has Manufacturing Been "Crowded Out"?', *Socialist Commentary*, January 1977, pp.4-5, p.4
69 Interview with Adrian Ham (15/08/02)
70 Interview with Roy Hattersley (31/10/02)
71 I am thinking particularly of the argument between the Croslandites and the Jenkinsites, which is a possible cause of the defection of several leading figures on the right of the Labour Party to form the SDP in 1981.

CHAPTER 8

CONCLUSION

In the previous chapters I have examined the nature of postwar British politics and economic policy, traced the development of the 1976 IMF Crisis and looked at the extent to which these events marked a turning-point in terms of both economic thought and policy. By way of conclusion, I wish to summarise my argument and to compare the conduct of policy between 1974-79 with the experience of New Labour in power since 1997.

Summary of Main Findings

I have argued that there was a postwar consensus. The notion of a postwar consensus was widely accepted in academic and political circles, and became a shorthand definition to describe the period from 1945 through to the early 1970s. However, in recent years the very idea of a postwar consensus has been questioned. A number of objections have been raised. Of particular importance were a number of studies which pointed to the ideological differences which existed between the Labour and the Conservative Parties after 1945. These studies provided sufficient evidence to accept that the political parties continued to hold different values. The Labour Party was committed to equality. In contrast, the Conservative Party rejected the value of equality. Instead, the Conservative Party held to its traditional values of nation, negative liberty, and 'One Nation' paternalism. However, the distinction between means and ends presented in the thesis allows for ideological divergence and policy convergence. In broad terms, the Conservative and Labour parties maintained a policy consensus based around a mixed economy, demand management and the welfare state. Evidence for this can be found in the high level of policy continuity following changes of political incumbency. Furthermore, the adversarial nature of politics in these years can be explained in terms of the means-ends distinction since the more controversial elements of legislation were those which were more closely integrated with political values.

Following on from the first point about the nature of consensus politics, it is possible to argue that there was a Keynesian framework which was adopted by both parties. There have been a number of arguments made against the notion that there was a consensus over Keynesian economics. These include an emphasis on the non-Keynesian nature of policy, the discontinuity over policy tools and techniques and the distinction between Keynesian economics and the economic theories of Keynes.   However, by defining the broad characteristics of Keynesian economics in terms of approaches to the state, policy objectives and the general use of policy tools and techniques it is possible to defend the thesis that there was a Keynesian consensus in economic policy. Keynesianism was established in the immediate postwar years following the failure of the Attlee Government's planning agreements, and was maintained by both Labour and Conservative governments after 1951.

However, the Keynesian framework was coming under attack by the early 1970s. On the left, this attack took the form of a reassertion of the importance of ownership and of the need for national economic protection.   Following the defeat of the Labour Government in the 1970 General Election, the Labour Party policymaking committees fell under the control of the left wing. In a number of policy documents, a range of measures which became known as the Alternative Economic Strategy (AES) were proposed.   These included compulsory planning agreements, the establishment of the National Enterprise Board, further public ownership, industrial democracy, and aid for the establishment of cooperatives.   However, the Labour Party leadership did not support these measures.   Therefore, despite the apparent manifesto commitments to the AES, the Government made little serious effort towards its implementation. This was significant since it led to charges of betrayal from the left, and a number of constitutional reforms were introduced in the Labour Party after 1979. The leadership can be held responsible for this since only Tony Crosland was prepared to argue against the AES while in opposition between 1970-74.

The Labour Party leadership could be more accurately said to have held a Keynesian stance when the Party was elected to government in 1974. Denis Healey initially embarked on a reflationary policy in line with Keynesian theory as a response to the oil shock. In this he was encouraged by the IMF, which advocated a reflationary policy to avoid international recession. However, this was opposed by the USA and West Germany, and particularly their respective financial authorities, which wanted to avoid additional inflationary pressures. From early 1975, therefore, the IMF placed pressure on governments to control prices. Between early 1975 and July 1976, the Labour Government therefore sought to reduce its public sector borrowing requirement and to bring down pay increases in order to reduce inflation, as advocated by international opinion. A significant number of policy changes can be seen to have been introduced before the autumn of 1976, including incomes policy, cash limits and public expenditure cuts. These changes were, then, introduced before the IMF arrived in London. They were introduced for two reasons. The first is that the Government, particularly the Treasury ministers, believed that they were necessary to restore the health of the domestic economy. The second is that international pressure was exerted on the British Government. This was both indirect by the markets on sterling following the attempt to halt the appreciation of sterling in March 1976, and directly by the US financial authorities in the negotiations for the June stand-by.

Keynesianism was also challenged by the emergence of economic liberalism, which amounted to a critique of state intervention and argued in favour of free markets. Three elements of economic liberalism were particularly relevant to the discussion of the IMF Crisis: monetarism, crowding-out theory and supply-side theory. Monetarism consists of two separate theories. The first is the theory that inflation is caused by excessive growth in the money supply. The second is the theory that there is a long-term, or natural rate, of unemployment. Although some have argued that monetarism is politically neutral, I have argued the contrary position, that monetarism is an integral part of economic liberalism. Supply-side theorists argue that there is a clear relationship between tax rates and incentives, and that there is a need to restore the effeciency of the private sector by reducing trades union power, workers rights and other 'barriers' to the operation of the free market. Crowding-out theory consists of two parts. The first is that public sector borrowing reduces the amount of investment capital available to the private sector. The second part states that the growth in the public sector takes labour away from the private sector. These ideas were already developed by the time of the IMF Crisis, and had reached a wide audience through the press, think-tanks etc.

Keynesianism was represented in Cabinet most clearly by Tony Crosland. Although Crosland was not opposed to reducing the rate of increase in public expenditure, he was opposed to cuts in December 1976 for three reasons. Firstly, public expenditure was necessary to meet welfare objectives. Secondly, public expenditure was necessary to avoid further increases in unemployment. Finally, therefore, there was no economic case for public expenditure cuts. Instead, cuts were being introduced to obtain international confidence. Crosland disliked making policy on the basis of international confidence and sought other ways to obtain international support including the threat of military withdrawal from Germany and Cyprus, withdrawal from the EEC and import measures. Despite some initial support, Crosland was left almost isolated and was forced to back down. This was because Callaghan voiced his support for Healey, and because senior ministers found it difficult to accept Crosland's arguments on the troops, the EEC and import deposits.

The AES was pushed most strongly by Tony Benn. Benn favoured widespread import quotas, planning agreements, tax increases and other parts of the AES. Benn made his case during the Cabinet debate over the July measures and again in November-December. However, the Benn strategy was rejected in Cabinet on December 1. This can be seen in terms of power realities and intellectual weaknesses. Benn failed to carry the full support of other left-wing ministers, and his position was rejected by other members of the Cabinet. The defeat of the Benn paper also demonstrates the use of Prime Ministerial power, since Callaghan subjected the paper to scrutiny by the Policy Unit and passed questions to Cabinet ministers. On December 1, the Benn paper failed to withstand the scrutiny of Cabinet.

Peter Shore is usually regarded to have been a left-wing member of the Cabinet. However, I have argued that this is incorrect. Shore did meet regularly with the left-wing group of Cabinet ministers, and he did present a paper to Cabinet advocating import deposits. However, his analysis was predicated on Keynesian assumptions of economic activity. Shore still held to demand-management policies, but also wished to see temporary import measures to protect domestic industry. The import measures were only defended in terms of the elimination of the balance of payments deficit. His position is best seen as a form of 'left-Keynesianism' - i.e. demand-management plus temporary import deposits - rather than the full AES, which held to more permanent import measures. Again, Shore was defeated by his failure to win over sufficient Cabinet support and weaknesses in his argument, especially the concession that import deposits would be, of themselves, deflationary.

The 1976 IMF Crisis is often seen as the point at which monetarism was introduced. In contrast, other commentators have argued that monetarism was accepted by the Labour Government before the Crisis, with the events of the autumn of 1976 marking a symbolic declaration of support for the new strategy. Instead, it can be argued that the Government did not introduce monetarism in 1976. Three policy reforms did take place in this area. The first was the publication of monetary targets. The second was the increased use of monetary techniques in macroeconomic policy. The third was the increased emphasis placed on anti-inflationary measures, even if this resulted in an increase in unemployment in the short term. However, none of this equates to the introduction of monetarism. Monetary targets were introduced for cosmetic reasons: that is to obtain international confidence. The greater use of monetary techniques can be seen as a response to a more integrated international economy in which fiscal measures were constrained by economic recession. Even the greater emphasis attached to the reduction of inflation can be viewed in Keynesian terms, since price stability was seen as crucial to long-term full employment by Keynes and by the 1944 White Paper. In order to show that the Government held to the monetarist line after 1976, it would have to be shown that they had abandoned wage control, reflationary budgets and direct intervention in the labour market, but these things were maintained. Moreover, the Labour Government did not accept the 'natural rate' hypothesis, or the quantity theory. At the very most it can be said that the Government was an 'unbelieving monetarist' one, but this fails to identify the main influences on policy at this time.

It is, however, possible to argue that the Labour Government, or at least the Chancellor of the Exchequer, accepted elements of the crowding-out theory and used the economic liberal supply-side argument in political debate. In terms of the crowding-out theory, Healey argued that there was a need to free resources for use by the private sector by cutting the PSBR. In this view, he was expressing the argument made by Bacon and Eltis, and some of the monetarists, rather than the Cambridge Economic Policy Group. He was supported in this debate by Alan Lord and Derek Mitchell in the Treasury and by Edmund Dell in Cabinet, but opposed by Tony Crosland and Roy Hattersley. Healey also argued for the need to cut the rates of direct taxation and to restrict the increase in the value of welfare payments to the out of work since they acted as a disincentive to work. Healey was therefore expressing the supply-side theory, and was supported by Dell and by Reg Prentice. Arguing most strongly against this position was Tony Benn. The conduct of industrial policy can be seen to have been influenced by supply-side theory of an interventionist rather than economic liberal form.

I have been able to utilise a broad range of sources in conducting my research. Indeed, in terms of interviews, I have been able to access many more participants than I originally thought possible. There are, however, two limitations in my research. These concern the public records and the Callaghan papers. After briefly discussing each, I wish to add one further methodological consideration.

The public records covering the IMF Crisis are all subject to the 30-year rule under the Official Secrets Act. They will therefore not be available to researchers until January 1, 2007. Public records will cover all of the relevant Cabinet discussions, correspondence between ministers, and between ministers and officials, and departmental briefs. There is, therefore, a great deal of information still to be released on the IMF Crisis. In this sense, my own study is no more restricted than other studies of the IMF Crisis. Indeed, it may be argued that the release of official papers in 2007 will add little new to the information already available. Researchers are fortunate that the Cabinet discussions are already widely known. This is so for two reasons. The first is that Cabinet discussions were widely leaked at the time of the IMF Crisis. Indeed, the discussions were so widely leaked that it can be said that the debate over the IMF application was one of the most open in postwar history. Secondly, ministers, officials and advisers were keen to tell their own version of events both to myself and to other researchers. It may also be added that researchers in America are not subject to such constraints, and the US records have been made available in Britain through the work of Mark Harmon.[1] The value of the public papers will therefore be in tracing the development of ideas within the Treasury. A similar problem exists with the Callaghan papers, now placed in the Bodleian at the University of Oxford. There are two restrictions on the Callaghan papers. The first is that as a former Cabinet minister, the Callaghan papers are also subject to the thirty-year rule. The second restriction on access is that Callaghan has placed a condition on the archive that they may not be used until after his death.[2]

One final point concerns a wider methodological implication of this study. I wish to argue that political scientists need to make use of primary source materials and add greater contextualisation to their work in general. There is a need to move away from large-scale generalisations and notions of 'hypothesis-formulation' and 'hypothesis-testing'.   Instead, there is a need to return to a more historical approach, which predated the emergence of political science as an academic discipline in British universities in the 1960s, but which has generally been neglected since then.[3] History is absurd in the strictest sense that it lacks any meaning. Events occur without sequence, and outcomes may be unintentional. A couple of examples have already been discussed in the thesis: namely the conduct of monetary policy in early March 1976, which started the run on the pound, and the introduction of cash limits.[4] A full understanding of the IMF Crisis, like any historical episode, therefore requires greater contextualisation: a detailed narrative and an analysis of that particular historical episode. Such an argument has been presented by philosophic conservatives[5], although there does not appear to be a necessity for such a methodological approach to be the preserve of a particular political outlook.[6]

New Labour

In the course of my research and writing on the 1976 IMF Crisis, I have been struck by the significance of these events for New Labour in power since 1997. The conduct of policy after 1976 was constrained to some extent by the limits placed on policy by the IMF agreement. However, the Government was able to spend more than it had anticipated after the restoration of economic growth in 1977. Had the Government called the Election in the autumn of 1978 it may well have won, but its electoral prospects were virtually destroyed by the 'Winter of Discontent'. Following the election of the first Thatcher Government in 1979, Labour moved rapidly leftwards and embraced more of the AES as official policy. It was only with the disasterous 1983 General Election that the Party moved back towards the centre-left. It was to take a further fourteen years before Labour was to be re-elected. Any comparison with the events of 1976 can therefore be only tentative and in the space available only brief. The political, economic, social and international context within which New Labour operates is very different from 1976. That said, I wish to make three brief points here.

Firstly, the IMF Crisis, it seems to me, is of major symbolic importance for New Labour. This can be seen in the emphasis Gordon Brown places on 'stability', of the need to maintain international financial confidence. Such references are observable in many of Brown's speeches, pamphlets etc. Such utterances may well reflect the fact that New Labour operates within a global economy, one much more integrated than that of 1976. It may also reflect the fact that the Major Government lost public support following the exit from the European Exchange Rate Mechanism in 1992. Yet it also reflects the fact that New Labour is keen to distance itself from the Party's past, which included frequent sterling crises of which 1976 was the most dramatic.

My second point is that New Labour accepts, to a much greater degree than any previous Labour government, the role of the market. New Labour in power has not reversed the trades union measures introduced by Thatcher and Major. Moreover, it has not reversed any of the privatisations and in some ways can be said to have increased the role of the private sector in public services – through Public-Private Partnerships and the Private Finance Initiative. New Labour appears to have abandoned any serious concern for substantive inequalities, involving as it does large-scale intervention to offset the unequal outcomes of market activity.[7] In providing, or at least in seeking to provide, life-long educational opportunities with supply-side measures to create more equal starting points, New Labour appears to be accepting market outcomes as just.

Finally, New Labour takes a more favourable view of monetarism than the 1974-79 Government did. Although Gordon Brown talks of a 'post-monetarist' policy[8], I think that the macroeconomic framework, with its emphasis on targets, is influenced heavily by monetarist theory. Emphasis is placed on the inflation rate and the Bank of England given the responsibility to meet it. In short, targets are more central to New Labour's macroeconomic framework than they were to Healey's.

[1] Harmon, M.D., *The British Labour Government and the 1976 IMF Crisis*, (Macmillan, Basingstoke, 1997)

[2] Correspondence from Helen Langley, archivist, Modern Political Papers, Bodleian Library, University of Oxford

[3] Kavanagh, D., 'Why Political Science Needs History', *Political Studies*, XXX, 1991, pp.479-495; pp.480-481

[4] A further example was the fact that Gerald Ford had lost the Presidential election in November 1976, and, as a consequence, had less influence than may at first be assumed. It can be speculated that he could have forced the Treasury and the Federal Reserve to back down had he won the election in November.

[5] See Oakeshott, M., 'Rationalism in Politics', 'Political Education', and 'On Being Conservative', all in his *Rationalism in Politics and Other Essays*, (Methuen, London, 1962) and Cowling, M., *The Nature and Limits of Political Science*, (Cambridge University Press, Cambridge, 1963)

[6] See, for example, Johnson, N., *The Limits of Political Science*, (Clarendon, Oxford, 1989), who argues that, "historical inquiry is the only method of illuminating the record of political endeavour and results." See also, Bedolla, M., 'Historical Method: A Brief Introduction', in Crabtree, B.F., and Miller, W.L., (Eds.), *Doing Qualitative Research*, (Sage, California, 1st Edition, 1992), pp.163-173

[7] See Hickson, K., 'Equality' in Plant, R., Beech, M. and Hickson, K., (Eds.) *The Struggle for Labour's Soul: Understanding the Political Thought of the Labour Party since 1945* (Routledge, London, 2004)

[8] See in particular, Brown, G., 'The Conditions for Full Employment', Mais Lecture (19/10/1999)

APPENDIX

THE 1976 IMF CRISIS: A CHRONOLOGY

1974

February
7   Heath calls General Election
28   General Election

March
4   Heath resigns
6   average 29% increase in Miners wage
7   end of 3-day week
26   Healey's first budget – reflationary.   Higher
            taxation   and spending

May
14   Healey speaks to CBI – financial aid to private
            sector
20   Benn reports on industrial strategy to Labour
            Party- TUC Liaison Committee

June
26   TUC approves Social Contract

July
22   Mini-budget - £200m added to demand.
            £340m to PSBR
25   Benn provides financial aid to establish
            Scottish Daily News
31   1971 Industrial Relations Act abolished

August   Treasury begins work on cash limits

| 14 | White Paper 'The Regeneration of British Industry' |

October

1	Healey suggests extension to oil surplus but gets little international support
10	General Election
17	Jack Jones calls for pay restraint

November

| 12 | Budget, £1500m aid to industry. Corporation Tax cut, £800m added to PSBR |

December

| 6 | Equity stake in British Leyland |
| 31 | Government purchases share in Burmah Oil |

1975

January

| 31 | Industry Bill |

February

| 11 | NUM – 35% pay rise |
| 19 | 29% average pay rises in 1974 |

April

15	Deflationary budget
18	Inflation – 25.4%
23	Healey says that further cuts may be necessary
24	Government takes majority share in British Leyland

May

| 9 | Crosland makes 'the party is over' speech |
| 17 | Jack Jones calls for flat rate pay rise |

June | debate over pay policy

| 5 | EEC referendum |
| 13 | Inflation – 36.3% |

July
1   Cash limits introduced
9   TUC accepts £6 per week pay policy
11   White Paper 'The Attack on Inflation'
24   unemployment level goes above 1M

August   Healey tells ministers of need to cut public
               expenditure
1   £6 pay policy introduced

September
3   TUC Conference accepts £6 pay policy
28   Labour Conference accepts £6 pay policy

October
28   Treasury proposes limited depreciation

November
5   Industrial Regeneration plans announced
7   Cabinet agrees to apply for $2 billion loan from
               the IMF
15-17   Rambouillet Summit

December
17   Formal application for the first IMF loan

1976

January
1   IMF grants $2 billion loan to Britain
16   UK borrows full amount of gold tranche
23   SDR1, 000 million oil facility claimed

February
12   Unemployment measures introduced, £220
               million
19   PEWP - £1 billion cuts 1977/8, £2.4 billion cuts
               1978/9

March

4   Bank sells sterling
5   Bank cuts interest rates
10   Government defeated on PEWP. £=$1.91
11   Government wins confidence motion
16   Wilson resigns

April

1   £=$1.88
5   Callaghan elected PM
6   Budget – extension of cash limits. Tax cuts
                linked to agreement on 3% wages settlement
7   Labour loses majority
29   Inflation halved in 9 months (30% to 13%)

May

5   Wage agreement
12   SDR700 million remainder of first tranche
                drawn
28   £=$1.76

June

2   £=$1.72. $300 million reserves used
4   Government initially welcomes agreement on
                stand-by
5/6   Yeo visits London – tells Healey that loan will
                be for 6 months maximum
7   Stand-by credit of $5.3 billion agreed
27   Puerto Rico Summit. Callaghan tries to gain
                the support of Ford

July

2   Meeting of EY Committee. Crosland opposed,
                and is criticised by Dell. Benn produces paper
                advocating AES
3   Healey asks for cuts
6   Cabinet discusses Healey's proposals for three
                hours. Social democrats support Benn
13, 19, 20, 21 Specific measures debate
22   £1 billion cuts plus £1 billion National
                Insurance Employers Surcharge. Mitchell tells

Healey that £1 billion is insufficient to restore confidence

August

1   New pay policy implemented
13   July visible trade deficit reaches £524 million

September

7   NEC produces paper calling for nationalisation of major banks
8   Seaman's strike
9   Bank of England stops supporting £
10   MLR raised by 1.5% to 13%
16   Bank tightens monetary policy
23   Cabinet. Healey says of need to go to the IMF
27   Conference rejects expenditure plans
28   £ falls to $1.63. Healey refuses to attend IMF summit. Callaghan's conference speech
29   Healey announces IMF application
30   Healey visits Conference. Callaghan telephones Ford and Schmidt, and talks about military commitments and import controls

October

7   MLR increased by 2% to 15%, after Healey threatens to resign
9/10   Schmidt visits Chequers
13   Healey discusses plan for import controls. Decision deferred
24   Sunday Times claims terms already agreed. Causes further fall in £
25   Callaghan appears on Panorama. Talks openly about introducing import measures and withdrawing the troops from Germany and Cyprus
26   Unemployment falls to 1.25 million. Cabinet discusses the PEWP
27   NEC rejects further expenditure cuts. Bundersbank formulates plan for reserves.
28   Healey tells Benn that Callaghan got Treasury approval for Panorama interview

November

1	IMF team arrives
2	Ford loses US Presidential election
3	EY Committee
4	First meeting between Healey and IMF team. Figures for PSBR not ready. Labour loses two by-elections. PEWP discussed in Cabinet
5	Treasury forecasts £11.2 billion PSBR in 1977. Later estimated down to £10.5 billion. Callaghan telephones Schmidt, who offers unlimited but vague support
10	First full meeting between IMF team and Treasury to discuss PSBR figures. CPRS paper discussed in Cabinet
11	Cabinet discusses PEWP. Harold Lever to visit USA. Jack Jones accepts need for cuts.
14	Lever visits USA
17	EY Committee
18	Government tries to reduce money supply. Meeting at No.10 Dell and Crosland disagree
19	Formal negotiations begin
22	First meeting of social democrats, without Crosland, and of left-wingers.
23	Healey asks for £1 billion cuts plus £500 million from sale of BP shares. Cabinet fails to support Healey. Meetings between Treasury and IMF; Whittome, Callaghan and Healey. Callaghan calls Ford and Schmidt
24	Hill approaches Morrell about possible deal. Rejected by Bennites. Crosland and Hattersley write paper on import deposits. Benn, Cripps and Morrell write paper on AES
25	Kaldor tells Benn of secret Treasury plan for import deposits. Cabinet discusses Crosland/Hattersley paper.
26	Pohl visits London
28	Simon visits London
29/30	European Council Summit

30	Schmidt informs Callaghan of refusal to help further without first taking IMF loan. Crosland informed of this
December	Early December, plans for ending of reserve currency status of £ produced.
1	Witteveen visits London. Argument with Callaghan. Cabinet discusses and rejects plans by Benn and Shore. Crosland paper discussed. Jack Jones and Hugh Scanlon support Callaghan. Meeting of social democrats – support withers away, only Hattersley left. Crosland informs Callaghan of his support.
2	Cabinet accepts loan and principle of cuts
3	Further disagreement between IMF and Government over extent of cuts
4	Negotiations reopen as IMF more moderate
6	Cabinet begins to negotiate cuts
7	Healey still hopes for safety-net agreement. Figures of £1 billion cuts + £500 million from sale of shares for 1977/8 and £1.5 billion for 1978/9 agreed in Cabinet
9	Yeo calls Mitchell offering talks on reserves
11/12	Letter of Intent formulated by Treasury and IMF delegation
12	Mitchell met Yeo and Burns about reserves
14	Cabinet accepts Letter of Intent. Mitchell met Pohl about reserves
15	Letter of Intent read to Parliament. Includes expenditure cuts, increase in indirect taxation, targets for DCE
15	Meeting of Parliamentary Labour Party
21	Labour win vote as Conservatives abstain – 219-51
29	£ rises to $1.71

1977

January	
3	IMF grants $3.9 billion

10	Bank of International Settlements grants $3 billion for Bank of England reserves
11	Healey announces agreement on reserve status of £ to Commons

BIBLIOGRAPHY

A. Interviews

Tony Benn MP	(telephone)
28/02/2000	
Dr. Martin Holmes	(Oxford)
23/03/2000	
Lord Morgan	(Oxford)
22/05/2000	
Lord Lipsey	(London)
12/10/2000	
Lord Donoughue	(London)
12/10/2000	
Lord Hattersley	(London)
31/10/2000	
Baroness Williams	(London)
21/11/2000	
Sir Nick Monck	(London)
18/01/2001	
Rt.Hon. Denzil Davies MP	(London)
23/01/2001	
Lord Shore	(London)
30/01/2001	
Lord Rodgers	(London)
19/03/2001	
Albert Booth	(London)
02/05/2001	
Sir Samuel Brittan	(London)
20/01/2002	
Lord Hunt	(London)
21/01/2002	
Adrian Ham	(London)
15/08/2002	

I also attempted to interview the remaining surviving members of the Cabinet, but they declined to be interviewed. I did, however, receive written answers from Jim Callaghan and Denis Healey. In addition, Peter Jay and Wilfred Beckerman supplied written answers.

B. Manuscript Collections

1. Private Papers

Tony Benn, unpublished diaries – private possession
Anthony Crosland papers – British Library of Political and Economic Science, London
Peter Thorneycroft papers, University of Southampton Library, Southampton

2. Other Papers

Institute for Contemporary British History IMF Witness Seminar 1989, papers and correspondence, (British Library of Political and Economic Science)
Labour Party: National Executive Committee, minutes and reports (Museum of Labour History, Manchester)
Labour Party: Parliamentary Labour Party, minutes and reports (Museum of Labour History, Manchester and the Office of the Parliamentary Labour Party, London)
Labour Party: 1976 Labour Party Conference Report (Museum of Labour History, Manchester)

C. Official Papers

Hansard, Parliamentary Debates, 5th series, 1976, vols.903-923
Hansard, House of Lords, Official Report, 1976, vols. 374-378
The Attack on Inflation, Cmnd. 6151, (HMSO, London, 1975)
The Attack on Inflation: The Second Year, Cmnd. 6507(HMSO, London, 1976)
Cash Limits on Public Expenditure, Cmnd. 6440, (HMSO, London, 1976)

The Regeneration of British Industry, Cmnd. 5710, (HMSO, London, 1974)

An Approach to Industrial Strategy, Cmnd. 6315, (HMSO, London, 1975)

Public Expenditure White Paper, February 1975, Cmnd. 5879, (HMSO, London, 1975)

Public Expenditure White Paper, January 1976, Cmnd. 6393, (HMSO, London, 1976)

Public Expenditure White Paper, January 1977, Cmnd. 6721, (HMSO, London, 1977)

Economic Trends, March 1977, No. 281, (CSO, London, 1977)

D. Newspapers

The following newspapers have been consulted during the course of my research:

Guardian, Observer, Sunday Telegraph, Sunday Times, Telegraph, Times

E. PhD Theses

Bernstein, K., *The International Monetary Fund and Deficit Countries: The Case of Britain 1974-77*, (Unpublished PhD Thesis, Stanford University, USA, 1983)

Mullard, M., *Explanations of Public Expenditure Changes in Britain Since 1968*, (Unpublished PhD Thesis, Southampton University, 1984)

F. Biographies, Memoirs, Diaries

Adams, J., *Tony Benn: A Biography*, (Macmillan, London, 1992)

Barnett, J., *Inside The Treasury*, (Andre Deutsch, London, 1982)

Benn, T., *Against the Tide: Diaries 1973-6*, (Arrow, London, 1989)

Callaghan, J., *Time and Chance*, (Collins, London, 1987)

Crosland, S., *Tony Crosland*, (Cape, London, 1982)

Dell, E., *A Hard Pounding: Politics and Economic Crisis 1974-6*, (Oxford University Press, Oxford, 1991)

Dell, E., *The Chancellors*, (HarperCollins, London, 1997)

Dell, E., and Hunt, J., 'The Failings of Cabinet Government in the Mid to Late 1970s', *Contemporary Record*, 8/3, Winter 1994, pp.453-72

Donoughue, B., *Prime Minister: The Conduct of Policy Under Wilson and Callaghan*, (Cape, London, 1987)

Hattersley, R., *Who Goes Home? Scenes From A Political Life*, (Little, Brown and Co. London, 1995, 2nd Edition)

Healey, D., *The Time of My Life*, (Penguin, Harmondsworth, 1990, 2nd Edition)

Jefferys, K., *Anthony Crosland: A New Biography*, (Cohen, London, 1999)

Jenkins, R., *A Life At The Centre*, (Macmillan, London, 1991)

Jones, J., *Union Man: The Autobiography of Jack Jones*, (Collins, London, 1986)

Kellner, P., and Hitchens, C., *Callaghan: The Road to Number 10*, (Cassell, London, 1976)

Morgan, K., *Callaghan: A Life*, (Oxford University Press, Oxford, 1997)

Pearce, E., *The Lost Leaders*, (Little, Brown and Co. London, 1997)

Pearce, E., *Denis Healey*, (Little, Brown and Company, London, 2002)

Pimlott, B., *Harold Wilson*, (HarperCollins, London, 1992)

Pliatzky, L., *Getting and Spending: Public Expenditure, Employment and Inflation*, (Blackwell, Oxford, 1982)

Rodgers, W., *Fourth Among Equals*, (Politicos, London, 2000)

Wilson, H., *Final Term: The Labour Government 1974-76*, (Weidenfeld and Nicolson, Joseph, London, 1979)

G. Books and Articles

Addison, P., *The Road To 1945:British Politics and the Second World War*, (Cape, London, 1975)

Addison, P., 'Consensus Revisited', *Twentieth Century British History*, 4/1, 1993, pp.91-94

Amery, L., *The Conservative Future: An Outline*, (Conservative Political Centre, London, 1946)

Arblaster, A., 'The Old Left' in Plant, R., Beech, M. and Hickson, K., (Eds.) *The Struggle for Labour's Soul: Understanding the Political Thought of the Labour Party since 1945* (Routledge, London, 2004)

Artis, M., and Cobham, D., (Eds.) *Labour's Economic Policies 1974-1979*, (Manchester University Press, Manchester, 1991)

Bacon, R., and Eltis, W., *Britain's Economic Problem; Too Few Producers*, (Macmillan, Basingstoke, 1978, 2nd Edition)

Barnett, C., *The Audit of War*, (Macmillan, London, 1986)

Barry, N., *Hayek's Social and Economic Philosophy* (Macmillan, London, 1979) Barry, N., *The New Right* (Croom Helm, Beckenham, 1987)

Bedolla, M., 'Historical Method: A Brief Introduction' in Crabtree, B. and Miller, W., (Eds.), *Doing Qualitative Research*, (Sage, California, 1992)

Beer, S., *Modern British Politics*, (Faber and Faber, London, 1965)

Borg, W.R., *Educational Research: An Introduction*, (Longman, London, 1963)

Bosanquet, N., 'Has Manufacturing Been "Crowded Out"?', *Socialist Commentary*, January 1977, pp.4-5

Brittan, S., *The Treasury Under the Tories*, (Penguin, Middlesex, 1964)

Brittan, S., *The Economic Consequences of Democracy*, (Temple Smith, London, 1977)

Brittan, S., *How to End the Monetarist Controversy*, Hobart Paper 90, (Institute of Economic Affairs, London, 1981)

Brittan, S., *The Role and Limits of Government: Essays in Political Economy*, (Temple Smith, Middlesex, 1983)

Brittan, S., and Lilley, P., *The Delusion of Incomes Policy*, (Temple Smith, London, 1977)

Britton, A., *Macroeconomic Policy In Britain 1974-87*, (Cambridge University Press, Cambridge, 1991)

Brown, G., 'The Conditions for Full Employment', Mais Lecture (19/10/1999)

Browning, P., *The Treasury and Economic Policy 1964-85*, (Longman, London, 1986)

Bulpitt, J., 'The Discipline of the New Democracy: Mrs. Thatcher's Domestic Statecraft' *Political Studies*, XXXIV, 1986, pp.19-39

Burk, K., et.al., 'The 1976 IMF Crisis', *Contemporary Record*, November 1989

Burk, K., *The Americans, the Germans and the British: The 1976 IMF Crisis, Twentieth Century British History*, 5/3, 1993, pp.351-369

Burk, K. and Cairncross, A., *Goodbye Great Britain: The 1976 IMF Crisis*, (Yale University Press, New Haven, 1992)

Butler, D. and Kavanagh, D., *The British General Election of February 1974* (Macmillan, London, 1974)

Butler, D. and Kavanagh, D, *The British General Election of October 1974*, (Macmillan, London, 1975)

Butler, R.A., *The Art of the Possible*, (Purnell, London, 1971)

Cairncross, A., *The British Economy Since 1945: Economic Policy and Performance 1945-1990*, (Blackwell, Oxford, 1992)

Calder, A., *The People's War: Britain 1939-45*, (Cape, London, 1969)

Canto, V., Joines, D., and Laffer, A., 'Tax Rates, Factor Employment, Market Production and Welfare', in Canto, V., Joines, D., and Laffer, A., (Eds.), *Foundations in Supply-side Economics: Theory and Evidence*, (Academic Press, New York, 1983)

Clark, D., *The Conservative Faith in a Modern Age*, (Conservative Political Centre, London, 1947)

Coates, D., *Labour in Power? A Study of the Labour Government 1974-79*, (Longman, London, 1980)

Coats, A.W., and Colander, D., 'An Introduction to the Spread of Economic Ideas', in Colander, D., and Coats, A.W., (Eds.), *The Spread of Economic Ideas*, (Cambridge University Press, New York, 1989)

Cockett, R., *Thinking the Unthinkable: Think-tanks and the Economic Counter-revolution 1931-1983*, (HarperCollins, London, 1994)

Congdon, T., *Monetarism: An Essay in Definition*, (Centre for Policy Studies, London, 1978)

Congdon, T., 'Monetarism and the Budget Deficit', in Congdon, T., *Reflections on Monetarism: Britain's Vain Search for a Successful Economic Strategy*, (Edward Elgar, Aldershot, 1992)

Conservative Party, *The Industrial Charter: A Statement of Conservative Industrial Policy*, (Conservative Central Office, London, 1947)

Conservative Party, *The Right Road for Britain*, (Conservative Central Office, London, 1949)

Coopey, R., Fielding, S., and Tiratsoo, N., *The Wilson Governments 1964-70*, (Pinter, London, 1993)

Cowling, M., *The Nature and Limits of Political Science*, (Cambridge University Press, Cambridge, 1963)

Cox, N. 'Public Records' in Seldon, A., (Ed.), *Contemporary History: Practice and Method*, (Blackwell, Oxford, 1988)

Crawford, M., 'High Conditionality Lending: The UK' in Williamson, J. (Ed.) *IMF Conditionality*, (Institute for International Economics, Washington, 1983)

Cripps, F., 'The British Case – can the left win', *New Left Review*, 129, 1981, pp.93-97

Crosland, C.A.R., 'Insiders and Controllers', in Crosland, C.A.R., *The Conservative Enemy: A Programme for Radical Reform in the 1960s*, (Cape, London, 1962)

Crosland, C.A.R., *The Future of Socialism*, (Schocken, London, 1963, 2nd Edition)

Crosland, C.A.R., 'Socialism Now', in Leonard, D., (Ed.), *Socialism Now and Other Essays*, (Cape, London, 1973)

Deakin, N., *In Search of the Postwar Consensus*, (Welfare State Programme, LSE, London, 1988)

Denham, A., and Garnett, M., *British Think-tanks and the Climate of Opinion*, (UCL, London, 1998)

Denzin, N.K., *Sociological Methods: A Sourcebook*, (Aldine, Chicago, 1970)

Desai, M., *Testing Monetarism*, (Pinter, London, 1981)

De Vries, M.G., *The International Monetary Fund and Deficit Countries 1972-78: Cooperation on Trial*, 3 Vols., (International Monetary Fund, Washington, 1985)

Dexter, L.A., *Elite and Specialised Interviewing*, (Northwestern University Press, Evanston, 1970)

Downs, A., *An Economic Theory of Democracy*, (Harper and Row, New York, 1957)

Dutton, D., *British Politics Since 1945: The Rise and Fall of Consensus* (Blackwell, Oxford, 1991)

Eatwell, R., *The 1945-51 Labour Governments*, (Batsford, London, 1979)

Eltis, W., 'The Need to Cut Public Expenditure and Taxation' in Minford, P., Rose, H., Eltis, W., Perlman, P., and Burton, J., *Is Monetarism Enough? Essays in Refining and Reinforcing the Monetary Cure for Inflation*, (Institute of Economic Affairs, London, 1980)

Englefield, D., 'Parliamentary Sources' in Seldon, A., (Ed.), *Contemporary History: Practice and Method*, (Blackwell, Oxford, 1988)

Evans, B., and Taylor, A., *From Salisbury to Major: Continuity and Change in Conservative Politics*, (Manchester University Press, Manchester, 1996)

Fay, S. and Young, H., *The Day The Pound Nearly Died*, (Sunday Times, London 1978)

Finer, S., (Ed.), *Adversary Politics and Electoral Reform*, (Wigram, London, 1975)

Forrester, T., 'Neutralising the Industrial Strategy', in Coates, K., (Ed.), *What Went Wrong: Explaining the Fall of the Labour Government*, (Spokesman, London, 1979)

Fraser, D., 'The Postwar Consensus: A Debate Not Long Enough', *Parliamentary Affairs*, 53/2, 2000, pp.347-362

Friedman, M., 'The Role of Monetary Policy', *The American Economic Review*, LVIII, March 1968, pp.3-15

Friedman, M., 'The Counter-revolution in Monetary Theory', Wincott Memorial Lecture, 1970, and IEA Occasional Paper No.33, (Institute of Economic Affairs, London, 1970)

Friedman, M., 'Unemployment Versus Inflation? An Evaluation of the Phillips Curve', IEA Occasional Paper 44, (Institute of Economic Affairs, London, 1975)

Friedman, M., 'Inflation and Unemployment: The New Dimension in Politics', IEA Occasional Paper 51, (Institute of Economic Affairs, London, 1976)

Friedman, M., 'The Line We Dare Not Cross: The Fragility of freedom at 60%', *Encounter*, November, 1976

Friedman, M., 'The Future of Capitalism', Federation of Swedish Industries, Stockholm, 1977

Friedman, M., *Tax Limitation, Inflation and the Role of Government*, (Fisher Institute, Dallas, 1978)

Friedman, M., *Monetarist Economics*, (Blackwell, Oxford, 1991)

Friedman, M., and Friedman, R., *Free to Choose*, (Pelican, London, 1980, 2nd Edition)

Gamble. A., *Britain in Decline: Economic Policy, Political Strategy and the British State* (Macmillan, London, 1981)

Gamble, A., *The Free Economy and the Strong State: The Politics of Thatcherism*, (Macmillan, Basingstoke, 1988)

Gamble, A., 'Ideas and Interests in British Economic Policy', *Contemporary British History*, 10/2, 1996, pp.1-21

Gamble, A. and Walkland, S., *The British Party System and Economic Policy 1945-83*, (Clarendon, Oxford, 1984)

Godley, W., and Cripps, F., *Macroeconomics*, (Fontana, London, 1983)

Greenleaf, W.H., *The British Political Tradition*, Vol.2, 'The Ideological Heritage' (Methuen, London, 1983)

Hadjimatheou, G. and Skouras, A., 'Britain's Economic Problem: the growth of the non-market sector', *Economic Journal*, 89, June 1979, pp.392-401

Hajer, M., *The Politics of Environmental Discourse*, (Oxford University Press, Oxford, 1995)

Hall, P., 'Policy Paradigms, Experts and the State: The Case of Macroeconomic Policymaking in Britain', in Brooks, S., and Gagnon, A., (Eds.), *Social Scientists, Policy and the State*, (Praeger, New York, 1990)

Hall, P., 'Policy Paradigms, Social Learning and The State: the case of economic policymaking in Britain', *Comparative Politics*, 25, April 1993, pp.275-296

Hamilton, N. 'The Role of Biography' in Brivati, B., Buxton, J., and Seldon, A., (Eds.), *Contemporary History Handbook*, (Manchester University Press, Manchester, 1996)

Harmon, M.D., *The British Labour Government and the 1976 IMF Crisis*, (Macmillan, London, 1997)

Harmon, M.D., 'The 1976 UK-IMF Crisis: The Markets, the Americans, and the IMF', *Contemporary British History*, 11/3, Autumn 1997, pp.1-17

Harris, J., 'Enterprise and Welfare States: A Comparative Perspective', *Translations of the Royal Historical Society*, 5th series, 40, 1990, pp.175-195

Hayek, F.A., *The Road to Serfdom*, (Routledge, London, 1944)

Heclo, H., *Modern Social Politics in Britain and Sweden*, (Yale University Press, New Haven, 1974)

Heffernan, R., *New Labour and Thatcherism*, (Macmillan, London, 2000)

Hickson, K., 'Economic Thought' in Seldon, A. and Hickson, K., *New Labour, Old Labour: the Wilson and Callaghan Governments of 1974-79* (Routledge, London, 2004)

Hickson, K., 'Equality' in Plant, R., Beech, M. and Hickson, K., (Eds.) *The Struggle for Labour's Soul: Understanding the Political Thought of the Labour Party since 1945* (Routledge, London, 2004)

Hickson, K., 'The Postwar Consensus Revisited', *Political Quarterly*, April 2004

Hodgson, G, *Labour at the Crossroads: The Political and Economic Challenge to the Labour Party n the 1980s*, (Robertson, Oxford, 1981)

Hogg, Q., *The Case for Conservatism*, (Conservative Political Centre, London, 1948)

Holland, S., *The Socialist Challenge*, (Quartet, London, 1975)

Holmes, M., *Political Pressure and Economic Policy: British Government 1970-1974*, (Butterworth, London, 1983)

Holmes, M., *The Labour Government 1974-79: Political Aims and Economic Reality*, (Macmillan, Basingstoke, 1985)

Hoover, K., and Plant, R., *Conservative Capitalism in Britain and the United States: A Critical Appraisal*, (Routledge, London, 1989)

Hoskyns, J., 'Conservatism Is Not Enough', *Political Quarterly*, 55, 1984, pp.3-16

Hutton, W., *The Revolution That Never Was: An Assessment of Keynesian Economics*, (Vintage, London, 2001, 3rd Edition)

Jackson, P., 'Public Expenditure', in Artis, M., and Cobham, D., (Eds.) *Labour's Economic Policies 1974-1979*, (Manchester University Press, Manchester, 1991)

Jay, P., *A General Hypothesis of Employment, Inflation and Politics*, IEA Occasional Paper No.46, (Institute of Economic Affairs, London, 1975)

Jefferys, K., 'British Politics and Social Policy During the Second World War', *Historical Journal*, 30/1, 1987, pp.123-144

Johnson, N., *The Limits of Political Science*, (Clarendon, Oxford, 1989)

Jones, H., 'The Postwar Consensus In Britain: Thesis, Antithesis, and Synthesis', in Brivati, B., Buxton, J. and Seldon, A., (Eds.), *The Contemporary History Handbook*, (Manchester University Press, Manchester, 1996)

Jones, H., and Kandiah, M., (Eds.), *The Myth of Consensus: New Visions on British History 1945-64*, (Macmillan, Basingstoke, 1996)

Joseph, K., *Stranded on the Middle Ground*, (Centre for Policy Studies, London, 1976)

Kandiah, M., 'Books and Journals', in Brivati, B., Buxton, J. and Seldon, A., (Eds.), *The Contemporary History Handbook*, (Manchester University Press, Manchester, 1996)

Kaul, C., 'The Press', Seldon, A., (Ed.), *The Contemporary History: Practice and Method*, (Blackwell, Oxford, 1988)

Kavanagh, D., 'The Heath Government' in Hennessy, P. and Seldon A., (Eds.) *Ruling Performance*, (Institute for Contemporary British History, London, 1987)

Kavanagh, D., 'Is The Postwar Consensus A Myth?', *Contemporary Record*, Summer 1989, pp.12-15

Kavanagh, D., *Thatcherism and British Politics: The End of Consensus?*, (Oxford University Press, Oxford, 1990, 2nd Edition)

Kavanagh, D., 'Why Political Science Needs History', *Political Studies*, XXX, 1991, pp.479-495

Kavanagh, D., 'The Postwar Consensus', *Twentieth Century British History*, 3/2, 1992, pp.175-190

Kavanagh, D. and Morris, P., *Consensus Politics from Attlee to Thatcher*, (Blackwell, Oxford, 1989)

Keegan, W., and Pennant-Rea, R., *Who Runs the Economy?*, (Maurice Temple Smith, London, 1979)

Kellner, P., 'Anatomy of the Vote', *New Statesman*, 9 April 1976

Kerr, P. 'The Postwar Consensus: A Woozle That Wasn't' in Marsh, D., (Ed.) *Postwar British Politics In Perspective*, (Polity, Cambridge, 1999)

Kerr, P., *Postwar British Politics: From Conflict to Consensus*, (Routledge, London, 2001)

Kuhn, T., *The Structure of Scientific Revolutions*, (University of Chicago, Chicago, 1970)

Labour Party, *Labour's Programme for Britain: 1973*, (Labour Party, London, 1973)

Labour Party, *Let Us Work Together: Labour's Way Out of the Crisis*, February 1974 General Election Manifesto, (Labour Party, London, 1974)

Labour Party, *Britain Will Win With Labour*, October 1974 General Election Manifesto, (Labour Party, London, 1974)

Lash, S., and Urry, J., *The End of Organised Capital*, (Polity, Cambridge, 1987)

Leijonhufvud, A., *On Keynesian Economics and the Economics of Keynes: A Study in Monetary Theory*, (Oxford University Press, New York, 1968)

Longstreth, F., 'The City, Industry and the Economy in Contemporary Capitalism', in Crouch, C., (Ed.), *State and the Economy in Contemporary Capitalism*, (Croom Helm, London, 1979)

Ludlum, S., 'The Gnomes of Washington: Four Myths of the 1976 IMF Crisis', *Political Studies*, XL, 1992, pp.713-727

MacIntyre, A., 'A Mistake About Causality in Social Science', in Laslett, P., and Runciman, W.G., *Philosophy, Politics and Society*, 2nd Series, (Blackwell, Oxford, 1972)

Marlow, J., *Questioning The Postwar Consensus Thesis: Towards An Alternative Account*, (Dartmouth, Aldershot, 1996)

Marquand, D., *The Unprincipled Society: New Demands and Old Politics*, (Cape, London, 1988)

Matthews, R.C.O., 'Why Has Britain Had Full-employment Since The War?', *Economic Journal*, No.311, Vol. LXXVIII, 1968, pp.555-569

McKenzie, R., *British Political Parties*, (Heinemann, London, 1955)

Middlemas, K., *Politics in Industrial Society*, (Andre Deutsch, London, 1979)

Mitchell, A., and Wienir, D., *Last Time: Labour's Lessons From the Sixties*, (Bellew, London, 1997)

Morgan, K.O., *The People's Peace: British History 1945-89*, (Oxford University Press, Oxford, 1990)

Mosley, P., *The Making of Economic Policy: Theory and Evidence from Britain and the United States Since 1945*, (Harvester Wheatsheaf, Brighton, 1984)

Mullard, M., *The Politics of Public Expenditure*, (Routledge, London, 1993, 2nd Edition)

Oakeshott, M., 'Rationalism In Politics', in Oakeshott, M., *Rationalism In Politics and Other Essays*, (Methuen, London, 1962) pp.1-32

Oakeshott, M., 'Political Education' in Oakeshott, M., *Rationalism In Politics and Other Essays*, (Methuen, London, 1962) pp.112-133

Oakeshott, M., 'On Being Conservative', in Oakeshott, M., *Rationalism In Politics and Other Essays*, (Methuen, London, 1962) pp.168-192

Oliver, M., 'From Anodyne Keynesianism to Delphic Monetarism: economic policy-making in Britain 1960-79', *Twentieth Century British History*, 9/1, 1998, pp.139-50

Ormerod, P., 'The Economic Record', in Bosanquet, N., and Townsend, P., (Eds.), *Labour and Equality: A Fabian Study of Labour in Power*, (Heinemann, London, 1980)

Pimlott, B., 'The Myth of Consensus', in Smith, L.M., (Ed.), *The Making of Britain: Echoes of Greatness*, (London Weekend Television, London, 1988)

Pimlott, B., 'Is The Postwar Consensus A Myth?', *Contemporary Record*, Summer 1989, pp.12-15

Plant, R., *Modern Political Thought*, (Blackwell, Oxford, 1991)

Plant, R., 'Blair and Ideology', in Seldon, A., (Ed.), *The Blair Effect*, (Little, Brown and Company, London, 2001)

Przeworski, A., *Capitalism and Social Democracy*, (Cambridge University Press, Cambridge, 1985)

Ramsden, J., 'Adapting to the Postwar Consensus', *Contemporary Record*, November 1989, pp.11-13

Raspin, A., 'Private Papers', in Seldon, A., (Ed.), *Contemporary History: Practice and Method*, (Blackwell, Oxford, 1988)

Roberts, B., *Biographical Research*, (Open University Press, Buckingham, 2002)

Rose, R., *Do Parties Make A Difference?*, (Macmillan, London, 1980)

Sabatier, P., 'Towards Better Theories of the Policy Process', *Political Science and Policy*, Vol.24, 1991, pp.147-156

Sabatier, P., 'The Advocacy Coalition Framework: Revisions and Relevance for Europe', *Journal of European Public Policy*, 5/1, 1998, pp.98-130

Sabatier, P., and Jenkins-Smith, H., *Policy Change and Learning: An Advocacy Coalition Approach*, (Westview, Boulder, 1993)

Sedgemore, B., *The Secret Constitution*, (Hodder and Stoughton, London, 1980)

Seldon, A., 'Consensus: A Debate Too Long?', *Parliamentary Affairs*, 47/4, 1994, pp.501-514

Seldon, A., 'The Heath Government in History' in Ball, S., and Seldon, A., (Eds.), *The Heath Government 1970-74*, (Addison Wesley Londman, New York, 1996)

Seldon, A., 'Elite Interviews', in Brivati, B., Buxton, J. and Seldon, A., (Eds.), *The Contemporary History Handbook*, (Manchester University Press, Manchester, 1996)

Seldon, A., 'Ideas are Not Enough', in Marquand, D., and Seldon, A., (Eds.), *The Ideas That Shaped Postwar Britain*, (Fontana, London, 1996)

Seldon, A., and Pappworth, J., *By Word of Mouth: 'Elite' Oral History*, Methuen, London, 1983)

Sharples, A., 'Alternative Economic Strategies: Labour Movement Responses to the Crisis', *Socialist Economic Review*, 1, 1981, pp.71-91

Shaw, G.K., *Keynesian Economics: The Permanent Revolution*, (Edward Elgar, Aldershot, 1988)

Smith, D., *The Rise and Fall of Monetarism*, (Penguin, London, 1987)

Stedward, G., 'On The Record: An Introduction to Interviewing', in Burnham, P., (Ed.), *Surviving the Research Process in Politics*, (Pinter, London, 1987)

Stone, D., 'Causal Stories and the Formation of Policy Agendas', *Political Science Quarterly*, 104/2, Summer 1989, pp.281-300

Strange, S., *Sterling and British Policy: A Political Study of an International Currency*, (Oxford University Press, London, 1971)

Thompson, N., *Left In the Wilderness: The Political Economy of British Democratic Socialism Since 1979*, (Acumen, Chesham, 1979)

Tomlinson, J., 'Why Was There Never A "Keynesian Revolution" In Economic Policy?', *Economy and Society*, 10/1, February 1981, pp.72-87

Tomlinson, J., *British Macroeconomic Policy Since 1940*, (Croom Helm, Beckenham, 1985)

Walter, A., *World Power and World Money: The Role of Hegemony and International Monetary Order*, (Harvester Wheatsheaf, London, 1993)

Walters, A., 'Money in Boom and Slump: An Empirical Inquiry into British Experience Since the 1880s', Hobart Paper 44, (Institute of Economic Affairs, London, 1971)

Wanniski, J., 'Taxes, Revenues and the "Laffer Curve"', *Public Interest*, 50, 1979, pp.3-16

Whitehead, P., *The Writing on the Wall*, (Michael Joseph, London, 1985)

Whitehead, P., 'The Labour Governments 1974-79', in Hennessy, P., and Seldon A., (Eds.), *Ruling Performance*, (Institute for Contemporary British History, London, 1987)

Wickham-Jones, M., 'A Calendar of Events', in Artis, M., and Cobham, D., (Eds.) *Labour's Economic Policies 1974-1979*, (Manchester University Press, Manchester, 1991)

Wickham-Jones, M., *Economic Strategy and the Labour Party: Politics and Policy-making 1970-83*, (MacMillan, Basingstoke, 1996)

Wickham-Jones, M., 'New Left' in Plant, R., Beech, M. and Hickson, K., (Eds.) *The Struggle for Labour's Soul: Understanding the Political Thought of the Labour Party since 1945* (Routledge, London, 2004)

Zis, G., 'The International Status of Sterling', in Artis, M., and Cobham, D., (Eds.) *Labour's Economic Policies 1974-1979*, (Manchester University Press, Manchester, 1991)

Index

Adam Smith Institute (ASI), 188

advocacy coalitions, 164-165

Alternative Economic Strategy (AES), 12, 50-53, 54, 55, 67, 81, 82, 93-94, 99, 105, 128, 132, 133, 134, 138, 161, 162, 166, 169-175, 184-185, 195, 201-204, 216, 222, 224, 225, 228

Amery, Leo, 30

Apel, Hans, 66

Approach to Industrial Strategy, An (1975), 53, 216.

Anderson, John, 20

Attlee, Clement, 17, 19, 211, 222

Austrian school, 177-178

Bank of International Settlements, 88, 89, 151

Barnett, Joel, 88, 92, 94, 95, 124-125, 126, 145, 147, 149, 209

Basnett, David, 86

Benn, Tony, 3, 8, 10, 24, 33, 53, 54, 59, 79, 81, 83, 93-94, 100-101, 116, 118, 127, 128, 130, 132, 133, 134, 135, 136, 137-138, 139, 140, 142, 143, 147, 153, 166, 171, 198, 202, 203-204, 206, 207, 208, 216, 224

Berrill, Kenneth, 207

Bevan, Aneurin, 21

Beveridge, William, 19, 24

Blair, Tony, 29

Booth, Albert, 94, 133, 134, 135, 142, 202, 203, 212

Bretton Woods system, 37, 41, 61-62

Brittan, Samuel, 177, 180-182, 188, 213

Brown, George, 40, 48-49

Brown, Gordon, 228

Burns, Arthur, 88, 89, 119-120, 137, 151

Butler, R.A., 20, 21, 30.

Callaghan, James, 3, 10, 48-49, 79, 80, 81, 82, 83, 84, 88, 89, 90, 91-94, 95, 96, 100, 101-106, 115, 116-117, 117-120, 121-124, 128-129, 129-130, 131, 132, 133, 135, 136, 137, 138, 140, 141, 142, 143, 144, 145, 146, 147, 148, 149, 150, 152, 153, 195, 198, 202, 204, 205, 206, 207-209, 211, 212, 214, 216, 224, 226-227

Cambridge Economic Policy Group (CEPG), 171, 173, 203, 214-215, 226

Carter, Jimmy, 119, 151

cash limits, 57-58, 84-86, 105, 125, 163, 199-200, 201, 209, 212, 223

Central Policy Review Staff (CPRS), 135, 207

Centre for Policy Studies (CPS), 187-188

Chamberlain, Joseph, 175

Chamberlain, Neville, 18

Churchill, Winston, 18, 20